CENTENARIANS

THE BONUS YEARS

CENTENARIANS

❧ THE BONUS YEARS ❧

LYNN PETERS ADLER, J.D.

FOREWORD BY WALTER M. BORTZ II, M.D.

HEALTH PRESS
SANTA FE, NEW MEXICO

.ϟ

DEDICATION

This book is dedicated to all the centenarians I have known
and to my husband, Jim, who together made it possible.
May he also live to be 100, and may I be around to give him the party.

Frontispiece: Ernest Windesheim, MD, age 100. Reprinted with permission
from the Oakland Tribune. Photograph by R. Williams.

Copyright © 1995 by Lynn Peters Adler, J.D.

Published by Health Press
P.O. Drawer 1388
Santa Fe, NM 87504

Library of Congress Cataloging-in-Publication Data

Adler, Lynn,
Centenarians : The Bonus Years
Lynn Peters Adler
p. cm.
ISBN 0-929173-02-3
1. Centenarians—United States. I. Title.
HQ1064.U5A6315
305.26'0973—dc20

Cover and Book Design by Jim Mafchir

Contents

Foreword

THE stories of this book represent a mirror into which we look to see our future. The centenarians' images which reflect back to us from these pages are prophetic. We look deep and see ourselves thirty of fifty or seventy years from now. We like what we see, but we are challenged, too. These lives are full to overflowing. They ask us to follow and learn. In *The Republic*, Socrates wrote "It is good that we should ask the old who have gone before us along a road which we must all travel in our turn the nature of that road." Victor Frankl comments "life achieves meaning when it serves as an example to others."

The road, the process, to 100 is not predestined. These 100-year-olds exhibit, more than any other single quality, self-determination. They were not given 100 years, they earned them. They each built their own road. The worked through their losses and won. Each person recorded here has caught the brass ring after a century of twirls on life's merry-go-round. Each is proud and is right in displaying boldly a credential that, until recently, only a few would dare to contemplate.

The first step to 100 is to believe. The "will to believe" is strongly evident. Scribian wrote "the Universe resounds with the joyful cry 'I am'." The centenarians have had the opportunity to cry "we are" for a long,

long time. They took their first steps a long, long time ago. It was a time when our country had thirty-eight states: McKinley was president; women didn't vote; the Spanish-American War; Indian treaties; X-rays were discovered; bloomers, fedoras; Kitty Hawk was a few years away; the telephone was new; no radio, no tv; the first automobiles; and Adolf Hitler and Charlie Chaplin were little boys. Life expectancy was 45 years. There were few centenarians then. Now there are many.

Kenneth Manton, eminent demographer at Duke University, looks into his mirror and finds if we take care of ourselves in ways which we already understand that in a few years our average life expectancy should be 100 years. Therefore, a century becomes no longer a curiosity, worthy of Willard Scott's notation, but a norm, a standard. Lynn Adler's centenarians are the evidence. They show how. But it is the why that matters. Why be 100? The how is the easy part, the why is the hard part. These ages give hints as to the why, but that answer isn't yet in.

When all of us, not just these elect few, can fill our 100 years with joyful meaning, then our species will have earned its name of sapient. Until we know and live the answer to "why 100?", we live lives of restricted extent and content. John Gardner challenges us with the motto, "life liberty, and the pursuit of *meaning*." The centenarians have been in the business of validating this goal for longer than anyone else.

Let us then read, learn, and live more fully as a result.

Walter M. Bortz II, M.D.
Clinical Associate Professor,
Stanford University Medical School
Former President, American Geriatrics Society

Preface

THIS book is *by and about* centenarians, people 100 years of age and over. It is the story of their contributions, challenges, and triumphs. Centenarians give us insight into what it is like to live 100 years or more, and their lives tell us about a part of our country's evolution. Their recollections add flavor and meaning to recorded history; they are our living links to the past.

I came to write this book because of my long-standing interest in and love for people who are very old. I would like others to recognize the importance of our elders' role in our collective and personal histories and to appreciate them as individuals. Further, I wish to call attention to the needs of people of advanced age with the hope that they will receive a higher priority in society.

It has long distressed me to observe that the older a person becomes the more it seems he or she is shunned by society, particularly in America, where youth is revered. There is a positive side to aging, and there are many people of very advanced age who are interested in remaining a part of the world around them and who want to remain active and engaged in life to the greatest extent possible. Centenarians help dispel the stereotype of advanced age as *merely* a time of physical decrepitude and emotional deterioration, and a general disinterest in life. By honoring and highlighting centenarians—who are at the pinnacle of old age—I hope to persuade others to think about the very eldest members of society (those eighty-five and over) in a more kindly light and recognize their rightful place in society.

Shortly after moving to Arizona at the beginning of 1985, I began a volunteer program to identify and to honor the state's eldest citizens. The centenarian program was adopted first by the Phoenix Mayor's Aging Services Commission, of which I was a member, thanks to the support of former Mayor Terry Goddard. He approved the then novel concept of seeking out and honoring the eldest citizens as a way of fostering greater community involvement with people of advanced age. The following year, while serving as a volunteer program coordinator for the Year of Action for Seniors for the Governor's Advisory Council on Aging, I was able to expand the program statewide. In succeeding years, as a member of the Governor's Council and chairman of the Centenarian Program, this concept was established regionally throughout the state and the program's activities and scope increased.

In 1988, I conceived the idea of a human interest questionnaire to be sent to all Arizona centenarians. Michael Baker, Ph.D., Executive Director of the Dorothy Garske Center (a private, nonprofit foundation in Phoenix dedicated to enhancing the well—being and autonomy of older adults), helped develop this questionnaire and applied his skill and research background to the project. The responses to this Arizona survey were then published in the December 1988 issue of the Garske Center's newsletter, *Lifestyle News*, and distributed throughout the state, thus furthering the goal of greater awareness of centenarians.

To continue this effort nationwide, I founded the National Centenarian Awareness Project. In 1989, as the cornerstone for this book, I contacted centenarians throughout the United States. Questionnaires were mailed to 3,000 centenarians, and approximately 350 responded. What they had to say was intriguing. The richness of the material far exceeded my greatest expectations. Centenarians related personal experiences and historical recollections, and spoke of their values and beliefs. They offered opinions on the quality of life and on the challenges of living long.

The responses to what I believe is the first-ever human interest survey of America's eldest citizens came from the centenarians themselves. Although most required help in writing, surprisingly, about one-quarter of the replies came back in the centenarian's own hand. From this beginning, lively correspondence of cards and letters developed, as did telephone calls, personal interviews, and visits. To facilitate communication, I installed a toll-free telephone line in my home. As time went by, many centenarians and their families and friends contributed other material about their lives, including newspaper articles, diaries, and photographs.

A heartwarming benefit from the survey was that it also furthered communication within the families of centenarians. Many relatives remarked that the survey became a catalyst for recollecting and recording details of their family history—details that might otherwise never have resurfaced. One daughter wrote: "I learned so much of mother's life that I never knew—she opened up to tell the stories of her early life and times and of the personalities of my ancestors. It was so interesting and enlightening and gave me a greater sense of who I am and of the family I come from. I tape recorded our conversations so I can share them with my children, and keep her words for their children." Another wrote to say: "My mother and I completed the questionnaire just five days before her death at age 103. We enjoyed the hours we spent together, talking, reminiscing. The memory of this time spent with her is one I will cherish all my life."

Centenarians in this book give a picture of what life is like at this great age. They do not attempt to give a quick answer to the commonly asked journalistic question, "How did you live to be so old?" They offer what they believe has worked for them, and their suggestions are subjective and varied. Most, however, share the traits common to centenarians who have been the subject of scientific research studies: having longevity in their families, keeping physically and mentally active, eating and drinking in moderation, maintaining an optimistic attitude, and developing successful coping skills to overcome life's vicissitudes. My personal observation is that many centenarians have an admirable ability to keep going, to reassess and cope with life at every turn despite their ever-increasing limitations and disabilities. They maintain a positive yet realistic outlook while reaffirming their desire to live and their love of life. In this remarkable *spirit* lives the common thread.

Through the stories and voices of the centenarians themselves, this book seeks to explore the characteristics and circumstances that help achieve a good quality of life for those who live long. It is a portrayal of the special qualities and contributions, and the special needs and problems, of the very old. It is not intended to be an academic or professional study about aging; nevertheless, I am grateful to those professionals who have reviewed my thoughts and supported my effort to bring these ideas to the attention of the general public. This is by no means a comprehensive analysis of all aspects of aging: rather, it is a look at those aspects most frequently mentioned by the centenarians themselves. Thus, it is a personal view compiled from the thoughts, feelings, and opinions of centenarians, from their families, friends, and caregivers, and from my own observations. Answers to what would most improve the quality of their lives today came from these personal sources: better vision, hearing, health, mobility, living conditions, increased socialization and companionship, and financial security. Taken together, these responses create the "Centenarian Wish List," a compendium that provided further impetus for this book.

The motivation for this work was to provide a forum for centenarians so their voices could be heard. As the book evolved, I realized that I was writing it for four audiences: first, the centenarians themselves, to give them and their families a connectedness with their peers. Second, those who are beginning or who are already in old age; my hope is that they will draw inspiration from today's centenarians as the possibility of living to a very advanced age becomes a closer reality. Centenarians are role models for all who will follow, but particularly for those nearer to them in age. The third audience is anyone with an elderly person in their lives, whether their relationship is close or distant, occasional or constant. For this audience, it is my hope that the book will be helpful in recognizing the needs and in improving the lives of their elders now. And last, but certainly not least, is everyone who would like to live to be 100. Hopefully, the models of centenarians here will give assurance that such longevity is becoming more possible and often desirable, as well as raise thought-provoking issues to be addressed for and by future centenarians.

This book is written in two parts: Part I, "Celebrating a Century of Life," introduces centenarians as individuals, and includes memories of their pasts and of life in America, along with the values and beliefs that were part of this life and that contribute to their spirit today. Part II, "The Challenges of Living to Be 100," focuses on their contemporary lives, their problems and their triumphs, and offers insights into the challenges of living long and the rewards.

Inherently, this book is the product of the centenarians who participated in this endeavor. It is their book and I am but the means through which their stories and ideas received expression; any errors in the book are my responsibility. The most rewarding personal experience of my involvement and interest in centenarians over the years is that now most of my best friends are 100 and over. I would like you, the reader, to get to know them, too.

❧

Acknowledgments

MANY people have contributed generously to this work. Foremost are the centenarians themselves, whose names appear in the Centenarian List, and their families and friends, who contributed invaluable material and insights. This assistance, which they were generous to give, greatly enlarged the horizons of this book.

I gratefully acknowledge the overall contribution of Paul Rousseau, M.D., Chief of Geriatrics, Hayden Veterans Medical Center, Phoenix, Arizona; the substantive contributions of Walter M. Bortz II, M.D., Palo Alto, California, one of the country's leading geriatric physicians, noted author and lecturer on healthy aging, and former president of the American Geriatrics Society; Rabbi Samuel Seicol, Chaplain at the Hebrew Rehabilitation Center for Aged in Boston, and Chairman Elect of the American Society on Aging Forum on Religion, Spirituality and Aging, for his contributions to chapter 6; John Boyer, M.D., Professor of Internal Medicine, University of Arizona, for his contribution to chapter 7; and Michael Baker, Ph.D., Executive Director of the Dorothy Garske Center, Phoenix, for his research assistance and consultation on chapters 7, 8, and 9.

I wish to express my appreciation to Jane Shure, Information Officer at the National Institute on Aging, for the opportunity to participate in the National Centenarian Day Salute in 1987 and for sharing data and statistics on centenarians from that project.

Reba Wells, Ph.D., oral historian, lent her expertise to the early chapters of this book, and Betsy May Stern contributed the quilting information and shared her knowledge of its importance in both the past and present.

I will never forget and could never repay Jean Still for her dedication to this project. Her outstanding work and her donation of hundreds of hours of word processing the numerous drafts of the manuscript are an invaluable gift. In addition, her husband, Jerry, contributed production help at their Kwik-Kopy center in Phoenix. Their friend, Janet Cool, quietly provided backup support by being what she is—a good neighbor.

I want to especially thank Frances Trout, who initially volunteered to address seasonal greeting cards and became so entranced by the centenarians that she stayed with the project for more than a year, helping to contact centenarians, interviewing a few of them in person and others over the telephone, and corresponding with their families. She was also of help with historical details and suggestions for chapters 3 and 4 of this book. Her contribution is very much appreciated.

I also want to thank Richard L. Stern for his thoughtful critique and enthusiastic support of the initial chapters and for his contribution over the years of newspaper clippings of interest, plus his informative commentary. His son, Andy, helped with the initial research and computer work in designing the national survey and accompanying letter to centenarians. Diane Retsin, Marjean Sessom, and Linda Machutas provided administrative help in the beginning stages of this work.

I am grateful to Mary Hawkins for reading the first draft manuscript and giving thoughtful suggestions based on her years of experience as an editor and her perspective as an octogenarian.

I further wish to thank the following people for reading and commenting on various parts of the manuscript: my friends, Karlene Wood, Ann Hofbauer Enyedy, and Margaret Powell, D.C. for their thoughts and encouragement; professionals Padraic T. Spence; Leonard W. Poon, Ph.D., Director of the Gerontology Center and Professor of Psychology at the University of Georgia, and Principal Investigator for the Georgia Centenarian Study; Robert Volz, M.D., Chief of Orthopedic Surgery, University of Arizona; Rick Weber, State of

Arizona Council for the Hearing Impaired; David Beard, Arizona Department of Economic Security, Services for the Blind and Visually Impaired; Maria Fiatarone, M.D., Human Nutrition Research Center on Aging, Tufts University, and Assistant Professor of Medicine at Harvard Medical School; Charlette R. Gallagher-Allred, Ph.D., R.D., Ross Laboratories; David Mitchell, Ph.D., Department of Psychology, Southern Methodist University; Jo Ann McConnell, Ph.D., Senior Vice President of Medical and Scientific Affairs at the Alzheimer's Association, and her predecessor, Creighton Phelps, Ph.D.; H. Latham Breunig, Ph.D., retired chemist and statistician and former member of the National Council on Disability; E. Kresent Thuringer, R.D., specializing in mature adults, Sun City, Arizona; Mary Lynn Kasunic, M.S., R.D., Executive Director, Arizona Area Agency on Aging, Region I. Families USA Foundation, Washington, D.C., a nonprofit organization dedicated to preserving and strengthening the security and dignity of older Americans, provided much of the income information and statistics.

Assistance in contacting centenarians came from many people. My aunt, Marion Peters Strickland, was a marvelous asset and a faithful and dedicated participant from the beginning of this project; she continued even while battling cancer. In what was to be our last telephone conversation, she enthusiastically told me of a woman in our hometown who was about to turn 100. Thus, in her memory, Edna Butler became a last-minute entry in this book.

Many state agencies on aging lent their assistance: especially Dena Zimmer of the Lincoln Area Agency on Aging, who single-handedly saw to it that Nebraska's centenarians were well represented in this project; Jean Marro of the Union Country Division on Aging in Elizabeth, New Jersey, who interviewed centenarians in her area; Randi Chergilia, and caseworkers in the Dennisport, Massachusetts, Council on Aging; and Kathi McDonnell-Bissell, M.S., Executive Director, Milford Elderly Services, Milford, Connecticut. Anita Mauldin and Mary and Jerry Casey helped with several initial mailings and follow-up of cards and letters.

Heidi Ross included me in the centenarian activities at Eden Hospital in Castro Valley, California, in 1989 and followed through to make me aware of several centenarians who, as a result of her interest in them, appear in this book. Lila Locksley, a writer and editor in New York City, who had contacted me regarding the centenarians in this book, unselfishly shared her follow up interviews in 1993 with several of the centenarians. Her sensitivity and understanding of the centenarians she met make her a young and true friend of her elders.

So many others, unfortunately too numerous to list here, deserve thanks for sending names, information, and for help in contacting centenarians—their kindness and interest is sincerely acknowledged. I especially want to thank the families of Clyde Ice, Ida Fox, Helen Gibson Cope, and Ted Gibson for their efforts and for their friendship; and Betty Nelson, friend of Hedvig Peterson; Dolly Stoppel, friend of Grace Northrup; Flora Frye, friend of Robert Cushman; Mrs. Phillip Hubbart, friend of Marjory Stoneman Douglas; Stephanie Dragovich, friend of Beatrice Wood; and Milton Feher, friend of Claire Willi. Also, the families of Viola Greenwald, Virginia Ortega, James Holy Eagle, Mary Gleason, Abe Goldberg, Sarah Wilson, Mr. and Mrs. Benjamin Pruitt, Hazel Herring, the Reverend Joseph Penn, Bertha Bliven, Addie Hutmacher, Viva Johnson, Nina Rust, Suzie Cook, Frances Campbell, Ward Nance, Tom Beston, Roger Warfield, Angelo Maltas, Anna King, Thomas Katsenes, Ollie Pike, Hazel Fergus and Edna Butler; and the wives of centenarians, Mrs. Frederick Steeves, Mrs. Frederick Pohl, Mrs. Harris Christopher, and Mrs. Harold Steele, and Mrs. Collister Wheeler, for their extra efforts. To the families of my longtime friends, Roy Miller, Alma Hauetter, Mary Ogburn, Mary Griswold, Hattie McGuire, Lizzie Davis, and Ola Canion, my appreciation has been longstanding.

With this specific acknowledgment for the assistance from family and friends, I do not mean to overlook the contributions from so many of the centenarians themselves, such as Mrs. Lynn Billy Earley, Dr. Michael Heidelberger, Dr. Helen Langner, Dr. Donald Warren, Rose Tackles, Elva Sholes, Tempa Robinson, Mabel Dudley, the Reverend David Moore, Oscar Wilmeth, John Langham, Richard Johnson, Myrtle Little. . .the list here could go on and on. I trust that the personal relationship and contributions from so very many of my centenarian friends will be evident in the book itself.

I wish to thank the following institutions for allowing me to use photographs and information on the centenarians they knew: Hebrew Rehabilitation Center for Aged, Boston, Massachusetts (Eva Akabas); Pennswood Village, Newtown, Pennsylvania (Mary Brown); Fairfield University (Eli Finn); New York University Medical Center (Michael Heidelberger, Ph.D.); Alta Bates-Herrick Hospital (Dr. Ernest Windesheim); University of Toronto (Selma Plaut); Yale University School of Medicine, Office of Public Information (Dr. Helen Langner), and Hunter College, Office of Alumni Affairs and The _Milford Citizen_ and _Connecticut Press_; Carlton College, Office of Alumni Affairs and (Grace Northrup) and the Northfield, Minnesota, Historical Society and the St. Paul Historical Society; _The Chicago Tribune_ (Adeline Moran and Mildred Rieger); _The Houston Herald_, Missouri (Mr. and Mrs. Frank Rowels); _People_ Magazine (Cloris Leachman and Arizona centenarians); and _The Arizona Republic_ and (Pearl Sprague, Hedvig Peterson); and the Arizona Press Women's Network.

I wish to thank the Honorable Terry Goddard, former Mayor of Phoenix, for his initial support and participation in the centenarian program and JoAnn Pedrick, Ph.D., former Executive Director of the Arizona Governor's Advisory Council on Aging also Congressman Sam Coppersmith's Arizona staff. Tina Romano, training resources officer at the Department of Economic Security, Office of Human Resources, took several of the photographs used in this book, along with many others over the years such as Laurette Alexander and Frank Balaam, at centenarian events. Tina's interest and personal contribution deserves special recognition.

I would be remiss if I did not include in this public acknowledgment the behind-the-scenes work of my parents, Evelyn and Frederick Peters, who have devoted their own retirement years to assisting me with my avocation from its inception. They are having, as a consequence, an active retirement, helping not only with this project but with all my numerous centenarian events since 1985. They have worked long hours—often seven days a week—doing whatever had to be done. On a daily basis, my mother helped run my household, frequently cooking dinner, doing the marketing and errands, and much more. She also answered the phones and helped a great deal with centenarian contacts and finding new centenarians. In addition, she read all the material contributed by and about centenarians and carefully recorded the information. She has kept in touch with and befriended centenarians and their families through letters, phone calls, and personal visits over all these years. My father has done much of the work with the numerous mailings throughout this time, and he helped and participated at the many events honoring centenarians in Arizona. During this book project itself, he was instrumental in reading and sorting hundreds of newspaper clippings and other materials on centenarians. One day he remarked, "I've only got twenty years to go and I can be one, too!" He compiled the entire initial mailing of the survey and accompanying materials by hand and continues to help with the numerous follow-up mailings. In addition, he helped with household chores, and he kept the papers generated by this project under control. In short, my parents freed me to devote my time and energies to this work. Their unselfish dedication and constant encouragement helped me further my goals; it is a life gift only parents can give. For them, too, this has been a labor of love and, moreover, a lasting legacy, more meaningful to me than any material gift.

If my parents have been the grease keeping the wheels turning then my husband, Jim, has been the steam driving the engine. Without his financial support for my avocation over these years, all of my activities would have been severely curtailed. He has been my coach, my supporter, my legal counsel, and my unofficial editor. He, too, has devoted his time and resources over the past many years to making my dream come true. Without his help and support, this, and my other volunteer centenarian projects, could not have continued, nor could this book have been published.

My brother, Brian Peters, is the last entry in a long list of supporters; his help and suggestions were just what were needed at just the right times.

I wish to thank Maria Karagianis and Jon Swan for their contributions in editing sections of the interim manuscript and for their helpful suggestions, and Cia Elkin for her copy editing assistance of the interim draft. The overall assistance of Karen Enyedy Breunig in research and drafting during the first and fundamental stage of this project is also much appreciated.

A special thanks goes to Patrick Barry of Fulton, New York, and his wife, Ruth, for their ongoing contact, interest, and helpful information and suggestions on centenarians in general.

Finally, I must thank my publishers, George and Kathleen Schwartz, for their belief in this work and for their understanding and forbearance when an automobile accident interrupted my progress and substantially delayed this publication. And to all my centenarian friends who participated in this work, especially Billy Earley, and their families, friends, and caregivers: Thank you for staying with me, for believing in me, for your continual encouragement, and for sharing with me your wisdom and philosophy—to persevere, to never give up, and to follow my heart.

ও Part I ও

Celebrating a Century of Life

Prelude

GRACE Sumner Northrup was the first centenarian I ever met. It was around six o'clock on an evening in mid-September 1985 when I walked into her room at the nursing home wing of the Sun Valley Lodge Retirement Center in Sun City, Arizona. Grace was sitting on the edge of her bed, waiting for me. I introduced myself. She invited me to be seated in a nearby chair. She asked me to sit in the light so she could see me better and sit near her so she could hear me better. I was immediately impressed by her demeanor and beauty. Grace was sitting very erect with her hands folded in her lap. Her voice was cordial yet formal, as though she were receiving a visitor in her home. Her white hair was coiffed in soft curls. Her smile was warm and lit up her face—her blue eyes were clear, alert, and interested. In short, to my amazement, she didn't look a day over eighty.

Explaining that I had come to invite her to a party in October to honor the eldest citizens of the Phoenix area, I handed her the printed invitation. She asked me to read it to her. When I finished, she carefully put the card on the table beside her, turned to me, and asked, "A party?" "Yes," I said eagerly, straightening in my chair and preparing to raise my voice to deliver my message about the event. I revealed how

I had come up with the idea as part of a larger reception, of which I was chairman, cosponsored by the Phoenix Mayor's Aging Services Commission and the Governor's Advisory Council on Aging. I described how the Mayor had approved of my concept to honor our eldest citizens; how he had given me permission to conduct this and future recognition programs for people of advanced age under his auspices; and how he would be there to greet our special guests and have his picture taken with them individually. I explained that I had arranged special transportation and special tables up front, away from the crowd; that there would be special soft food that could be eaten conveniently and volunteers to serve it—including Brownie's and Girl Scouts—so the honored guests wouldn't have to stand in a buffet line; how I would take very good care of them and give them my personal assurance that all would be provided for; that she could bring a guest to accompany her; that even the band, the Ink Spots, would be there to play music from the thirties and forties; and, finally, that the news media would be there to cover the event and feature it in local television and newspaper pictures and stories.

When I'd finished, exhilarated but out of breath, Grace looked up at me and said softly, "Why, my dear, I'd love to come. But, you see, I cannot."

Disappointment overcame me, and I fought to retain my composure. Were all the naysayers right who had said, "What do you want to be bothered with those old people for? What does it matter to them?" The words, repeated by many, had stung me whenever spoken and had always brought tears to my eyes. I was stung again now and fought back the tears. Many had said it was too much effort to make special arrangements for the very old and frail, some of whom were in wheelchairs or in nursing homes—"Let them stay there. Why try to bring them out?" was their rationale. I had been told that people of such advanced age would not be interested in participating in any such event except perhaps on a very limited scale, and then only within the security and confines of their nursing homes or with family members.

However, Grace continued, explaining, "I must decline because I have nothing to wear."

I wanted to laugh, to cry with joy, to hug her. I was ecstatic, for suddenly I realized that this dear little lady, who had lived 100 years, was just like me—one of the millions of women throughout time who have lamented not having something to wear for a special occasion. Grace was 100, but she was, first and last, a woman. It was not them (the elderly) and us (the younger generations). We were the same, only at different places on the continuum of life. Her first thought upon being invited as a guest of honor to this new Century Club party was so typically female—it had nothing to do with the naysaying!

I learned a lesson then that has served me well: In no real way—other than the number of years lived—does a centenarian differ from anyone else. And, in a sense, one's age is unimportant until one reaches 100. Then it becomes an honor, a distinction. "Centenarian" is a title, as is "Mr.," "Ms.," "Mrs.," "Doctor," or "Reverend." As with "M.D.," "J.D.," or "Ph.D.," it is a title of accomplishment. With Grace Northrup, the idea I had been working to promote—that many of our eldest citizens, centenarians along with those age eighty-five or older, can and want to remain participants in society—became a reality for me. This realization bolstered my determination to give this special group of people the positive recognition they deserved. Our eldest citizens have been part of the fiber and fabric of our country and have contributed much to its greatness. They should not be forgotten and discarded now, just because they have grown old.

A few minutes later, Grace and I stood in her small walk-in closet, searching fruitlessly for an appropriate dress for her to wear. When I suggested this one or that, her comment was "Why no, that's just a housedress." I finally gave up and agreed that she had nothing appropriate to wear. I empathized with her because I'd felt the same way hundreds of times myself. I then asked Grace what kind and color dress she would like to wear if she had a choice (having already checked her size on the other dresses in her closet). I decided to go to a local dress shop, buy one for her, and have it sent to the nursing home anonymously; but while I was distracted with that thought, Grace, tackling the problem herself, came up with the solution: she would borrow one of the outfits she had given away.

That hurdle crossed, we settled down to visit for another hour. I learned that Grace Sumner had been born on May 14, 1885, and raised in Northfield, Minnesota, one of four children. She could trace her ancestors back to 1632. Her older brother had been "struck down with the deadly influenza epidemic of 1918, long before the wonderful lifesaving use of antibiotics became common."

Grace spoke fondly of growing up in the college town of Northfield, where her father was the town photographer, and of the cultural and intellectual advantages she had that she might not have experienced in another setting; the house she was raised in is now Summer Residence Hall, a part of the Carleton College campus. Grace graduated from Northfield High School in 1904 and from Carleton College in 1908. (I mentioned that although I had never been to Minnesota myself, my husband was also a graduate of Carleton College.) After graduating from college, Grace taught high school English in the nearby town of Mankato for a number of years. She met her husband there; Charles was a plumbing contractor. They were married in Grace's family home in 1913. She took an album from her bedside drawer and carefully removed a fragile, yellowed clipping dated July 4, 1913. In the dim light of her bedside lamp, we bent our heads, more than half a century apart in thought and experience, as I read aloud from the clipping that Miss Grace Sumner was married in a "simple but impressive" service in her family home. The ceremony was held in front of a "bower of white flowers and masses of foliage." In her cultured voice, Grace added some of the details of that special day and of her courtship in the early part of this century. She seemed to enjoy reminiscing and would laugh softly at some points in her own story. How appropriately Grace was named, I thought. The newspaper account of her wedding aptly characterized this lovely lady—simply elegant, with grace and beauty and dignity.

As we sat together, I had the feeling there was no distance between us. I was touched by a sense of oneness with her. At that moment Tennyson's well-known phrase, "I am a part of all that I have met," came to mind. I felt enriched by having met Grace Northrup and I looked forward to meeting more, many more, centenarians.

My husband, Jim, asked where I had been when I arrived home.
"Visiting with a Carleton alum of yours," I answered.
"Oh, really?" he said, interested. "What year?"
"A little before your time," I replied, "1908."

In subsequent visits with Grace and other centenarians, I began to have a greater appreciation of how far back in time 100 years of memories spans; I began also to develop a greater appreciation of the special qualities, the special needs and problems, and, above all, the special spirit of America's eldest citizens.

 ❧ *Lynn Peters Adler and Grace Sumner Northrup at the party;*
Grace was the first guest to arrive. Photo courtesy of the Arizona Governor's
Advisory Council on Aging. Photograph by Laurette Alexander.

❧ 1 ❧

Centenarian Voice

❧ AMERICANS have been fascinated by longevity ever since learning of Ponce de León's search in Florida, five centuries ago, for the fountain of youth. In this century, the search for longevity, and the good health that makes it possible, has been enhanced by discoveries such as antibiotics and other lifesaving drugs, heroic medical interventions, which include organ transplants, heart pacemakers and other life-prolonging devices, the emergence of preventive medicine, and a new focus on wellness. On an individual level, people are realizing that, to an ever-increasing extent, they are able to influence life-style factors that can lead to a healthier and longer life—perhaps even a life of 100 years or more.

Until recently, living to 100 was considered a rare phenomenon. Within the past few years, however, with several hundred people reaching the century mark each month, scientists and laypeople alike are beginning to look upon these oldest of the old as beacons guiding us to a new, longer lived age—possibly, the Age of Centenarians.

Moving toward the twenty-first century, this philosophy is within our grasp. As people live longer, America's concept of what it means to be old and the age at which one becomes old are changing. Members of the youth culture, which dominated our society during the 1960s and 1970s, saw age thirty as the beginning of the end of life and enjoyment. During the 1980s, forty was considered "over the hill." For the 1990s, there are sure signs that the "hill" is being pushed to age fifty and beyond, and with it the idea of middle age. Advertisements are portraying people at or nearing fifty as approaching the prime time of life.

Those in the generation ahead of them are also making their mark. In the media, people in their sixties are being depicted as enjoying life, taking care of their health, and looking forward to their later years. Films, often an indicator of society's taste and trends, have created new roles for entertainers in their seventies and eighties. With this has come the success of movies such as *On Golden Pond* (1981), starring Katharine Hepburn and Henry Fonda; *Cocoon* (1985) starring Wilford Brimley, Hume Cronyn, Jack Gilford, and Don Ameche in his Oscar-winning performance for Best Supporting Actor; and *Driving Miss Daisy* (1989), starring Jessica Tandy in her Oscar-winning performance as Best Actress, in addition, *Fried Green Tomatoes* (1992); and *Grumpy Old Men* (1993) starring Walter Matheau and Jack Lemon. Entertainer Bob Hope, who is over ninety, has continued to perform in television specials and to participate in golf tournaments. George Burns, at ninety-eight, has announced his intention to perform at Caesar's Place in Las Vegas for his 100th birthday. And at the 1991 Academy Award presentations, millions of viewers watched as 100-year-old producer/director Hal Roach was honored. There's no doubt about it—the trend is forming: Old age isn't what it used to be. Active aging is in!

We laud those now at the pinnacle of old age—centenarians—who have lived to celebrate 100 years or more. Today's centenarians are the survivors of a generation born in the 1880s and 1890s. The 1990 census counted 37,306 centenarians, 29,405 of them women. Over the past ten years, their numbers have doubled making centenarians the most rapidly growing age group within the fastest-growing segment of the United States population—those eighty-five and over. Some estimates place the number of centenarians today at 45,000, a number predicted to continue to increase dramatically in the near future, to 108,000 centenarians by the turn of the century and to 400,000 by the year 2025. Worldwide, by the year 2000, it is anticipated that there will be more than one million centenarians.

This is just the tip of the aging iceberg. The number of people living into their eighties and nineties is expected to increase dramatically as well. In fact, there are such great numbers of Americans living beyond what was once considered old age (sixty-five) that some sociologists have begun to delineate three tiers of aging: the young, the middle, and the old of "old age." French philosopher Simone de Beauvoir has artfully renamed old age "the third age." Her characterization seems to fit the demographics today. Adding to this, Betty Friedan, at seventy-two, has published *The Fountain of Age* (1993) to "unmask the mystique of aging." Ms. Friedan predicts a new movement in America "that will use the wisdom and resources of older women and men who by the year 2000 will be the dominant population group."

To be sure, the long-held stereotype of advanced age as a period of decrepitude and disinterest in life is breaking down. This stereotype is as obsolete as is the arbitrary age of sixty-five for the time in life when people become, or are considered, old. Centenarians are playing an important part in bringing about this change in attitude about the aging process and about what life can be like in old age: They are the vanguard of aging and highlight its future. As many centenarians you are about to meet in this book demonstrate, not only are people living longer, but they also are remaining physically active and mentally alert while retaining an interest in life into very great ages.

By their examples, centenarians are showing us what is possible, and what can be realized, if one not only lives long but ages well. Interestingly, many centenarians say they don't feel old—that age is, in large part, a state of mind. Underscoring this thought is the Reverend Roy Miller of Glendale, Arizona, who at 101 often remarked that he did not feel his age. The phrase "young at heart" readily comes to mind in the company of centenarians such as Roy, who was fond of saying "when someone says 'Go,' I'm ready."

On a more serious note, he often expressed his gratitude for the extra years, beyond the biblical "three score and ten, or fourscore" (seventy or eighty years, respectively; Psalm 90:10) that he was given to live, a sentiment shared by so many of his peers.

Moreover, like many of his peers, Roy did not look his age. This sounds humorous when speaking of a person who has lived so long, yet it is startling to see how good one can look after 100 years of living. "Keeping active definitely improves the way you look and feel," Roy advised, "and makes life merry."

❧ Roy Miller, Governor's Cup Walk, 1987. Photo courtesy of the Dorothy Garske Center, Phoenix, Arizona. Photograph by Don B. Stevenson.

Mrs. Lynn Billy Earley of Florence Arizona, has as her motto, "105 and still alive!" Born in New York City on December 10, 1888, Billy says, "There may be old men and women out there, but I'm not one of them." As a friend observed, "Billy takes care of her health. She goes to the doctor whenever necessary and to the dentist regularly; she takes care of her skin and everything!"

Billy appears frequently as a mentor throughout the pages of this book. Anyone who meets her remembers her indomitable spirit, lively sense of humor, and *joie de vivre*. "I refuse to let anything be a problem," she says affably. Yet, like many centenarians, Billy enjoys good general health but has one of the common physical impairments of advanced

✿ *Billy Earley, January 1993, in Washington, D.C., at*
Senator Dennis DeConcini's desk (D-AZ). Photo courtesy of Billy Earley.

age, near blindness. Nevertheless, she relishes life and stays active, both at home and on her frequent travels—most notably traveling to Hawaii in 1992 to attend the Pearl Harbor anniversary ceremonies and to Washington D.C. in 1993 to attend the presidential inauguration, including several of the receptions. In the spring of 1994, she visited Graceland and is headed next to New York City "because I want to see Greenwich Village again. I love Arizona, but I miss New York." Sharing her recollections of Greenwich Village eight decades ago, Billy adds "I'm a Greenwich Village person."

Unfortunately, not everyone ages well or ages evenly. For some, physical energy and mobility are diminished or impaired while they remain mentally sound. As 100-year-old Elizabeth Paukert of Faribault, Minnesota, tells: "I admire the other centenarians I read about in the newspaper and see on television who can get out to events and do things—I would like to very much. But I try to stay as active as I can, even with my [mobility] limitations. I belong to a volunteer network of other shut-ins through my church and I call people each day. I watch a lot of television and read the newspapers so I can keep track of what's going on in the world. Mentally, I'm very alert and I enjoy being with people; I would love it if I could get around." Aware of the importance of keeping their minds active, many others read newspapers, watch television news and programs, and do crossword puzzles. Some, such as Helen Gibson Cope, who remains both physically and mentally active, enjoy playing word games, especially Scrabble. "She still beats me," Helen's son-in-law and frequent opponent reports.

Then there are thousands of centenarians and others of advanced age who are in good physical health while suffering from debilitating mental diseases, such as Alzheimer's. One recent study suggests that the numbers of those afflicted with Alzheimer's disease are much higher than previously thought. For the eighty-five and over age group, nearly half may be suffering from this irreversible disease, which strikes most often in later years. Some centenarians suffer from other forms of memory loss and dementia, as well as from physical decline. "It appears that marked physical and mental decline is typical of the majority of centenarians," states Erdmore Palmore, Ph.D., in *The Encyclopedia of Aging* (1987), "but there are many exceptions, and many manage to remain alert and positive toward life, despite their [physical] declines."

Oscar Wilmeth of Phoenix, Arizona, is one of the many exceptions. At 102, he counseled: "You need to be open to learning new things. Most of all be optimistic—that's the most important thing. The trick [to life] is all in how you look at it."

From the examples of centenarians' daily lives we can redefine our own ideas about aging, both good and bad, and bad news heard early enough can be turned into good news. This heightened awareness can help shape the way we age and the way we live in our later years. As Walter M. Bortz II, M.D., one of the country's leading geriatric physicians, past president of the American Geriatric Society, noted lecturer on healthy aging, and author of *We Live Too Short and Die Too Long, How to Achieve and Enjoy Your Natural 100-Year-Plus Life Span*, states, ". . .the health of an older person is inextricably linked to the society in which they are aging. Medicine is a social science as well as a biologic one. The two interact intimately." In his opinion, "Until now, nearly everything we thought we knew about aging was wrong. Centenarians are an important part of establishing our true definitions; they are the evidence."

The active centenarians in this book are inspirations for all who wish

to live life to the fullest extent. They are our role models. The knowledge they possess is a tremendous resource. Centenarians know
things others do not. No one else knows what it is like to live so long;
they are the true experts. Others can speculate, researchers can study,
but a centenarian knows for sure, from experience. In order to discover
this knowledge, which they are most willing to share, we need to look
at what they are doing now and how they have lived in the past. Centenarians can be consulted about the aging process and how to cope
with it successfully.

The experiences of these survivors give hope and direction for our
future. They offer us encouragement. Centenarians instruct us to take
better care of ourselves and our health while we still have the chance.
For those who are interested in living longer, healthier lives, this book
contains examples of some who have achieved that goal. Most centenarians do not speculate in a serious way on the secret of their
longevity—they accept it as a gift from God or as a mystery of life. As
Billy Earley says, "You start with what you inherited and the rest is up
to you." Centenarian Dr. Ernest Windesheim concurs: "It's a matter of
good genes and healthful living." Mary Gleason adds with a twinkle
in her eye, "And a bit o'luck!"

Certainly, heredity plays a significant role. Most centenarians, but
not all, say either one or both of their parents lived to a "ripe old age"
for their generation. But then, they wonder, "Why me?" Of several
siblings in the typical centenarian's family, often there is only one to
survive to the century mark.

Longevity studies, by a number of scientific researchers and medical
doctors, list factors that appear to contribute to long life, such as a
favorable genetic makeup, simple diets with little animal fat, moderation in the use of tobacco and alcohol, physical activity, and a positive mental attitude. However, some centenarians have smoked for
decades and some have been overweight. Yet most share the basic
advice given by Eli Finn, 102, of Norwalk, Connecticut for anyone
wanting to live long: "Eat the right food, exercise, and remain mentally
curious."

In general, no particular ethnic group or nationality appears to have
a monopoly on reaching 100. There have been reports over the years
of so-called "pockets of centenarians" in certain parts of the world,
such as Soviet Georgia and Tibet. There, it has been said, the clean air
and low-fat diet promote longevity and result in greater numbers living

to 100. However, this claim is controversial. Centenarians in America live in all kinds of environments. Some live in the clean air of the Rocky Mountains. Others have survived 100 years in New York City.

Centenarians come from all walks of life. There are doctors, lawyers, clergymen, rabbis, farmers, entrepreneurs, factory workers, home-makers, teachers, nurses, nuns, aviators, and artists, to name a few. Some have lived their lives in the public eye, such as Rose Kennedy and George Abbott.

Most have lived private lives. Centenarians can be found in every area of the country—there is probably a centenarian living near you.

Concurrent with today's focus on longevity must come a concern for the quality of life in advanced age. What lies in store for people who live long lives? What will give enjoyment and meaning to added years? How can health and vitality be sustained? What can be done to achieve an acceptable life-style as increasing numbers join the ranks of the third age? These are necessary questions society must ask and then answer.

By looking at centenarians both individually and as a group, questions about the quality of life in advanced age are explored. Here, in this book, the centenarians themselves speak. This communication is a beginning and provides some insights into the answers. What centenarians have to say may be surprising.

The centenarian responses dispel some of the myths about the very old. To begin, contrary to one popular perception of old people, most centenarians neither yearn for the past nor live in the past. Most are oriented in the present, and while they appreciate aspects of life that they believe were better years ago, such as more time for socializing, neighborliness, companionship, and the absence of pervasive crime, violence, and drugs, these are the same conditions that people of every age would like to see changed about modern life.

"In the old days you had time, neighbors and family who cared for each other, and a greater sense of community," explained Mary Ogburn, 105. "Some things were better. But all in all, I like the new days best." Adds the Reverend Joseph Penn, 103, "Every day is a good day." This contemporaneity of today's eldest citizens is amazing. For instance, Lu Lu Doran, 105, who recalls the many years of cooking on the family's wood stove in Nebraska as she was growing up, comments on how much she enjoys the convenience of her microwave oven. Billy Earley's favorite gift on her 100th birthday was a cordless phone: "I can take it around the house with me," she says. "Everybody should have one of these."

Another surprising fact is the number of centenarians who are living independently; it is estimated that approximately one-quarter live alone, dispelling the view that nearly everyone of advanced age is institutionalized in a nursing home. As Agnes McDonald, 102, of Bridgeport, Connecticut, says, "I live alone and like it." More often than not, though, they live with family members. Also surprising was the number of men who had remarried in their mid-eighties, usually to "younger women," fifteen to twenty years their junior.

The centenarians in this book are a diverse group of individuals. Though they come from varied backgrounds and geographic areas and represent a wide variety of incomes and occupations, a common denominator among them is a history of hard work. Most believe that "hard work never hurt anybody" and report that they have done plenty of it. Another common denominator seems to be their individualism and a strong sense of self. This self-determination, they say, has helped them get through hard times and heartbreak, the losses of family and friends, and even illnesses that threatened to shorten their lives. Looking at it from their perspective, the ability to cope with losses, to remain optimistic and determined, and to renegotiate life at every turn, is a powerful life force.

Perhaps most surprising of all is the love of life, interest in living, and sense of fun so many express, even at the pinnacle of old age. These life-affirming attributes reverberate throughout the collective centenarian voice in the survey that was the cornerstone of this book (see Preface): "I enjoyed answering these questions and the memories they called forth." "I enjoy every day of my life." "I get up in the morning happy." "I'm never bored." "I love to laugh." "This was fun."

It is this sense of fun and love of life that form an essential part of the centenarian *spirit*, a spirit that leads contemporary centenarians to share the sentiment of Cora Belle Gilland, a Wyoming pioneer and mother of centenarian Ida Fox, who passed on this wisdom in her diary:

> *Age is the top of the mountain*
> *Nearer the sky so blue*
> *A long hard climb*
> *A bit of fatigue*
> *But oh—what a*
> *wonderful view!*

Today people are beginning to think about the possibility of living to be 100 years old. There are many books being written giving medical and dietary advice on how to do so. Newspaper articles regularly carry stories of centenarians on their birthdays, and of course, to his credit, weatherman Willard Scott has made the celebration of centenarians a daily event on national television. An Associated Press article, which ran near the end of 1991, reported that in a survey conducted for the Alliance for Aging Research, "most Americans questioned. . . said they want to live 100 years."

And yet, what do we know of what life is like at the century mark? What do we know of the problems, the challenges to getting there, and the obstacles that make so few able to achieve this goal at present? How do we know what needs to be improved to make survival more of a probability? Are Americans who think they would like to live to be 100 also thinking about the quality of those extra years beyond eighty, the bonus years, so to speak, and what needs to go into planning for such a possibility?

Beyond health and medical technology, is society ready for legions of people living to a very advanced age? And, finally, what kind of a welcome will our nation's elders receive from younger generations?

In this book, centenarians themselves tell what it is really like at the top, as well as along the way to getting there. The answers to the questions that need to be asked come from these experts; centenarians tell us what is good and what is not. For the rest of us—future centenarians—we have time to plan, to prepare, and to work to bring about the changes that will make the world of people of advanced age better for our future. Starting now.

As Billy Earley comments, "People say to me all the time 'Oh, I want to live to be 100, too.' But they don't have a clue what that means."

Listen, then, to what our elders have to say about what would improve the quality of life in the advanced years to which we aspire. They tell us what is needed from medicine, from research, from individuals, from society, and from ourselves, in order to make our lives at 100 plus, and the years leading up to the century mark, the best that they can be.

                                                               ❧

❧ 2 ❧

The Pinnacle of the Third Age

LIVING at the pinnacle of old age, centenarians can enjoy an unmatched view of life both past and present. Several thousand Americans have childhood memories that reach back to the 1890s and the beginning of this century. These time travelers recall childhood chores that included chopping wood for cooking and heating and cleaning the chimneys of kerosene lamps used for light. A horse and buggy was their transportation as teenagers or they walked, often many miles; long skirts and petticoats were the fashion for ladies, who also dressed "properly" for swimming, in long, heavy suits.

They vividly recall the major events and practical inventions from the early decades of this century. They were glad when they could "just push a button for lights and didn't have to clean the dirty chimneys," and they watched with fascination the development of aviation, starting with the Wright brothers' first flight in 1903. Several centenarians took their first airplane rides at state fairs in biplanes, a popular attraction, in the early 1920s. They recall the invention of the radio in 1906 and the early homemade crystal sets. Women report that, to them, the washing machine was the most valued labor saving invention of this century.

In 1913, motion pictures began with silent films. Live music was provided in the theaters; several women centenarians played the piano as accompaniment to Charlie Chaplin movies and many others. By the middle of the first decade, the availability of telephones increased communication, and some centenarians tell of their first automobile rides. A few are veterans of World War I, and all recall the deadly flu epidemic of 1918 that claimed more lives than were lost in the war.

In 1920, women gained the right to vote, a change most centenarians, but not all, favored. Eventually, those who resisted or disapproved of the change were won over to the idea. The introduction of penicillin in 1929 would help cut the mortality rate and contribute to longer life expectancy when it became widely available after World War II. Also beginning in 1929, the Great Depression is indelibly etched in the memories of their generation; centenarians hope and pray that such hard times will never again be experienced by Americans.

In 1930, the first television was introduced, but it was not until after World War II that it became widely affordable, they say. Many lost sons during the war and some of the women went to work outside their homes for the first time since World War I. By 1950, Americans were becoming more mobile. Several centenarians tell of their first commercial airline passenger trip, often to visit their children living in other parts of the country. Incidentally, the rock 'n' roll music introduced around 1955 has recently become a favorite of some oldsters because they can hear it better than that of the crooners of earlier times. Many centenarians were approaching the retirement age of sixty-five when the space program began in the early 1960s, and watched with amazement as the first manned space flight went up in 1961 and the first American orbited the earth in 1962.

By the mid-sixties, when Dr. Martin Luther King, Jr. received the Nobel Prize, centenarians were observing the beginnings of another era of social change. Later they applauded the 1969 moon walk, recalling the days when the moon was just a romantic image to them; but the young women wearing bikinis, miniskirts, and flowers in their hair received mixed reviews.

Whether they were for or against the suffragette movement of their youth, by 1970 most women agreed that equality of the sexes was a good idea. They watched with Deja Vu, this time on television, as thousands of women paraded on New York's Fifth Avenue celebrating fifty years of voting and urging passage of the Equal Rights Amendment.

In 1976, as America celebrated its 200th birthday, today's centenarians were approaching their ninth decade. By the 1980s, many caught on to the trend of using high technology inventions, such as microwave ovens and personal computers. They also witnessed the advent of high technology in the medical field. Many centenarians have benefitted from advanced medical technology, and they are glad to have these "modern miracles" available.

In 1986, one centenarian was invited to the 100th birthday celebration of the Statue of Liberty to represent all 100-year-olds that year, many of whom were greeted by the "great lady" as they came to America. In 1987, the ranks of centenarians had increased to such a significant population that President Ronald Reagan proclaimed July 1st as National Centenarians' Day. Subsequently, many more states began programs to identify and honor their eldest citizens and to include them in state and local celebrations.

Many of those reaching the century mark in recent years are pleased to have their birthdays announced on national television; newspapers, too, regularly include the comings and goings of today's eldest. Looking back over it all, centenarians are very much a part of American life.

The following stories of four centenarians illustrate the role historical developments played in their lives and also their remarkable involvement and sustained interest in contemporary life. Clyde Ice, Ted Gibson, Helen Gibson Cope, and Hedvig Peterson, as they celebrate reaching the century mark, present a picture of what life can be like at the top.

·⁊·

FLYING HIGH AT 100: CLYDE ICE

On his 100th birthday, Clyde Ice of Spearfish, South Dakota, celebrated by doing what he liked best—flying. In preparation, Clyde, who taught himself to fly in 1919, requested a special flight check from the Federal Aviation Administration (FAA). He chose as his copilot a former student whom he had taught to fly in 1939, when he took over as manager/owner of the Black Hills Airport and Flight School in Spearfish. The plane he chose for his centennial flight on May 28, 1989, was a restored 1940 J-3 Piper Cub trainer he had sold to this student in 1941. "The old J-3 flew as good as when I had last flown her forty-eight years ago," Clyde remarked. Apparently, Clyde did all right, too, even though he hadn't been at the controls for nine years. The FAA instructor passed him. "He got out, the co-pilot got in, and we went right up," Clyde recalls.

Following his celebration flight, Clyde went directly to the local Holiday Inn for his birthday party, where, seated on a stool, he personally greeted each of his 376 guests. The day's events mirror something of Clyde's vigor and charisma, along with the gusto with which he has lived his life.

Aviation has played a central role in Clyde's life and he instilled his love of flying in his four sons, all of whom made it part of their careers. He taught them to fly, and today he and his three surviving sons are known, affectionately, as "the Flying Ices." He also taught his daughter, Ginny, but much to his dismay, she did not share his enthusiasm. Clyde made up for this, though, by taking her son flying from an early age. His grandson went on to become a U.S. Air Force pilot.

Over the years, Clyde's love of flying has not waned, nor have his memories of the planes he's flown, the places he's been, and the experiences he's had. While growing up on a farm, Clyde first dreamed of being able to fly. "I used to watch the birds flying and gliding overhead, and I envied their freedom," he recalls. "I wished that someday I could do that." He paid keen attention to early-day pilots and followed their careers with interest, especially the barnstormers who would give rides at local fairs and perform wing walking and other stunts. As Clyde tells it, this is how he met up with his first airplane: "I never had a lesson—I had a couple of rides with a barnstormer, and that's all." After those rides, and the realization that the man was making as much as $100 a day in 1919, Clyde, who was selling insurance and cars at the time, decided his dream of freedom in the air could pay off financially as well. "I figured I could do it, too," he says. So he invested his savings in a slightly damaged army surplus Jenny, which he repaired. "When the fellow who was supposed to teach me to fly it didn't show up, I got in and figured it out for myself by moving the control stick back and forth and trying a few things. I flew it home, then and there."

His first wife, the mother of his four sons, didn't approve of his flying, and they were divorced when the children were still young. In 1929, Clyde remarried. Audrey, a schoolteacher, "traveled the country with him in his plane for about eight years before settling down to raise me," says Ginny. Adds Mrs. Ice, "It was fun for a while, but then I got tired of it—always being on the move. Clyde was a very safe pilot and I was never afraid."

During World War II, Clyde taught 2,000 U.S. Army Air Corps cadets to fly. At the beginning, he recalls, he even housed them and fed them. "I'd go into the Wyoming woods just over the border from the airport to shoot moose and elk." After giving the boys flying lessons all day, Clyde would cook moose and elk steaks for his students for dinner.

Clyde's flying career—which began as a barnstormer with his first plane, and including doing stunts, aerobatics, and wing walking, then continued as an airline pilot for Western Airlines' airmail route, and later as a charter pilot and instructor, and owner of a small airport—ended as a crop duster.

At eighty-three Clyde gave up crop dusting because, he says, "I was tired of getting up at four in the morning" and also because his feet were giving him trouble—poor circulation causing them to fall asleep. "I had to keep waking my feet up in order to land," he jokes ruefully. At age ninety-one, Clyde gave up flying altogether because of failing eyesight, but since then a cataract operation has corrected his vision. "My blood pressure is 120/67," he adds proudly—"It doesn't bother me at all to fly."

ᶘ *Clyde Ice after a flight on his 100th birthday, 1989. Photo courtesy of the Ice family.*

Off to a good start, Clyde's centennial year continued to be busy and active. He planted his usual large garden, selling beans and peas and other vegetables to nearby stores and preparing canned tomatoes for his family and neighbors. For the past many summers, Clyde has lived alone on his farm near the Black Hills airport. The quiet farm life, which he has always enjoyed in between his flying, was interrupted once again that fall with special flying events, this time in tribute to the pioneer aviator.

In September, Clyde flew with two of his sons to Reno, Nevada, for "Clyde Ice Day" at the large Reno air show. Later, he went for a ride with famous stunt pilot Bob Hoover. Still later that evening, "the Flying Ices" flew back to South Dakota in time for Clyde to appear at the state's Centennial Celebration. "We stopped once in Rapid City for gas and took right off again," said his son, Howard, who was piloting the plane. "We landed in Sioux City and Dad got to bed at three-thirty a.m.; he was up again at eight and ready to go to the ceremony where he was being honored as a South Dakota pioneer." What made the event so special was the attendance of President George Bush, who personally greeted each of the pioneers on stage. "I didn't want to miss that," Clyde added. "I think he's the greatest."

The paths of President Bush and Clyde Ice crossed again the following month when both were honored for their heroism and bravery as aviators at an invocation ceremony of the International Forest of Friendship in Atchinson, Kansas. This time Clyde and his three sons flew down in their twin engine Comanche for the impressive ceremony. President Bush was honored for his heroism as a World War II fighter pilot. Clyde was honored for his many decades of service as an aviator who had logged more than 40,000 hours of flight with a perfect safety record; for the hundreds of rescues and mercy missions he had flown; and for his contribution to the war effort, training army pilots. It is said of Clyde that throughout his life, he never refused requests to fly rescue missions for sick or injured people, and he would find the time to make food drops for snowbound people, and even for animals.

An unassuming man, Clyde shrugs off most of his daring rescues as things "any good pilot could do," calling his emergency missions "just plain old good neighbor deeds if an airplane was needed." There are two things about his flying career, however, in which he does take great pride. The first is his perfect flying record for what he calls "safe and sane" flying. "I never spilled a drop of blood; I never had an acci-

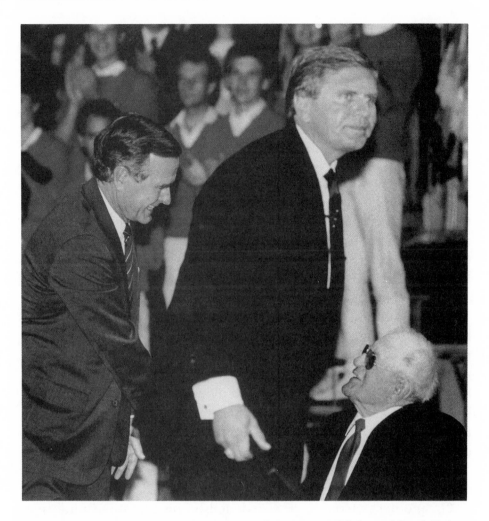

✺ *Clyde Ice at 100 with President Bush and Governor Nickelson of South Dakota at the state's centennial celebration, 1989. Photo courtesy of the Ice family and the South Dakota State Historical Society-State Archives.*

dent," he tells. The second source of pride is a rescue mission even Clyde admits no other pilot without his experience and knowledge of the terrain could have completed successfully (and which no one else in the area would attempt because of the personal danger involved).

Clyde modestly downplays the danger and the personal tragedy he was suffering at that time. He does not dwell on the irony that he was called upon to rescue two lives during one of the worst blizzards in South Dakota's history on the very day he was to bury his son and daughter-in-law, who were killed while attempting to land an airmail plane in the storm. It makes one wonder, was it a coincidence that the plane Clyde chose for his 100th birthday flight is the same model he flew during his proudest hour? Clyde does not venture an answer. He tells the story.

It was March 1947. A young ranchwoman had given birth prematurely in an isolated area 125 miles from Spearfish. The doctor could not reach her except by air, and no pilot, except Clyde, would attempt to fly. Without medical attention, it was likely both mother and child would die. "I realized I had to do it," Clyde says. "We took off at dawn." The wind was fierce, swirling the snow and buffeting the plane. "I couldn't see a thing," he recalls. "It was a total whiteout. I had nothing but my senses to rely on and my knowledge of the terrain. I knew the ranch and flew low to pick out landmarks. All the while, the wind threw the little J-3 around."

Clyde finally made a harrowing landing on a ridge near the ranch. "They [the ranchers] had to hold the plane down to keep us from being blown off the edge," Clyde tells. The doctor did what he could for the mother. Then with the tiny infant, "no bigger than a small jackrabbit," wrapped in a blanket, Clyde made the return flight to Spearfish, which he remembers as even more difficult than getting to the ranch. "My son Howard was waiting for us at the airport." Again, the plane had to be held down to keep from blowing over. "Doc took the baby to the hospital and we went to the funeral. The miracle is that baby survived. Today she has three children of her own. She sends me pictures of herself and her family from time to time and a birthday card each year."

On another personal note, Clyde tells of his pleasure in meeting fellow centenarian James Holy Eagle, a Lakota Sioux, at one of the South Dakota Centennial events in May 1989. It was an air show, at Ellsworth Air Force Base in Rapid City, where Chief Holy Eagle lives. Clyde was honored at the celebration by having the Number Five hanger named after him. "I'd never met Holy Eagle before," Clyde says, "but I had heard a lot about him over the years...I was friends with many members of the Lakota Sioux tribe, but Holy Eagle had moved away as a young man to go to college in the East, and then he lived in California for a long time, so he wasn't around much when I was. I was real pleased to meet him. He is a fine man."

Later that year, Clyde returned to Pinedale, Wyoming, near the South Dakota border, to spend the winter with his wife at their home near daughter Ginny and her husband. For years, Clyde had hunted

❧ *Clyde Ice with moose on hunting trip. Photo courtesy of the Ice family.*

in this area, but he hadn't hunted for moose in a long time. Deciding he wanted to continue his 100th-year celebration doing more of the things he loved, Clyde applied for a moose hunting permit. However, state officials sent back his application, saying the birth date must be wrong. One of Clyde's sons went to the capitol himself, explaining that the date was correct, 1889, and that his father wanted to go moose hunting. The application was refused because of his age. Clyde was finally able to get a permit by petitioning the governor's office for one of the five discretionary permits the governor is empowered to award each year.

As soon as Clyde received it, he set off with his sons on a hunting trip. The first day Clyde "bagged a moose with one shot from a

30C H&H (Holland and Holland) game rifle." The following day, he "bagged a three-point buck deer" the same way. During the winter, Clyde says he also enjoys tamer activities, such as reading and ice fishing.

Clyde's summer farmhouse is seven years older than he is. "I bought it in 1950," he tells, "to make a home for my elderly mother and aunt nearby." The farmhouse is within sight of "Clyde Ice Field" across Interstate 90 at the Spearfish airport. The small rooms are jammed with memorabilia, the artifacts of Clyde's life, leaving little space to move around. The walls are covered with dozens of plaques and certificates and citations: from the Flight Safety Foundation, a Certificate of Recognition (1969) for fifty years of safe flight; from the South Dakota Aviation Association (1982) for outstanding service; from the National Aeronautic Association (1969) a certificate of appreciation; an Honorary Military Airlife Award; South Dakota Transportation Hall of Honor (1983) to the "Patriarch of South Dakota Aviation"; the High Plains Aviation Award; the OX5 Aviation Pioneers Hall of Fame; and the South Dakota Cowboy and Western Heritage Hall of Fame, to name a few.

There are framed letters of recognition, too, and pictures and newspaper articles. One, a full front page from the *Sioux City Journal* in 1928, shows Clyde's favorite plane, a Ford TriMotor, he bought new that year. The caption reads, "Giant 15 passenger TriMotor lands here; huge ship is making a 12-month tour of the United States...and a new era unfolds in South Dakota." Clyde tells of how people would stand in line for hours to take a ten- to fifteen-minute ride. He believes this plane was the first of its kind to carry passengers and that he was the only pilot at that time to take up as many as five hundred in one day.

Clyde Ice was one of aviation's pioneers who shaped the post-World War I era, and his memory for details is impressive. He even remembers the serial number of the plane named "Wamblee Ohanka," Blackfoot for "Swift Eagle." Clyde smiles as he recalls the day his plane was blessed by the tribe's medicine man while on his tour that year. "They made me an honorary member of the tribe, naming me 'Chief Eagle Flies Against the Wind.' Then they all wanted to go for a ride. I made three or four trips—there were forty-three of them in all—and the medicine man had to go along each time."

It would take an entire book to capture the accomplishments and adventures stored in Clyde's memory and evidenced by the plaques

*❧ August 1928, Clyde Ice is named ''Chief Eagle Flys Against the Wind''
by the Black Foot Tribe. Photo courtesy of the Ice family.*

and citations on the walls, and to do justice to the spirit of this man.
Fortunately, one exists. *Sky Trails, The Life of Clyde W. Ice* was written
by Wyoming writer and historian Rhonda Coy Sedgwick when Clyde
was ninety-eight.

Intermingled with the certificates of achievement in aviation are
dozens of pictures of Clyde's family, some from long ago, some recent.
They bear witness to the importance of his family throughout his life
and of the pride Clyde has in them. Another wall is almost covered
with a huge collage of photos of Clyde and his planes and family over
the years, with the title "Happy Birthday Grandpa" (at age ninety-six).
The photos are grouped into categories and interests that define Clyde:
son, father, friend, helping hand, guide, adventurer, aviator, pioneer,
horseman, farmer, hunter. Centered at the top is a large portrait photograph of Clyde, with the simple caption: Gentleman.

Returning to South Dakota just before his 101st birthday, Clyde sold
the 1882 farmhouse. Then, two days later, he auctioned off a lifetime
of furniture and equipment, keeping only his personal belongings,
including the dozens of plaques, certificates of merit, awards for bravery and service, and the family photos.

‰ *A dashing Clyde Ice, Spearfish, SD. Photo courtesy of the Ice family.*

Clyde still has his driver's license and keeps an old pickup truck. He would like to buy a motor home with the proceeds from the sale so that he could travel during the summers, spending time with each of his sons, before returning to Wyoming for the winter. After years of freedom in the air and carving out his own unique life-style, Clyde thinks it would be hard for him to stay put year-round. "What I'd like to do is live in the motor home during the summer at my sons' places—still be independent and yet get some help as I need it from time to time," Clyde says. "The rub is, they won't let me drive the motor home myself."

Realistically, Clyde understands the limitations age has imposed, but that hasn't stopped him. "The biggest problem," he says, "is that my landing gear is worn out and I can't get around like I used to. But the rest of me is as good as it was twenty years ago."

❧

THE JOY OF BEING 100: TED GIBSON AND HELEN GIBSON COPE

Theodore Gibson celebrated his 100th birthday on the West Coast late in March 1988. His ninety-nine-year-old sister, Helen Gibson Cope, flew to Los Angeles from New York for a weekend of parties, with other family and friends flying in from all over the country.

The following year on the East Coast, in November, there was a 100th birthday party for Helen, who, like her brother, celebrated her centenary at a round of parties decorated in blue and gold, the colors of their shared alma mater—the University of Michigan in Ann Arbor. "Our mother and father and many other family members spanning four generations are alums also," Ted explains. "In our family, when the Michigan fight song is played everyone stands."

A few years before his 100th birthday, Ted Gibson had moved from his Connecticut home, where he had spent the previous thirty years, to California to live with his son and daughter-in-law. Although vastly different from the Northeast and his native Michigan, the California life-style is one this centenarian says he enjoys. From his perch on a hill in Culver City, in a ranch house overlooking Los Angeles on one side and the Pacific Ocean on the other, Ted says, "The setting is magnificent and the weather is wonderful, but what I particularly enjoy are the warm pleasures of having my family close by."

Helen Gibson Cope, who also moved late in life from her native

ॐ Helen Gibson Cope—Belle Haven Club Centennial.
Photo courtesy of her daughter Lois.

Michigan to Connecticut to live with her daughter, says she regretted giving up her Detroit apartment, her friends, and her car; but she finds life surrounded by her extended family and the new friends she has made pleasurable. For the last few years, she says, "I have lived in my daughter's lovely home. I have a comfortable bedroom and private sitting room, which I use as my study. I have my typewriter and my books and many of my antiques. . . . And I, too, have a view of the water—Long Island Sound. I take my daily walk around the broad porch that surrounds the house, so I get a lot of exercise. And there's a fine view of Greenwich Harbor, with all the sailing boats."

Both Ted and Helen consider themselves fortunate to live in such idyllic spots, thanks to the generosity of their families. "We take care of each other," son Jim Gibson tells. "Mom and Dad did a lot for us when we were first married and raising our family, and now it's our turn to reciprocate."

Ted and Helen are the oldest of six children. They are the only two still living. "I wish the others were here to see Theodore turn 100," said Helen at his party in California.

March 26, 1988, was declared Ted Gibson Day by the mayor of Culver City. During a dinner dance at the Marina Beach Hotel, Helen read a speech she had written in his honor. She recalled her brother's spunky wrestling matches with "husky farm boys" much bigger than Ted at their one-room schoolhouse in Port Austin, Michigan, overlooking Lake Huron, and their later high school years in Ann Arbor, where their parents moved to provide better educational opportunities for their children. In 1908, both Ted and Helen entered the University of Michigan. Helen graduated in 1912 with a bachelor's degree and returned to the University of Michigan for a master's degree in social work in 1939. Ted received two degrees, in chemistry and pharmacy, in 1913.

"Our mother taught Latin and Greek before her marriage," Helen continued. "In Greek, Theodore means *gift of God*. So I give you Theodore Thomas Gibson, gift of God, son, brother, husband, father, grandfather, and friend."

After the applause ended, Ted rose to speak.

"I'm especially pleased to have my little sister here with me tonight," he said, noting also that his greatest sadness was that his beloved wife of seventy-three years, also named Helen, was not with him at his 100th birthday party.

"I lost my beautiful, intelligent redhead last year," he explained. "She was just three years younger than me. She was the most understanding person I have ever known." Theodore recalled the summer between his sophomore and junior years in college, when he was selling aluminum ware in small towns in Michigan. "I walked into a bakery. She was bending down behind one of the counters. She stood up as I entered, a little sixteen-year-old girl with red hair and freckles. I loved her the first minute I saw her."

He told his guests that his late wife's devotion was one of the few things in life that truly amazed him. He said, "During many moves, changing jobs, with two young sons to raise, she never complained. It must not have been easy. She always believed in me, and her faith kept me going during some hard times."

◿ *Helen Gibson Cope in foul weather gear on board Frolic—a firm hand on the tiller.*
Photo courtesy of her daughter Lois.

Reviewing his life, he said surviving the deadly influenza epidemic of 1918 was also a source of amazement to him. Ted recalled people dying by the thousands. Parents died. Their children were left orphaned. Sometimes whole families were wiped out.

Traveling by train for two days from Kingsport, Tennessee, to St. Louis, Missouri, where he was to begin a new job as research assistant to the superintendent of the Monsanto Chemical plant there, Ted and his family fell ill with the disease. "At one station, the bodies of forty soldiers were piled up, awaiting burial." Unlike Ted and Helen's younger brother, a fighter pilot shot down and killed at the French and German border just seven days before the armistice, these soldiers had not died in World War I. Rather, they had been stricken by the influenza that claimed more American lives than were lost in the War.

Ted recalled that half those on the train got sick and by the time his family got to St. Louis, "We were all ready to pass out. Somehow we managed to get to the hotel. One son and I were the worst. We were taken out of the hotel early in the morning, picked up by the police wagon taking sick people to the hospital. The wagon made several stops along the way. By the time we got to the hospital, the wagon was filled. My son and I were split up and put into separate wards. I nearly died."

He said the memory of that night, when his temperature reached 107 degrees, haunts him. "A doctor came over to talk to me, and when I asked him if I was going to make it, he didn't answer. Rather, he gave me a red liquid to drink. I never tasted anything so good in my life because it was a lifesaving drink."

Ted said he also recalled that, during the night, the ward nurse "kept everyone laughing. She packed me in ice, saying she had had another patient just like me the day before and he died." Not sure if she was joking, Ted really thought he was going to die, but in the morning "my fever started to come down. I never did find out what that red liquid was nor did I find the doctor to thank him. It was a terrible epidemic. There was no cure for it. You either got over it or you succumbed to it. We were among the lucky ones—my son and I lived. But I was so sick that I couldn't appreciate the armistice celebration at the end of the war. All I wanted was for them to stop making all that noise in the streets because it made my head hurt worse." He said it took him two months to recover and that, fortunately, the company held his new job for him.

Ted's early jobs kept them crisscrossing the eastern United States. He went from Michigan to New Jersey; back to Michigan in 1915, where he was married; back to New Jersey; then to Kingsport, Tennessee, and then St. Louis. From there, Ted moved his family to Northborough, Massachusetts, when he was offered a promising partnership manufacturing red dye. "Before World War I," Ted tells, "there was no dye industry in the United States and all dyes were imported from Europe. We saw an opportunity here."

However, after five years of hard effort, Ted admitted defeat. "We were living on $100 a month. Things were pretty bad." Almost broke, he accepted part-time work as a park commissioner. Then, one day, "out of the blue," he received a telegram from a large chemical company with job offers at either their cellophane plant or their rayon plant, both near Buffalo.

"I didn't even know if cellophane was a solid or a liquid," Ted confides. "They had only been making it a couple of years." (In fact, cellophane was first manufactured in 1924; synthetic silk was first produced in 1910, then trademarked as "rayon," also in 1924.) So the Gibsons moved once again. He decided in favor of the cellophane plant "because I liked the looks of it better," and he worked there as a plant superintendent until 1927. "The chemicals made me ill," he tells. So, again, with his family in tow, he moved back to Michigan.

"I moved back at the beginning of the Depression to Michigan, when there were no jobs, and when chemists with doctorate degrees were earning as little as $100 a month." Ted couldn't find work in his field, so he took a job selling household appliances for five years. Fed up, in 1933, he took his wife's suggestion and contacted a former schoolmate of hers who was an executive at a chemical plant in Detroit. As Ted tells it, this was a monumental event in his career.

Through this contact, Ted was eventually invited to apply for one of two job openings at a pharmaceutical company in Chicago, but he was warned that he was competing with seventy other applicants. To prepare for his interviews, "and to get a jump on the competition," he says with a smile, "I went to Chicago and stayed around the plant for a couple of weeks and I found out how they sold the products." He was offered, and accepted, a job in Hartford, Connecticut, staying with the company ten years and becoming their top salesman in the process. "That's how the Depression brought about a change in my career—from chemistry to pharmaceutical sales."

Ted's natural ability as a salesman was another source of amazement to him. "I could sell anything," he recalled. After fifteen years, restless, he quit for a year to take life easy.

"About the time I was getting tired of loafing," he continued (it was 1947 and he was fifty-nine years old), "I ran into an old friend who worked at the Robbins Company in Richmond, Virginia. He asked me if I'd like his sales job." After several weeks, when the job offer didn't materialize, Ted called his friend who told him, apologetically, that his company "didn't want to hire me because I was almost sixty years old.

"I told him if he could arrange a meeting with the president, I would come at my own expense. The next day he called and told me that the owner said if I was such a fool as to spend my own money like that, to come ahead."

When Ted, dapper in a new suit, was ushered into Mr. Robbins's office, he recalls him saying, "You're not the Mr. Gibson who applied for a job. You must be his son."

"No," Ted replied. "I am the man who applied for the job."

Although company policy restricted new employees to those under age forty-five, and although Ted was almost sixty, the president, admiring his spunk, hired him.

"I repaid his faith in me by being his top salesman, competing with men twenty to thirty years younger; but they all loved me. I retired from the Robbins Company when I was seventy. Those were the happiest ten years of my career. I went back to a reunion for retired employees recently, and they said I was the best salesman they had ever had. For my 100th birthday I received a letter from the president and a check for $100."

After retirement, Ted decided to go back to college. "I didn't feel like seventy by a long shot," he says, "but I was turned down at the University of Connecticut because of my age." So he took a real estate brokers' course and passed the exam to sell real estate. "I sold a couple of houses but it didn't appeal to me so we stayed home, planted a large vegetable garden that we shared with the neighbors, traveled a little, and became fixtures in our community, always ready to welcome people with homemade cookies and neighborliness."

In 1982, "My son Jim asked us to move out here and we did. We took several trips with Jim and Dot." Ted still loves to travel and hasn't let a few medical problems slow him down, including a heart attack at ninety-eight when he had a pacemaker put in, a hip replacement, cataract surgery on both eyes, and two cancer surgeries. "I guess you could call me a bionic man," he says. "I'm in good health now, and I try to take care of myself. After the heart attack, I bought an exercise bicycle and I ride it at least a mile each day." Undaunted by these "minor adjustments," Ted maintains an optimistic attitude and a good sense of humor.

An avid reader, Ted likes "to keep in touch with what everybody's reading and I love to be around young people. I enjoy having my great-grandchildren stop in after school or Boy Scout meetings and having my grandson drop by for a chat. I'm thankful that I have my family and their friends close by—they bring them along, to meet me. My philosophy is, I want to be where there's action and young people."

When he'd finished speaking, Ted asked Helen to dance the first dance. "He danced every dance," she said later, "bright-eyed as ever, flattering all the girls. He had a wonderful time."

So did Helen, the following year, at her own 100th birthday celebration. Traveling from California with his son and daughter-in-law, Ted arrived on the eve of the festivities, just in time for a weekend family gathering, a formal dance at the yacht club, and a brunch on Sunday.

"The door opened and there he was. My brother and fellow centenarian, looking very fit and handsome as ever," said Helen.

At the party Saturday night, Ted rose to give a toast to his sister. Congratulating her on reaching the century mark, he began, "We had an Uncle David who lived to be 104. My intended goal is to beat that, and Helen's ambition is to catch up with me.

"I have known Helen for 100 years—longer than anyone has. At first there was just my parents, me, and then Helen in the family. After that, it seems there was a new baby every year for the next four years. Our parents got a rather late start having a family, but they made up for lost time. While a medical student at the University of Michigan, our father boarded at our mother's family home. Mother, meanwhile, had graduated from the University of Michigan in 1877. Her class was the second coeducational class in the school's history. She was teaching Latin and Greek in a high school in Ohio. They met during one of her vacations home. Our grandmother was very proud of her college-educated daughter since she herself had been denied admission to the university years earlier because she was a female. It was her goal to have her daughters receive the education she had wanted.

"Our parents married on July 4, 1887, and started a family tradition on their first wedding anniversary. Every Fourth of July since, there has been a Gibson family reunion in Michigan. Helen and I still attend regularly, and hundreds of relatives gather each year near Meade, Michigan, by Lake St. Clair. One of Helen's lasting contributions to this family has been her keen interest and work in our genealogy. In the 1940s she began to trace the family's history, and she and her husband traveled all over the country searching for Gibson family members. She compiled their stories as a history of the family. Helen has tallied 1,700 descendants of our grandfather, who came from England in 1833. This has been a labor of love, and we all thank her for it. Our family is richer because of her efforts. Helen recently passed this project on to my son Jim, who computerized her information.

"Helen taught both high school and college but is known primarily for her outstanding social work, her second career. During the Depression, Helen was a case worker in the Detroit Department of Public Welfare. Although she officially retired at sixty-five, in 1953, she is very much still the social worker to this day, visiting residents in the nursing home and contributing to the senior center programs and the church here, leading study and lecture groups. In Detroit, she was also active in church circles and taught Sunday school. Religion has always been important to Helen. She led the family prayers at home.

"Giving up driving and her own apartment in Detroit, leaving her friends and the many organizations she belonged to, and resigning from various boards and committees on which she was prominent in Detroit was difficult for Helen. At ninety-six, she had to start over again. Never content to sit at home, Helen joined new organizations here, in Greenwich, or branches of ones she was involved in before. She has kept in touch through letter writing with her old friends, made new friends, and has continued with her most cherished activity—travel. Unlike me, Helen loves to go abroad, often to exotic places. She loves adventure. Besides traveling all over the United States, she has been to Europe frequently and to Australia, New Zealand, Mexico, and the Middle East. She still travels, and her Christmas letter tells of her annual adventures.

"One trip stands out in my mind, however. At ninety-one, Helen went with a group from the American Association of University Women to Egypt. Not content to view the pyramids from the outside, Helen joined a group climbing the steep passageway to the upper chamber at the top of the Great Pyramid of Cheops. With only a rope to hang on to, Helen made the steep ascent over the worn stones. It was very hot outside and even hotter inside, with little ventilation, and people packed closely together on the long, arduous climb. This grueling exercise has been known to exhaust tourists half her age. When they finally emerged from the pyramid, while others took the tourist rides on waiting camels, Helen decided to investigate the digging activity beyond a high fence several hundred yards from the pyramids—an excavation of some sort. She found a rickety wooden ladder, with rungs tied with rope, and began to climb to see what was going on on the other side of the fence. Near the top, one of the rungs gave way, sending Helen back to the hard-packed sand in a hurry. As a result, she sprained her ankle and was unable to continue on with the group when they departed the next day for Upper Egypt. Left alone in the teeming city of Cairo, the ever-resourceful Helen arranged her own transportation back to the U.S. We were all greatly relieved to have her back safe and sound on American soil.

"I know Helen is anxious to have the floor, so I'm going to close now with a parting thought. If there were one way to characterize Helen over the century I have known her, I would say this: She is an individualist, independent—and likes to be her own boss."

"Thank you, Theodore," Helen said as she rose to address her guests. "This is indeed a happy day for me, and one I've looked forward to. I come from a long-living family. My brother has told you about Uncle David, who lived to be 104, but we also have a cousin who is almost as old as I am, and our maternal grandfather was over 100 when he died. I remember him as bright and outgoing to the end.

"My memory of historical events goes back to 1898 and the Spanish-American War, when I saw the soldiers returning home victorious as they got off the train in Port Austin. And I recall the suffrage movement, though I didn't take an active part. But I voted in 1916 for President [Woodrow] Wilson, before women won the right to the vote nationally, because I was teaching in Illinois where women could vote by state decree. I don't think many realize it, but several states gave women the vote before 1920 when the Nineteenth Amendment was ratified.

"I have always felt that voting was a basic right, that everyone should have and I felt women should become informed about the issues they were voting for. I have been interested in politics for many years. In Detroit, I was a member of the Republican Club and a senior citizen advisor to a Michigan congressman. Here in my new home in Greenwich, I've continued my affiliation with the Republican Club, the American Association of University Women, and have even found a local chapter of the University of Michigan Alumni Club. I celebrated the seventy-fifth anniversary of my graduation with them—they gave me a lovely party. Each autumn I watch at least one football game with them at Casey's Bar. I also enjoy the literature and history classes here at the senior center. Last year I led the women's Bible class at our church because all the usual leaders were busy remodeling the sanctuary. I learned a lot from preparing my lessons. I hope others found it stimulating, too.

"What I like about living here is the proximity to the wide variety of cultural events in New York City. We go to plays, opera, theater, ballet—it's all so accessible. I think one of the many advantages of modern times is the availability of cultural events and entertainment, for everyone, through television, radio, public libraries, and free concerts. And I enjoy having family nearby. There's one grandchild each in Boston, Philadelphia, Connecticut, and Washington. I often visit them by train. I love the train—it's my favorite mode of travel.

"When I was ninety-eight, I took part in a study on diet and nutrition in elderly people at Massachusetts General Hospital in Boston, after I noticed a tiny ad in the *New York Times* asking for volunteers and offering room, board, and a stipend for participating. Without telling anyone in the family, I sat down at my typewriter and wrote the researchers a letter and told them all about myself. They accepted me. As you can imagine, Lois had a fit. Everyone else in the family was horrified. When the time came, I was perfectly ready to take the train to Boston, but Lois insisted on driving me. I had a lovely room for two weeks overlooking the Charles River. We had meals that were specially made, and we were asked to perform certain mental tasks and exercises while our 'vital signs' were frequently checked. We were asked a lot of questions. It was interesting. My own view of longevity is that it's a combination of good genes, most importantly, but also important is one's attitude and a sense of humor. It's worked for me.

"I am still enjoying this wonderful life I've been given, every day. I was married when I was thirty years old and had one child, my lovely daughter, Lois. I married again when I was sixty, to an old family friend, a widower, five years older. Fortunately for me, both my husbands liked adventure, for as my brother told you, I do love to travel. Just in the last three years I have traveled with Lois twice to Mexico, once to Paris, and then a barge trip for a week in France and have visited many friends and relatives in other states. I look forward to more of the same. I would like to conclude with a little poem by Edna St. Vincent Millay ("Travel", 1921), a contemporary of mine, that rather sums up the way I feel at this time and place in my life:

> *My heart is warm with the friends I make,*
> *and better friends I'll not be knowing;*
> *Yet there isn't a train I wouldn't take,*
> *no matter where it's going!*

"May all the bright threads of our lives continue to be woven together across the miles and across the generations. God be with you one and all."

One hundred and sixty guests rose and sang "Happy Birthday" to

∂∑ *Helen Gibson Cope & Ted Gibson at her 100th Birthday Celebration.*
Photo courtesy of Lois and the Gibson family. Photograph by Marian Hesemeyer.

the triumphant centenarian. When they finished, Helen turned to Ted and said, "I'd like a copy of your speech, I liked what you said." "I can't give it to you," Ted replied. "Why not?" asked Helen indignantly, piqued at being refused any request on her 100th birthday.

"Because it's in here," her brother answered softly, smiling as he patted his chest over his heart.

Then they were off, hand in hand, to cut Helen's cake and to dance the first dance.

∂∑

VICTORY AT 100: HEDVIG PETERSON

On her 100th birthday, Hedvig Peterson of Tempe, Arizona, was absorbed in an arbitration hearing before the National Association of

Securities Dealers, which regulates firms handling over-the-counter securities. The defendant was an unscrupulous stockbroker, to whom she had entrusted her life's savings and who had been swindling her for several years. "Miraculously, they decided not to meet that day, August 17, 1989. So I was able to attend my birthday celebration," she said. The party was at the Tempe Women's Club, where she had been an active member for twenty-four years.

Hedvig stood at the podium, before the large group assembled to honor her. As she spoke of her life, enlarged photos corresponding to that time were brought out by her friends and placed beside her on the stage as a surprise. "Heddie" was delighted. "I was born on a farm in central Sweden," she began slowly, deliberately, only the rhythm and cadence of her soft, melodic voice suggesting her foreign birth.

"My father died when I was eleven years old. When I was thirteen, my mother brought me to America, so I could have a better education than in Sweden and more opportunity to make a better life for myself. It was 1903. We came by ship to England through the North Sea and then across the Atlantic to Ellis Island. I can still remember being very sick the entire time aboard the ship. We came second class and were down in the hold of the ship, and it rocked violently from side to side all the time.

"We were met in New York by my father's brother. We traveled by train to Lindsbork, Kansas (a small community of about 2,000 people twenty miles from Salina), where he had a general store that carried everything except coffins. In those days, twenty miles by horse and buggy took a long time, so his business was good. But after the cars came, it was like turning off a switch. The difference showed up immediately. People would then drive to Salina to shop and goods began to be shipped more readily from the Sears & Roebuck and Montgomery Ward catalogues. His store, like many others, went under. When we first arrived, my mother worked in the store. When the store failed, she had to keep house for people in order to support us. I have always been so glad that my mother was kind enough to bring me over here—Uncle Sam has been good to me. But my mother left her family in Sweden and never saw them again. She gave up a lot for me. The man she kept house for was wealthy and had asked her to marry him. As I grew older, I asked why she refused—he would have made her life so much easier. 'When I find someone I could love as much as your father, I'll marry again,' she told me. She never did.

"We couldn't speak English when we arrived in America, although someone on the boat taught me to say a few words—hello, thank you, and excuse me. Soon after we arrived, my mother sent me to work for a family on a farm two miles outside of town so I could learn English better. She thought being immersed in the language would help me learn the language tempo better—so different from Swedish—and she was right. The family was very good to me, but after several months I began having severe migraine headaches. The woman finally took me to the town doctor, who advised her to return me to my family, predicting I would drop dead at any moment. Years later, in 1923, I met her again on the street one day, and she greeted me by saying, 'Here is the girl who was going to die so young.' I still suffer from migraine headaches. I was told by a doctor that when I got older I wouldn't have them anymore. I wonder how old I have to get.

"Because my English was poor, I had to begin school in first grade, even though I was fourteen years old. At fifteen, I started the seventh grade, going on to eighth, and then finished high school in three years, often studying late into the night. At fifteen I also worked as a waitress after school. I took part in both debate and oratory in high school and later in college." It was a skill that came to serve her well in her later tribulations while fighting for her savings, she admits. "I graduated valedictorian of both my high school and college classes.

"In 1911, I entered Bethany College near home and my mother went to work as a cook there to pay my expenses. I finished college in three years on an accelerated schedule, but it was difficult. The school did not want to give me the extra courses. I had to really fight for it. They finally agreed to let me take an overloaded schedule, but with the stipulation that I had to maintain the grade of 90 in each subject to be able to continue at an accelerated pace. Believe me, I burned a lot of midnight oil. I graduated in 1914 at the age of twenty-three with a B.A. and a teaching certificate. While in college, I was also on the student council; there were ten young men and me. Even though I was the only female, I didn't let them intimidate me. Someone had to represent the women students; we were called girls then.

"I met my future husband, George Peterson, through my church. That was in 1914. I had just started teaching seventh grade in the same high school which I had attended. Eventually, a vacancy became available and I taught social studies and the Constitution. I enjoyed teaching high school students.

"Although we met in 1914, George and I were not married until 1923—he said it took him that long to decide. In fact, the war intervened. He went off to World War I and served in the medical corps in France, assisting a doctor. By the end of the war, he was so fatigued and undernourished that he came down with the flu during the epidemic of 1918. He was so weakened and run down that the doctor pronounced him dead of pneumonia three times. George's doctor, whom he had served with, delayed his own return after the end of the war and stayed until George regained his health. Finally, he was strong enough to make the journey back to Kansas. His heart and lungs were permanently affected. He was two years trying to regain his health once he returned, but he never fully did; he was unable to work on a consistent basis throughout his life.

"By June of 1923, he was well enough to be married and we moved to Mound City, Arkansas, where his parents had bought a farm thinking it would be good for George's health. I got a teaching job there and we stayed in Mound City for five years. Neither George nor I liked living on the farm, and George was terrible at being a farmer, but it was what his parents wanted. That first winter the barn caught on fire and George said, 'Here goes everything.' It is strange, but often in life it seems the things that look bad or disastrous at the time over the long run are good and lead down another, better path. We couldn't leave Arkansas because of my teaching contract, but we did move into town. George got a job in the office of a timber company. When my contract was finished I didn't renew it and I didn't work some of the time we were there. We carried on as normal, with George working and me staying home as typical young married people, but then his health broke and on doctor's advice, we moved to Arizona with $200 in our pockets. At the same time the Depression hit.

"When we arrived in Arizona in 1929, I was unable to get a teaching job, or any other work for that matter, because I was a married woman. At that time, jobs were so scarce that married women were not allowed to work because it was thought it would take a job away from a man with a family to feed. However, George was too ill and weak to work. We traveled all over the state trying to find work, finally settling in Oracle Junction, in the southern part of the state, where the school supervisor gave me a job as a rural schoolteacher even though he wasn't supposed to. He said he felt that at least one member of the family ought to be permitted to work. We later bought a small piece of land and built a cabin on it with our own hands, a little at a time, as we had the money. We raised chickens and loved life. We stayed in Oracle because it was good for George's health. The air was very pure although the altitude was high. Later I became the principal of the school, which had only five teachers. The Mexican children in the school were often hungry and malnourished. I enlisted the help of nearby farmers who volunteered to bring daily lunches for the children. The school and children also benefitted from George's many talents; he was an early role model for the modern teacher's aid.

"We lived in Oracle for twenty-six years. During that time, in 1941, I earned my master's degree in history, from the University of Arizona. I was fifty-two. Shortly after I retired at the age of sixty-five, we traveled to California to visit a relative, and on the way we stopped in Tempe, Arizona, to stay with friends. By that time, the altitude in Oracle was starting to bother George. We liked Tempe, a college town next to Phoenix, and decided to return and buy a small home near Arizona State University.

"In 1961, we visited Sweden and other parts of Europe. It was the trip of a lifetime, which we had planned for many years. This was the first time I had been back to my birthplace because until then we hadn't had the money to travel. The trip didn't seem hard on George, and we both enjoyed it very much. I am so glad we did it because he died in 1965.

"Travel is important, especially for teachers, so they can expose their students to other cultures from their own experiences. I believe I was a better teacher because I came from Sweden and had a broader view of the world. I still enjoy traveling and take as many trips as I can each year. Often, I go by bus or plane to visit relatives in California and recently went to Alaska with three women from the Club.

"After George died, I got my driver's license at the age of seventy-six. I joined several local organizations, including the Tempe Women's Club. I am also active in my church and in a number of education associations. Also, I began doing volunteer work for the Cook Theological Training School. I have always enjoyed the study of religion and history, and I like to stay current on world and state affairs. I still live alone, cook, and clean my house. I only walk four blocks a day now, with a cane, and ride a stationary bicycle. And I like to play bridge. Although George and I never had children and I have no really close relatives, I am blessed with many friends of all generations. They are good to me, and I thank you."

Hedvig looked around her, smiling, and left the podium to enjoy the company of those friends who say she is a precious treasure they would like to keep forever. The feeling is mutual. Hedvig has a hand-carved wooden plaque in her attractively decorated home that states her position: "Friends are the flowers in the garden of life."

The following day, Hedvig was back at the arbitration hearing in Phoenix with her local lawyer and special counsel from New York, but this time the setting in which she told a part of her life story was an adversarial one.

"I had been keeping my small savings in the bank for years earning interest. All I had was the money we had saved and the money from the sale of our homestead in Oracle. I have always been a saver. Then I became concerned about inflation and wondered, with living so long, if my money would last. So I took my money out of the bank and gave it to a stockbroker my cousin had known for several years. I told him to invest the money safely, not to take any risks with it because it was all I had. I specifically told him not to buy stocks on margin because I could lose everything. Things went along all right for the first couple of years, but then I began to notice a lot of transactions on my monthly statements and fees taken out for them. After a while, I became concerned when I could see no advantage to those transactions. There were so many in each month. I wasn't earning any money and I was losing capital by paying the fees. Whenever I would ask the stockbroker he would tell me that everything was as it should be and that I just didn't understand the stock market or its transactions. After a time, I began writing to the company asking for someone to look into this. Each time I would receive a patronizing letter telling me everything was aboveboard and that I just didn't understand how to read the statement. Then one Friday afternoon last year, I received a certified letter telling me I had to pay $8,000 on the following Monday morning because the market went down and I had stocks on margin. A friend happened to be visiting at my home and she knew a woman stockbroker here, with the same large national firm as my own, so we went to see her immediately. This stockbroker said she would look into what this man had been doing with my account over the years. I transferred everything I had left to her as soon as the paperwork could be done; within a year, I would have lost all my savings and I would have been penniless. On Monday I had to pay the $8,000."

The arbitrators ultimately awarded Hedvig $225,000 as compensation for the money she had lost over the years and an unprecedented $1 million award for punitive damages. Out of the proceeds of her award, Hedvig's lawyers received a third, plus reimbursements for expenses related to the arbitration. The rest of the money is being given to charities, already selected. "I guess the large amount is to teach people a lesson," explains Hedvig.

"He took advantage of me because of my age, my failing eyesight [she uses a magnifying glass to read] and he knew that if I died no one would know how much money I had had and wouldn't do anything about it. We oldsters have to be careful. There are a lot of unscrupulous people trying to take advantage of us, and they often succeed. I wanted someone to take charge of my investments for me, someone I could rely on. But when I inquired about things, I could never receive a direct explanation. If my case will help someone else to come forward or encourage others to be persistent and not let themselves be placated or intimidated by the people handling their money who tell them they just are too old to understand, then all the uncertainty, effort, and unpleasantness I have gone through will have been worthwhile.

"I do not wish this man any harm, however. In my youth, my parents had faith in God and they started us out with the understanding that to do right is better than to do wrong. They showed me from a young age that you must forgive the person you were playing with who hurt you. One's formative years are so important. I don't expect too much of some folks who had a different beginning than I had. It is my job as a religious person to forgive. I could have harmed myself by becoming angry. I could have ruined my health over this. I could have been so upset that I died because of what he was doing to me. As far as something bad happening to him, that would give me no satisfaction. If anything can be done to change him, that is what I would like. I don't have bad feelings about him, but I do feel that he should be stopped from taking advantage of other people. I have heard that he is still working for the same brokerage house and is now advising people and handling people's finances at a retirement center here in Tempe. That worries me. I am so afraid he'll do the same to someone else. I don't believe he's learned a lesson.

"If I had my life to live over again," says Hedvig, "I would study law and finance so that I could be better prepared to protect myself." What Hedvig has accomplished, however, without such training, is remarkable. Throughout her life, she has been an advocate for the disadvantaged. She represented the views of women students at Bethany College as the solitary female on a male-dominated student council. She respected her husband George for the special person he was, accepting his physical limitations. She worked toward equality of education and health for minority children in her Oracle school. Now, at age 100, she has become an advocate for better treatment of older adults. Her viewpoint: "The fact that they just want to forget the old people in this country is a crime."

✺ *Hedvig Peterson. Photograph by Jacques Barbey,*
reprinted with permission from The Arizona Republic.

❧ 3 ❧

Our Living Links to the Past

Over the past 100 years there hasn't been anything I have not found interesting historically—scientific and astronomical findings, technology and modern conveniences, radio, black-and-white to color movies and television, communications, transportation—and the space shuttle. I would go to the moon tomorrow if they would take me!

—Mrs. Lynn Billy Earley at 100

By talking with centenarians such as Billy Earley, we begin to realize just how long ago 100 years actually is, and we begin to develop an appreciation for the tremendous changes that have occurred in America during their lifetimes. In fact, centenarians' lives span nearly half of our nation's history. Many of the historical events or eras of social change that most of us know only from history books were real-life experiences for centenarians, and they are here today to tell us about it. As Ted Gibson reminds us, "I only missed the Civil War by twenty-three years."

Sit with them for a while and they will tell you stories of their lives. You will be experiencing our country's history, its development, its customs, its moral attitudes, and its social trends. You will learn interesting details of our heritage, and you will carry a memory of what was said that is lasting and unique.

Take, for example, Louis Kelly, 103, of Scottsdale, Arizona, whose earliest memory imparts a vivid image of one way people lived and traveled long ago: "I can recall it as clearly as if it were yesterday," he says, "and I can see it in my mind's eye. I was standing in a covered wagon looking out the back; my younger sister was asleep on the bedding on the floor beside me. I realized that my father was driving the team of horses and that his wagon belonged to us—that this was our home. My mother was on the seat beside him holding my four-month-old brother in her arms."

❧

EARLY YEARS AND SETTLING THE WEST

In 1890, the Kelly family was traveling from Saunders County in eastern Nebraska, near Omaha, where the children were born, northwest to the Black Hills of South Dakota. Louis's father had heard there was work on the railroad then under construction near what is now Custer National Park. "We would camp along the way," Louis continues. "My parents slept in a tent at night with the baby. My sister and I slept in the wagon. It was a converted farm wagon, not the Conestoga type or prairie schooners so often pictured in Western movies. These were used much earlier and were much larger. People have a romanticized vision of all covered wagons being like the one in the movies, but the covered wagon we had was a covered farm wagon. Our family was very poor—as were many of the families who were migrating and looking for work or a better place to live. It was common for people to simply use their farm wagons to move the family. Bowed stays were attached to the brackets provided on the sides of the wagons and canvas sheets were attached to the stays to provide protection from the elements. Thus, they became covered wagons. A farm wagon was much smaller than the covered wagons in the movies—usually twenty-six inches deep; a dining room table is twenty-nine inches high, just to give you some idea. Sometimes people would take two wagons, if they had them, and enough horses, in order to accommodate all the household items. Often older children walked beside them to save space for the family's possessions. Our wagon, like many others, didn't have springs. But the ground on our route—to the Niobrara River and from there up into the Black Hills—must have been soft, making the ride pretty comfortable. I don't now how long it took us. I think wagons traveled between two and four miles an hour in those days.

"When we got to the site, my father did find work laying the track for the railroad. I remember a big Irish woman, the camp cook, cooking in large pots over an open fire, with my mother helping her. I remember her serving the men, seated at long tables made out of rough planks of wood. I knew that after the men were fed, it would be my turn. My parents stayed just one summer and left in the fall. We then traveled in the wagon to Fremont, Nebraska, near Omaha, settling for several years near my mother's family. There were five girls in my mother's family; all of them, my mother included, had been school-teachers. Several other children were born to my parents during those years, but they did not survive long. A couple of them, as was common in those days, died in infancy.

"I worked on various farms with my father and attended school intermittently as I grew up. We depended on corn for our cash crop. I can tell you all about the farm machinery, such as it was in those days, and how the crops were planted and harvested and sold. And how nothing would be wasted. After the corn kernels had been removed, the dried cobs were burned for heat and the dried husks were used to stuff mattresses. I can remember my mother hauling out the mattresses each year in the spring and taking out the old stuffing and filling them with new dried husks. Then they would be nice and thick for a while until they mashed down and became lumpy and uncomfortable.

"In 1906 my father bought a large farm in Red Willow County, near McCook, the county seat in western Nebraska about sixty miles from North Platte. He intended for me to be a farmer. I remember standing out at the windmill in 1909 when I was about twenty-two and telling my mother that I didn't want to be a farmer; that I was leaving for the city to try to make my way in life and that my younger brother Wayne could take over on the farm. Unfortunately for my parents, he left soon after I did, and my sister was the only one who turned out to be a life-long resident of McCook.

"I went to Kansas City, Missouri, because I didn't have any relatives there—I wanted to make it on my own. I found a job working for a mail-order business for thirty dollars a month and a room for two dollars and fifty cents a week, which I shared with a reporter who worked nights, so it cost us each one dollar and twenty-five cents a week. A cup of coffee and a sweet roll for breakfast cost five cents—I ate it at the streetcar transfer each morning on my way to work. Dinner was fifteen cents. When I got a small raise, I sometimes paid thirty-five cents for a really good dinner. . . .I remember the first time I could afford a grapefruit for dessert—it was a real treat. I made my way in life from there. After a few years in Kansas City, I joined the Spiegel Company in Chicago and continued to work in the mail-order business as a furniture buyer for twenty-seven years.

"Remarkably, all three of us children traveling in the family's covered wagon that spring day in 1890 have lived to be 100. Sister Dorothy stayed in McCook, Nebraska; baby brother Wayne, who spent most of his life as a railroad engineer, moved to Seattle, Washington, to be near one of his children. I think we may be the family with the most oldest in the U.S.," Louis concludes.

⚬

More changes and innovations have occurred during the lifetimes of today's centenarians than during any other period of history. For instance, at the time of their birth, Native Americans were still fighting in an effort to keep control of their remaining territories in the West. Centenarians are as old or older than the last ten western states that completed the coast-to-coast expansion of this country; many share their centennials with the states in which they live. They recall the feeling of national pride prevalent when they were growing up—the feeling of being part of a young and growing country.

Many people were going west to homestead in search of fulfilling the American dream of owning land, a home of their own, and of making a better life for themselves and their children. Centenarian Bill Sutton tells how, at the age of nineteen, after eloping with his sweetheart, he headed from Arkansas to Texas to make his fortune. "Perthena's parents did not want us to marry—maybe they thought she was too young, maybe they just didn't like me. So in June 1907, I picked her up with one horse and we went to Fort Smith, Arkansas, to be married. We left immediately for the train depot twenty-five miles away, riding double through a heavy rainstorm. We stayed in Texas that year. The following year we moved on to Oklahoma and settled there for forty years. First I had a cotton farm but lost everything to the boll weevil, so I gave up farming for oil field work and made a good living. When I retired from the oil fields, I returned to Texas to help my son in his oil business. I live in Texas now, as I'd planned originally."

⚬

Completion of the railroads helped a great deal to open up the new western frontiers. For the first time, people could travel in relative safety and convenience as individuals, not having to rely on traveling in groups, as had the earlier settlers of the wagon train era. "The first transcontinental railroad was completed in 1869," Ted Gibson reminds us. "The occasion was marked by the well-known driving of the

Golden Spike at Ogden, Utah." Other smaller lines, such as the one Louis Kelly's father worked on in South Dakota, allowed access to western states that were situated off the main line.

The federal Homestead Act of 1862 gave settlers ownership of land, usually parcels of 160 acres. After they had occupied it continuously for five years and had made certain "improvements," such as permanent buildings, the land was theirs to keep; they had only to pay the taxes. Adding improvements and occupying the land were commonly called "proving up on the land." So alluring was the idea of acquiring land simply by developing it and living on it that people came from distant places to take advantage of the U.S. government's offer. Homesteading helped to develop many of the new western states as the federal government had intended, and some centenarians participated in this adventure.

Sarah Isaacson Ingle of Watford City, North Dakota, tells that her grandparents came from Norway and were among the first to take advantage of the Homestead Act. They settled in Wisconsin, as did many Scandinavians. Sarah was born in 1889 in River Falls. Several of her aunts and uncles then set out from Wisconsin for the Dakotas to homestead. In 1909, Sarah and her mother, following the path of these family members, moved to North Dakota, where she now lives. "I had been teaching for two years in Wisconsin after graduating from the Normal School with a teacher's certificate in 1907," she tells. "My mother and I came to North Dakota to visit with her older daughter, my half sister. I found out I could get a nine-month term of school teaching in North Dakota plus forty-five dollars a month—more than I was earning in Wisconsin. In addition, I could homestead the land. That decided me. My mother took up a homestead right away, near my sister's place; I had to wait a year until I was twenty-one.

"I met my husband through my homestead. He was already settled on the land nearby, seven miles southeast of Johnson Corners. Earl and I were married at Schafer in January of 1911. We started married life in Earl's one-room log house. The following spring we built a fourteen-by-twenty-foot house on my claim and lived there until after proving up the land. Then, because of a water shortage on my homestead, we moved back to Earl's homestead, moving the house and other buildings with us. We sold my claim and invested the money in buying a nearby homestead. To swing the deal, Earl mortgaged his own homestead, too. Then poor crops set in and we were unable to keep up the payments on the new place, so we lost the whole works.

"Life wasn't easy. There were everlasting debts, and when we got a few good years, all the surplus was used up in paying up back debts. Eventually, we did get a farm of our own. We grew our own vegetables, raised our own meat, and even had to make our own soap. We had four children; our first two were born on my homestead.

"Our third child was our 'war baby,' born in 1917. We called her that because she kept my husband out of the war. When Earl was called up that year to appear before the draft board, he got a friend, who had a brand new Ford car, to take me to Schafer where Earl and I were to appear to request an exemption because of the children and me. Well, something went wrong with the car and Earl's friend didn't come and didn't come. I don't know who was more nervous—Earl, waiting for me at the draft office in Schafer, or me, waiting at home and fearing it would be too late by the time I got there and my husband would have been drafted into the war. Finally, the car and driver came along, and we made it to Schafer all right. That was my first ride in an automobile, and I was thankful for its speed.

"In about 1925, I got a gasoline-powered washing machine, which was a great improvement over the washboard. In 1946, we got a bottled gas refrigerator, followed by electricity in 1951. All three were greatly appreciated. I think electricity for the farms, we were dairy farmers, was the best thing that ever happened for the farm people because they could enjoy the modern conveniences that the city people had. And before that it was great to have a radio, which we got when we acquired a thirty-two-volt windcharger along with—if I remember correctly— one light hanging from the ceiling in the living room. I lived alone on the farm after Earl died. I celebrated my ninety-ninth birthday on that farm before I had to give it up."

Another North Dakota homesteader, Anna Strand of Crosby, was among the many foreigners who came to America to take advantage of this opportunity. In 1907, at the age of twenty-seven, she came from Norway with her cousin. "An uncle living in North Dakota encouraged us to come," she recalls. "At first we came to eastern North Dakota by train from the East Coast, spending the first year there with my uncle. Not long after arriving, I was working in a hotel in Ambrose. One day a drunken cowboy rode his horse into a saloon next door to the hotel. After some rowdiness in the saloon, he led his horse out the back door and began shooting in the air. I had never seen anyone wearing horse chaps before. He mounted his horse and rode down the street. A lot of the townspeople, including me, came out and watched him, attracted by the commotion. As he was leaving, someone shot and killed him. Everyone in the town was so afraid his two buddies would shoot up the town, but nothing happened. The newspaper article of the incident was critical of the killing and said he was only a cowboy on a spree and not deserving of being killed. This was one of my first impressions of the West.

"After a year, my cousin and I moved to northwestern North Dakota, where my uncle helped us homestead on adjoining quarters of land. Our shacks were only a few yards apart. We lived near each other until she passed away many years later. During the Depression I lost my homestead, but later managed to pay the back taxes so I won ownership of it again—and I still have it."

With the opening of spur lines to the transcontinental railroad, new towns and communities formed continuously during the centenarians' younger years. Some thrived. Others became extinct or obsolete within short periods, victims of rapidly changing times. Among the many centenarians who have homesteading stories to tell is Jesse Holman of Dodson, Montana, who recalls her opportunity to settle in the territories and new states. "I came to Montana to take a homestead in 1914," she says. "I enjoyed the sight of Montana, so I stayed. And I still love Montana."

While many settlers took advantage of this great opportunity, not all were able to stay. Some, like Johanna Gustafson and her husband, went back to where they came from, forced to return by hard times. Born in Chicago in 1886, they married in 1907 and then traveled by train to Chickasha, Oklahoma, to farm, but the dust storms and the harsh life overcame them. Three years later, after a particularly devastating dust storm, they left with only their farm wagon (which they converted into a covered wagon) and drove back to Chicago with one team of horses and one riding horse, their sole possessions. "We always slept in the wagon and cooked outdoors," Johanna tells. "Sometimes we accepted invitations to share a meal with farmers along the way." For the Gustafsons, it was a relief to leave the difficulties of a pioneer's life in a young state—Oklahoma was admitted in 1907—and return to the conveniences and more settled life-style in the city.

Others came, persevered, and prospered. Hazel Herring's new life in the West began in Indian territory in Oklahoma a few years before statehood. "My father moved around a lot, always in search of greener grass. We left my birthplace of Niles, Michigan, when I was about eight and moved to Iowa. Then in 1900, when I was about twelve, we moved again to eastern Oklahoma—Indian territory. Papa leased a farm 1.5 miles from the town of Westville, and we moved into a house owned by an old Indian family. The house was oddly built and inconvenient, but none of its inconveniences meant anything to Papa. He was going to make big money from cheap land.

"The people in the area were nice but very different. The customs and the speech were so strange to us that we children thought it was all a lark. The roads were paths through the woods or dry creek beds full of rocks. When a tree fell across the path it wasn't cleared; everyone just went around it until eventually the road had many a crook and turn. Oftentimes we would see Indians going to town, with the man on the horse and the woman walking behind carrying a

❧ *Hazel Irwin Herring as a schoolteacher at age 20, in Sallisaw, Oklahoma, 1909. Photo courtesy of Hazel Herring.*

basket of eggs to sell. The Indians close to us had intermarried with the whites. The full-bloods lived farther from town. In full-blood schools they used Cherokee books in which Sequoya's alphabet was used." [Sequoya, a Native American scholar, invented an alphabet for his language in the 1800s, enabling Cherokees to learn to read and write.]

"Soon after our move, I was old enough to start high school, but there was no high school for miles around; so rather than miss school, I repeated the eighth grade courses again in a new brick school that had been built in Westville. It was a good thing I did. I got excellent grades, and the learning helped me get started on a teaching certificate at Talequah when I was sixteen. I began teaching in one-room country

✄ *Hazel Akeley (Fergus) at age 9, with her brother and sister,*
taken shortly before the family migrated from Presque Isle, Maine
to central Montana in 1899. Hazel later married into the Fergus family,
prominent ranchers after whom a county was named.
Photo courtesy of the Fergus family. Photograph by Smart.

schoolhouses in Indian territory at seventeen. Each summer I would return to Talequah to upgrade my teaching certificate so I could qualify to teach in a better school. After statehood in 1907, I attended Central Teacher's College in Edmund, Oklahoma, to qualify to continue teaching. By the time my father gave up trying to farm and moved to Sallisaw, a town forty miles south, I was able to get a position teaching fifth grade in the Sallisaw school, which was in a new brick building. I was able to live at home with my family, and this advanced position drew the princely sum of fifty-five dollars a month. But it was more than the money—I enjoyed being at home and also enjoyed teaching in town.

"By the next fall, I was teaching the third grade in Sallisaw. On Thanksgiving Day 1909, I met Dick Herring, my future husband, who was in the hardware business. He had come from England with his parents several years before and settled in an English community in Pennsylvania. He and a cousin came west to start a hardware business. He was handsome and had an English accent, which I liked. I liked him from the start, and he said he had had his eye on me for some time. And so, on the first day of January when Papa and Mama and my sisters moved to Palm Springs, California, where Papa planned to raise date trees, I stayed in Oklahoma. Dick and I were married in October 1910. After so many hardships of moving around with Papa and teaching in country schools, I could hardly believe my good fortune in having a nice, four-room home, which we rented. My husband furnished our home before the wedding and had it all ready to move into. I remember he even had the table set for our first breakfast. I gave up teaching forever to become a full-time wife and mother and to settle down permanently here. At 103, I still live in Lawton, Oklahoma."

For the family of young Ben Pruitt, however, moving to new territories and states was a way of life they enjoyed. Born in 1888 in Cedar Creek, Missouri, Ben was named after President-elect Benjamin Harrison. The early years of Oklahoma figured prominently in the early years of Ben's life, too. Ben's father took part in the Oklahoma land rush when Ben was just a year old. His father established the first permanent general store in Pawnee, Oklahoma, around 1893.

Life in several other states also figured prominently in Ben's formative years. His father moved the family often in search of new land and new mercantile opportunities. The states included Arkansas, Idaho, and as far west as Oregon. Ben's family opened many general stores

❧ *Above: Gladys and Ben Pruitt with their first two children,
Hal and Irene, 1916. Photo courtesy of the Pruitt family.
Below: Ben, Ernest and Commie Pruitt in baseball uniforms,
1912. Photo courtesy of the Pruitt family.*

in booming new areas only to close them or sell them after the early rush of people to the area ended. They would then move on to new opportunities. As they grew older, Mr. Pruitt would often leave one or more of his children behind to run the store for a few months or years while he forged ahead to open new ones.

In one such venture, Ben was sent to Arkansas, where he met his future wife, Gladys, when she came to the Pruitt's store with her brother to purchase supplies. After a long courtship they married in 1913 when Ben was twenty-five and his bride a year younger. They moved to the new state of Washington to run the family store and later moved again to Oregon, where they celebrated their seventy-eighth wedding anniversary. Mr. and Mrs. Pruitt are one of the very few centenarian couples in the country.

↪

THE BEGINNING OF MODERN TIMES

Meanwhile, Sarah Payne Wilson, who was born in New York City in 1888, tells of her life growing up in a metropolis. "My family lived on West 43rd Street near Times Square. I attended school until the eighth grade and then continued with music lessons, piano, and organ. I developed a good singing voice and loved going to the theater and concerts, to Delmonico's and other popular restaurants, and to Broadway plays, such as the George M. Cohan musical *45 Minutes from Broadway* (starring Victor Moore in 1906). I liked following the lives and careers of actresses such as Ethel Barrymore, who played the lead in *The Doll's House* (1905). I had one brief fling in show business myself when I had a spot in the chorus line of a touring company. We traveled the Midwest for six months."

"I hadn't planned on such an exciting life," Sarah continues. "Actually, I wanted to be a manicurist and a hairdresser. But one day in 1905, a family friend called and suggested I answer an ad in the paper for a model at a department store. I did, and I got the job. I modeled for stores and also for magazines and for Butterick Patterns. In 1907, the Gibson Girl look became popular and was soon touted as the model of femininity. Small waistlines were a fashion must, and many women had to rely on extremely tight corsets to achieve the look. I didn't—I had a perfect figure."

Billy Earley, who grew up in Cleveland and who spent her early adulthood in Boston and New York, recalls the fashion revolutions of

꙰ *Sarah Payne Wilson as model, circa 1907.*
Photo courtesy of the Wilson family.

these days. "Around 1913, the introduction of the V neck caused quite a stir." According to Billy, this departure from collars covering the entire neck raised the dander of many influential people, clergymen, who called it indecent exposure, and doctors, who warned it was a health hazard." The newspapers had a field day with all the controversy and began calling even blouses with a very modest opening at the neckline 'pneumonia blouses.' It was pretty exciting and, of course, everyone wanted one," she tells. Soon they became generally accepted, as did shorter skirts (about eight inches from the ground) around 1915, Billy recalls.

It was really the World War I years that changed the way women dressed, many centenarians explain. With women doing work for the war effort, comfortable clothes and shorter skirts became the everyday garb and the fashion. Many women stopped wearing corsets. The fashion of one-piece dresses that hung from the shoulders, unbelted, became popular. "They were more comfortable to work in, and for home wear, too," Billy says.

"By this time, I had retired from my brief career as a model and was—much to my parents' relief—a full-time wife and mother living on Long Island," Sarah adds.

Centenarians such as Sarah Wilson and Billy Earley to this day take great pride in their appearance and dress fastidiously and stylishly. Their generation has seen fashion change from the bustle to the bikini and from the days of tightly corseted figures, which sometimes caused women to faint from the constraints, to the free-flowing freedom and sometimes near nudity of today's fashions. Billy Earley laughs as she describes the fashions of her youth. Holding up her bathing suit "vintage 1912" that she has donated to the Historical Society in Florence, Arizona, she says, "Any deviation from *this* was immodest! With it we wore black stockings held up by garters, and a bathing cap—really more like a dust cap—and flat shoes, even in the water. Some women went so far as to wear bloomers under their bathing suits. I didn't because when it got wet, you could sink. Our house was in Cleveland Heights and I did most of my swimming in Lake Erie."

The changes are mind-boggling. Centenarians recall the days when the automobile was new and how the "devil wagon," as it was first nicknamed, would frighten the horses it met on the road, upsetting many carriages. They took part in the enthusiasm and the excitement of the early decades of aviation. "We grew to maturity along with it," says

✑ *Billy Earley at the Pinal County Historical Society Museum with
her vintage 1912 bathing suit. Photograph by Don Stillman,
Old Corral Photo Studio, Florence, AZ, courtesy of Billy Earley.*

Louis Kelly. "In the early days, folks would run out of their houses and
peer up at the sky to watch the new invention pass low and noisily
overhead. Children were fascinated by the shadow the plane made
along the ground as it flew over the farmlands and towns. Often they
would run after it, trying to catch up with the plane's shadow. Some
people were superstitious and thought that if you looked up at the
plane, it would fall from the sky. When you think of it, we centenarians have gone from marveling over a short ride in a barnstorming
plane to taking jetliners for granted. Why, some of these planes now-

adays hold more people than lived in the towns we grew up in.

"There was so much happening at once in the early years of this century that our individual experiences were quite different, even though we're around the same age," Louis continues. "Probably looks like a hodgepodge to people hearing about it now. For instance, city people had electricity very early, by the turn of the century, and access to the modern inventions it brought about, while farm people, depending on where they lived in the country, didn't have electricity until years later—sometimes, in remote areas, decades later. And some of us were still riding in farm wagons and using horses for transportation while others were riding streetcars and taking their first automobile rides in their father's or neighbor's vehicles. It took a long time for the whole country to get caught up together in modern times."

Maude Jones, who spent most of her life in Yuma, Colorado, agrees, adding that whether or not a family had modern devices also depended on the family's finances. She recalls that her neighbor ordered a brand new Sears Motor Buggy from the Sears Roebuck Catalogue in 1913 and gave all the neighbors rides. However, it was a few years later before her father bought his first car, "a used 1912 Hupmobile."

Ranching and farming families across the country relied heavily on Sears and other mail-order catalogues, such as those issued by Montgomery Ward and the Spiegel Company. Anticipating the arrival of the season's new catalogues and perusing the "wish book," as it was sometimes called, was an experience rural Americans across the country shared. It was an experience looked down upon by city dwellers at that time since they had the availability of more up-to-date goods purchased from stores, centenarians say.

Nevertheless, "the mail-order catalogues were a boon to those living far from any city," explains Maude. "The Sears and Roebuck catalogue advertised everything from violins to farm machinery. It was a big book, not just a few-page brochure. It was sent free to anyone who asked for it." Sears has printed a 1908 replica edition that pictures the kind of first washing machines described by many centenarians. "I remember the washing machines clearly because it made work so much easier," Maude says. "It was a round wooden tub on three legs and was worked by a handle pushed back and forth in a semicircle; I think it was called a thrasher. [The advertisement in the 1908 catalogue lists a similar machine at six dollars and thirty-eight cents and says it is 'so easy to use, even a child could do it.'] Later, we got one turned by a crank on a wheel," Maude remarks, "and that was easier still."

Other memories Maude has of her early housekeeping days include the rationing of white flour during World War I. "We had to buy a certain amount of whole wheat flour, which we hated at that time." Other centenarians, too, recall having to bake with the dark flour and spoke of the awful taste. "One time I just couldn't stand the awful-tasting stuff anymore and I baked a cake with white flour. It was a frivolous thing to do, and I didn't enjoy it. Instead, I felt guilty because we weren't supposed to use it," Maude tells.

Edwin Ray Vestal of Elyria, Ohio, has recollections of World War I that are more immediate. "I remember World War I because I was in it," he says. He remembers crossing the English Channel in a troop carrier where the soldiers were packed so tightly it was impossible to sit down. "We stood for twenty-four hours," he recalls, "with no food. Our only ration was a quart of water each." Before leaving for France, he stuffed his pack with lots of toilet paper. "My buddies wondered why my pack was so wide," he laughs. "I could have gotten a lot of money for that toilet paper because no one else had any. It's funny, the things you remember from a time like that." His buddies are mostly gone now and he has very few veterans of World War I with whom to share his memories.

Although he wasn't a soldier, Harry Steele, 102, who now lives in Sun City, Arizona, also has memories of World War I. While working as a reporter at the *Chicago Tribune*, the opportunity arose to cover the war in Europe for one of the wire services. Harry, who was in his mid-twenties, jumped at the chance to be a war correspondent. He recalls the perils of getting his stories from the front lines "back to civilization" to report them, telling that he rode in boxcars of troop trains, and sometimes—as incredible as this seems—he rode underneath the boxcars, hanging on—any way to get his story out.

Harry's dedication to the news business paid off. After the war, he went back to the newspaper and later became editor, a position he held for twenty-five years.

✑

Centenarians talk about what life was like before the invention of the radio, television, and motion pictures; for home entertainment, they relied on reading, social gatherings with neighbors and friends, storytelling and reading out loud to each other, singing, playing piano, and playing games. They speak of the excitement of the times, as innovations in communication and entertainment became a part of their daily lives—their own "Age of Enlightenment," as Louis Kelly dubbed it. "The beginning of the radio in the late 1800s began the revolution in communications," he says with certainty.

"The first radios I recall were called crystal sets. They were introduced about 1901 and you could build them yourself if you were handy. The vacuum tube, which made radios able to be mass produced, had not yet been invented. Early 'crystal' receivers, as they were called, operated without electricity or batteries, and the signals they picked up were very weak. If someone had one, however, all the neighbors would gather around at night. The operator, usually the owner and builder, used a crystal detector, which was a metal wire coming into contact with a metal sulfide crystal, to pick up the signal—that is, try to pick up the signal. They were very fickle. Sometimes you could spend the whole evening searching for one and give up, disappointed." Still, many centenarians remember the thrill of hearing a voice from miles and miles away coming through the headphones when the signal was picked up.

The early radio programs were mostly music: dance orchestras, such as the Cliquot Club Eskimos playing popular music of the time, lively and with a catchy beat, centenarians recall. The first electric radios came out after World War I. A popular program was the dance orchestra, the A and P Gypsies in 1923. By the end of the 1920s, programs were more sophisticated and included drama hours, such as the "Everready Hour" and "Great Moments in History". In 1928, there was the "Music Appreciation Hour" over the Blue Network with Walter Damrosch, which was very popular, centenarians say. The only other was called the Red Network.

"When we were young, the moon was an image for romance and love songs and nursery rhymes," Louis muses. "Imagine seeing men walking on that moon, brought to us through the miracle of technology. It's amazing—'awesome' as my college student great-grandson would say. I think it's the most incredible thing I've witnessed in all these 100 years. And brought right into our living rooms through television."

ஃ

HISTORY REPEATS ITSELF

In addition to the explosion of innovations and new technologies, centenarians have also seen the repetitive cycles of history and social change. Louis Kelly continues: "Young people today, like my great-grandson, assume that what's happening in the world at the time they perceive it is something new, a new development. But after you've been around for a few decades, you begin to realize that while scientific development and technology change rapidly and offer brand-new innovations, like the atomic bomb at one extreme and television at the other—much of what goes on in other areas of life, in politics, for example, or in human behavior, has occurred before, though maybe played out in a different way.

"I remember in the first decade of this century there was controversy over the government's involvement in South American countries, especially Panama and Nicaragua, with some people supporting America's presence there and other people opposed. Also, people forget that another president besides John Kennedy was assassinated in this century. People in my generation recall President William McKinley. In fact, we have vivid memories of him because he traveled the country in a special presidential train for several years, first when he was running for president and then for reelection. We were kids at the time and many of us lived near the railroads or in the towns and cities where he stopped. He was very popular, and whole schools would turn out to see him wave from the back of the train or speaking to crowds in the streets. We may not have understood what he said, but we sure knew he was our president, and we remember what a black day it was in this country when he was assassinated in 1901 at the Pan-American Exposition in Buffalo, New York.

"There are literally hundred of examples. I could go on and on," Louis Kelly says, with a mischievous gleam in his blue eyes, "but I won't. It just seems natural, though, the older you get and the more you've seen happen, the less excited you get about the next similar occurrence. When the assassination attempt was made on President Reagan's life early in his presidency in 1981 and James Brady was so badly wounded, I thought back to 1933 when in Miami, Florida, newly elected President Franklin D. Roosevelt was the target of an assassin's bullet, which missed him and killed the mayor of Chicago, who was in the presidential party. And, come to think of it, in the 1920s there was outrage over the discovery of colleges giving scholarships for athletic ability only in order to build winning teams. Not so different from today, is it?"

Louis is proud of his prodigious memory. He remembers not only events of history but most of the dates also. With no formal education, he is a self-taught man. At eighty-eight, Louis began writing accounts of his lifetime of reading, calling them interpretative historical papers. In all, he has completed fifty-nine articles, which he's copied and distributed to friends over the years. He has now put his collection of writings together, entitled *The Joy of Understanding*. "I've heard it said many times over that a person must know the past to understand the present and to know the future. That's what I've tried to do."

.⅍.

Elizabeth Davis, who spent most of her years in Prairie Grove, Arkansas, near Brentwood where she was born, agrees with Louis's cycles of history theory, citing the recurrent interest in traditions as another example. One such tradition that is enjoying a resurgence of attention is quilting, Mrs. Davis's particular area of expertise. Almost Louis's age of 103, Lizzie Davis learned to piece quilts at the age of six, "and I'm still at it, sure enough," she tells with an enthusiastic grin. When asked about what interests, pastimes, or hobbies they have had through the years, the majority of women centenarians mention quilting. Many, like Lizzie, still piece quilts, giving their creations as gifts to family members, donating them to church organizations for needy families and sometimes, like Lizzie, selling them to earn money.

"For many years, the art of quilting fell into disregard," says quilt expert Betsy May Stern, originally of Nashville, Tennessee, and now of Scarsdale, New York. "For the past several years, there has been a revival of interest, and women of all ages are once again quilting and collecting quilts." Quilting is achieving new attention with museum displays, newspaper articles about the values of quilts, state and local historical projects, quilting clubs, books and documentaries, and even as children's toys. Recently, a magazine article appeared on "smart toys" that are designed to develop creativity in children. One of the boxed kits of supplies and instructions was called "Quilting Bee." "The old quilts, especially from the nineteenth century, are now worth a lot of money," continues Betsy. "Some are in museums; others are being sold. These are antiques, which have become boutique items, selling for between five hundred dollars and one thousand dollars each."

Then there are other quilts that fall into the craft category, such as the ones Lizzie Davis and Cora Meek, 100, of Matoon, Illinois, still make and sell. "Someday they'll be antiques, too," says Lizzie, whose favorite patterns are the Wedding Ring, Dutch Rose, and Flower Garden.

Betsy explains: "Quilts provide a glimpse into history, a way to see the past. We can tell a lot about the time a quilt was made and its creator by the stitching and the fabrics used. Quilts allow us to look into the lives of the women who made them. If we know the person who made a particular quilt, we can look at the quilt and evoke memories; if we don't know the quilt's creator, then we can have fun speculating." It was also a way for women to get together just for fun and for companionship.

"When I first started quilting, all those years ago," adds Lizzie, "the purpose was practical: to make warm bed covers, which our large families needed." Nevertheless, centenarian women tell how they tried with whatever materials they had to make their quilts pretty and to tell a story. "Most didn't have museums and art galleries to go to look at pretty things, so they tried to make them," Betsy adds. "I've always felt a sense of pride walking into a room and seeing a quilt I've made on the bed. It's brought back a lot of fond memories," Lizzie confirms.

What Lizzie Davis has described captures the true beauty of quilts. As Betsy observed, "They are not just a link to bygone days but are also a way to reach into the future. As quilts are handed down from generation to generation, traditions are passed along with them. For example, when the American West was settled, families would leave the East for homes in far-off states, usually never to see family or friends again. When the families departed, they would often receive a friendship quilt as a way to take a 'piece' of each family member along. Through such things old ties were maintained."

Lizzie continues: "I left Arkansas when I was eighteen; in 1906, my husband and I moved to Texas. We had seven children. When my husband died suddenly in 1929, I had no means to support them. I moved back to Arkansas and lived with my parents. I worked as a bookkeeper and made and sold quilts to earn extra money until I remarried in 1941. I was also a charter member of our church, and I started something called the Willing Workers Club. A group of us women made quilts and

› *Elizabeth Davis at 100 continues her favorite pastime-quilting. Photo courtesy of her daughter Robye.*

sold them to raise money for community projects. I've made a lot of quilts in my time, a lot of quilts. I'm still making them. I still am piecing the top pieces of quilts and selling them for twenty-five dollars for a double and thirty-five dollars for a queen-size bed. I still give a lot of them away, too. Each time a family member has a new baby, I give the child a quilt. I live with my daughter now in Yuma, Arizona, and I'm glad I can earn a little money to help with my expenses. I guess you could say that quilting has been a major part of my life. I'm glad to see younger people appreciate and enjoy it, too."

The treasure trove of centenarian reflections and memories captures some of the flavor of the past. Their legacy, in part, is a portrayal of American life from the early years of the twentieth century.

"Centenarians and others of advanced age are our living national treasure," Jane Shure, Information Officer for the National Institute on Aging, says. "They are custodians of tradition, culture, and history. Their personal stories are an important part of our nation's history, yet their wisdom and experiences are seldom recorded. Hopefully, the country's fascination with longevity will focus attention on the contributions of all our elders. . . . Their unique and personal links to our common heritage and their enriching stories and memories are a valuable asset."

❧ 4 ❧

The American Experience

The century after the Civil War was to be an age of revolution—of countless, little-noticed revolutions, which occurred not in the halls of legislatures or on battlefields...but in the homes and farms and factories and schools and stores, across the landscape and in the air—so little noticed because they came so swiftly, because they touched Americans everywhere and every day....A new democratic world was being invented and was being discovered by Americans wherever they lived.

—Daniel J. Boorstin
The Americans

IF all the knowledge and experiences of our nation's eldest citizens could be recorded, what a wonderful mural we would have of the past century, reminiscent of scenes depicting American history on the walls of public buildings painted during the Great Depression by Works Progress Administration (WPA) artists. This program was initiated by Franklin Delano Roosevelt—centenarians' choice as their favorite president. The mural of past memories centenarians have to offer covers a range of experiences as vast as America itself: It cannot be seen in its entirety. Perhaps the sum of experiences of our nation's eldest citizens can best be thought of as viewed through a kaleidoscope, that fascinating novelty object so popular in the homes of Americans when centenarians were young. Each turn of the kaleidoscope produces a different—yet correlative—pattern, as does each centenarian's story.

Today's centenarians continue as our living links to the past by adding to our national story their experiences as immigrants, pioneers, and adventurers. Some epitomize the pluckiness, courage, and hard work of the millions of other immigrants who came here, from all around the globe, seeking a better way of life. Listen, for instance, to

Mary Gleason, who arrived at Ellis Island in steerage from Ireland, and Isidor Zeitz, a Russian Jewish immigrant, whose first job in America was in a toy factory making teddy bears on the Lower East Side of Manhattan for three dollars a week. Hear, too, the dramatic voice of Dr. Ernest Windesheim, a centenarian living in California, who speaks of fleeing from Hitler's Germany—leaving behind family, possessions, and his life's savings—to begin again in America.

The lives of people who were pioneers figure centrally, too. Many centenarians were pioneers in one sense or another, whether in helping to settle new western states such as the Pruitt family, or in founding industries and businesses, like the Greenwalds and the Ortegas.

And then there were the adventurers and missionaries who went forth from this country to live for a time in distant lands, taking American ways, religion, and language with them; returning with a broader perspective of the human condition and a deeper appreciation for the wealth of opportunity in America. Emma Dorsey, born in Ohio in the heartland of America, journeyed to Asia to teach in Japan. The Reverend Joseph Penn grew up in Maryland and then became an African missionary. There's also the amazing story of Brullio Valle, who now lives in Texas, but who was born in Mexico, kidnapped by bandits as an eight-year-old child, and rescued three years later by the infamous rebel leader, Pancho Villa.

Each story is unique. Yet whether born in American or elsewhere, this generation shares a common theme as our living links to history— perseverance before obstacles, ingenuity, a vision of a better life, the capacity for hard work, and determination to succeed. We are fortunate to have those who have lived so long in our midst to enliven history for us. They speak to us of our collective past.

❧

Consider, for instance, the lives of Viola Greenwald, born near the thunder of Niagara Falls, married to an entrepreneur of German descent, and Virginia Ortega, a Spanish-speaking woman also married to an entrepreneur, born near the Sangre de Cristo mountains of New Mexico. Their lives are woven of the unique strands of their own particular culture and heritage and were shaped by their husbands' entrepreneurship. As different as they are, their stories tell of a shared American experience, and each story contributes to the Americana we know today.

Viola Greenwald, who at 103 still lived in Niagara Falls near where she was born, begins: "At first, my life was fairly routine. Nothing special. I went to school and as a child sold flowers, which my widowed mother grew in her garden and made into bouquets, to tourists at the falls." In 1914, Viola married Max Greenwald, a house painter whose parents had emigrated from Germany; the Greenwald family owned considerable property around Cayuga Creek, which flows into the Niagara River, about five miles upstream from the falls. The young couple had two children, Max, and Ruth, and the family lived comfortably, if routinely. Viola supplemented their income by growing and selling strawberries at a roadside stand.

"Just after World War I, however, everything changed. Max couldn't find enough work to support us. I was terribly worried. What I didn't know then was that this difficulty would alter our lives forever."

Max built a one-room store, about the size of a garage, on the family property across the street from the house, near the bank of Cayuga Creek. At first, he sold only dry goods, bread and staples, but soon he put in a gas pump, figuring correctly that with all the tourists coming to the area, it would be a good business. Then he learned of and added a milkshake machine—the first in the area, and "business really took off. People would drive up for gas and a milkshake, then sit in their cars and drink the shake. The shakes were delicious," Viola recalls, "and really caused a sensation. Meanwhile, I was the bookkeeper."

Before long, it occurred to Max that people needed something to eat with the milkshake. He approached Viola with the idea of opening a hot dog stand. He had heard that people were doing a gold mine of business in New York City and that the idea would catch on quickly in Niagara Falls, too. "I was skeptical and opposed the idea of disrupting the grocery business to go into a new venture I had never heard of. I asked him, very sarcastically, 'What's a hot dog?' thinking that would end the conversation and the idea." Instead, Max told her a hot dog was the nickname for the German "dachshund" (little dog) sausages, called little dogs because of their size in comparison with some of the larger German varieties. In New York, people had begun putting them on soft milk rolls like a sandwich. The name "hot dog," he explained, had been coined by a cartoonist covering a baseball game at the New York Polo Grounds. There were concessionaires at the ball park even then, selling cold drinks and ice cream, but no one was buying them this particularly cool April day. The concession owner got the idea to

❧ *Greenwald's Hot Dog Stand, circa 1923. Photo courtesy of the Greenwald family.*

sell something warm instead and sent his employees out to buy up all the dachshund sausages and rolls they could find in the neighborhood. He then had his men hawk the warm sausages from portable hot water tanks: "Get your dachshund sausages while they're red hot!" so the story goes. Hearing this, the cartoonist in the press box drew a picture of a sausage barking, lying in a roll. Since he wasn't sure how to spell "dachshund," he wrote "hot dogs!" as the caption. The cartoon was a success and the coined expression stuck.

"'The point is, Viola,' Max told me, 'hot dogs are very successful in New York City and I think they will be here, too.'" Although miffed, Viola knew it was futile to argue with her husband, who set about with enthusiasm converting the grocery store into a hot dog stand; he even added a boat dock so people in rowboats and canoes could paddle up for a hot dog and a milkshake.

Viola recalls, "All the while I tried to ignore it. On the first day the stand opened, I refused to go. But as it got close to noontime, I kept looking out the front windows to see more and more people pulling up in front, then walking out with milkshakes and the hot dogs, sitting in their cars, and even on the lawn and on the dock, enjoying them. It was too much for me to resist. So I put on my apron, walked across the street, and was there for the next fifty years.

"I'm glad the business was a success. Max loved it. Over the years, he was always adding something new, enlarging the stand, putting in indoor seating, adding a jukebox and colored lights outside, all the way down to the dock. Taking a sweetheart to the Greenwalds' by canoe or rowboat became the popular date in the 1920's and 1930's." Viola remembers "a lot of sparking going on, along with the hot dogs and shakes. The local folks began calling the Greenwald place the LaSalle Country Club, naming it after that area of the city, since almost every-one ended up there on a Saturday night."

Viola retired when she was eighty-five and sold the business, but she still has the fondest of recollections. "Everyone knew us, and we met wonderful people from all over. I have nice memories, and so do they, of good times at Greenwalds. Every so often, someone will say to me that they remember when they used to come to the stand; and they tell my daughter Ruth, too—they still remember the wonderful strawberry pies she introduced. We were an institution in Niagara Falls. The first hot dog stand in Western New York. I still get cards and letters from people we met over the years," Viola says with pleasure. "And what's more important, it was fun."

Two thousand miles southwest of Niagara Falls, seemingly a world away, lives Virginia Trujillo Ortega, matriarch of the weaving dynasty that made her family and the small Northern New Mexico village of Chimayo, internationally known. Virginia is of Spanish descent, with Spanish being her native language; her son, David, serves as her interpreter.

"Spaniards from New Spain, now Mexico, settled in the Chimayo area in 1696; the first Ortega was born here in 1729. In the mid-1700s the Ortega family bought land around Chimayo's old plaza, and we still own much of that land." Mrs. Ortega goes on to explain that one of her ancestors, Concepcion Trujillo, came to the area as a military man long before there was ever a dream of New Mexico becoming part of the United States. [It was part of the settlement of the Mexican War that

⁊ *Ortega Family, circa 1909. (Left to right) Nicacio Ortega, Ricardo Ortega (baby),*
Virginia Ortega, Bonificia Ortega, Joe Ramon Ortega, Francisquita Trujillo.
Photo courtesy of the Ortega family.

the New Mexico territory was ceded to the United States in 1848.]
When New Mexico became the forty-seventh state in 1912, Mrs.
Ortega's brother-in-law, Victor, was a member of the new state's first
constitutional convention, she tells proudly.

In 1900, Nicosio Ortega, Virginia's husband, built an adobe house
for his fifteen-year-old bride; it is a house Virginia lived in all her life.
The surrounding countryside, with its bucolic scenery, in the foothills
of the mountain range, is juxtaposed against the thriving industry at
work in and around the Ortega home. The house has been added onto
over the years, she explains, to accommodate their growing family and
growing business.

"During the first two years of our marriage," Virginia tells, "my
husband had to go to Colorado to find work because our little rural
communities were economically depressed. He would send money
home for me, and my father or brothers would see that my needs were
provided for."

Similarities between the Ortegas and the Greenwalds begin to surface when Virginia Ortega tells proudly how her husband's business sense and hard work brought economic success to their family and to the community of Chimayo.

About 1912, the story goes, a Californian familiar with the area's Spanish heritage came to the village to purchase blankets from the village weavers. Virginia's husband agreed to supply them, and organized about thirty weavers among his friends and family to make the blankets. Nicosio bought the yarns and other materials needed by the weavers and they set to work; if the work passed his inspection, he paid the weaver. He then shipped the blankets to California from Española, about ten miles away via the narrow-gauge railroad line. Business got so good that, like Max Greenwald, Nicosio soon expanded, opening a general store, the first one in Chimayo, in 1914.

The weaving business grew from its fine reputation for craftsmanship, Virginia Ortega says proudly, and from some of the prominent, satisfied customers they have had over the years. Significantly, a blanket made in 1934 was given to President Roosevelt. As newspapers and magazines picked up the story of the Chimayan weaving, the Ortega family business thrived. Customers from all over the world sent orders for blankets. Tourists were attracted to Chimayo to see the weaving and to enjoy the Spanish flavor of the area. As she puts it, "When the Spaniards came to the New World, they brought with them two special things: their God and their loom. This is a good life we live here in Chimayo."

Son David adds: "We have had eight generations of weavers in the family, now that my grandchildren are in the business. My mother has been a part of the business for all these years; she helped us all by overseeing the business in every way. In the old days, when the company expanded, she took over paying the weavers my father hired, and she helped market the blankets, vests, pillows, purses, and coats that we made. My father built the weaving shop next to our home. She ran the grocery store as well while raising her family. Most importantly, she kept the family happy, and the business prospered."

By promoting weaving and employing many villagers, the Ortegas became community leaders, just as the Greenwalds became well known in Niagara Falls. Both families gained prominence from humble grass-roots beginnings thanks to their entrepreneurship and by drawing upon their family cultural backgrounds.

❧ *Virginia Ortega on her 104th birthday with an Ortega blanket in the background. Photo courtesy of the Ortega family, 1990.*

❧

PIONEERS

Another turn of the kaleidoscope brings into focus those centenarians who were pioneers, helping to open and settle new territory for America's expansion, some right in the places where they were born. One such pioneer is Wilma Jeffers McGloughlin, born in Soldier, Idaho, in 1888, two years before it became a state. Wilma taught school for ten years before her marriage in 1915. She and her husband, Forest, lived on a ranch in Tikura, in Silver Creek, for thirty years before moving to Boise. In 1982, at the age of ninety-four and a widow, Wilma traveled by pickup truck with her daughter, pulling a twenty-foot trailer containing all her possessions. "I moved into an apartment about a mile from my daughter in Kellogg. I live alone and I take care of myself, but we have dinner together every night. Idaho is my home," she says. "I've never lived anywhere else." In her home state, Wilma is honored as a pioneer.

Among those pioneering far from home is Hattie Allen. Born on a farm in Minnesota in 1886, she moved with her family to Washington two years after it became a state in 1889, and then went on to Valdez, Alaska, in 1907, fifty-two years before it became a state. There she owned a general store. "I moved to Alaska because I could earn a lot more money there than women were making in the States," she tells. Mrs. Allen, who now lives in Palmer, fifty miles north of Anchorage, was also honored by the state as an Alaska pioneer.

Hattie Allen recalls her first memory at the age of five. "We were moving to Washington by train from Minnesota. Everyone was hanging out the windows at one of the stops. We were happy. A bunch of Chinese men walked by. They had long pigtails. They talked different and were dressed different. I reached out and pulled a pigtail. The man turned around and talked fast to me. I made a face at him. My mother pulled me in from the window and gave me a good lickin'. You'd thought I'd started a war or something. I can see it yet. Of course, later, I learned about prejudice, and realized why I had been wrong. When I got to Alaska at the age of twenty-one, there were all kinds of people coming and going there. It was a lesson that served me in good stead."

Moving the eyepiece of a kaleidoscope, an infinite number of colorful patterns appear, ever changing. So, too, the ever changing variety of individuals and experiences. Margarita Padilla was born in Albuquerque in the New Mexico Territory in 1889. Her grandparents came from Spain in the mid-1800s, settling in the area to raise cattle and sheep. Both her grandfather and father had died by the time she was eight years old. Margarita's mother then decided to move to the eastern part of the Arizona Territory, where two grown sons and an older daughter had gone a few years earlier to work in the cattle business.

"We made the trip in a homemade covered wagon," Margarita tells, "pulled by burros and leading a cow." The group consisted of her mother, grandmother, a sister-in-law, her ten-year-old brother, and Margarita. "It took several weeks of rather uneventful travel," she continues, "covering only a few miles a day. We met wagons going both ways so we never were all alone very long. There were no road maps—no guideposts. I don't know how my mother ever found the way. For three women to undertake this, what courage it must have taken," she says with admiration. "I was too young to sense the danger. My only recollection is of being bored."

The family arrived safely in St. John's, Arizona, and soon everyone was working. "Even the children helped out," Margarita says. "My mother and grandmother, following the Spanish tradition, did not believe in educating daughters, so I never attended school at all. My mother sewed and ironed for other people and sold homemade tamales. I used to help her and learned a skill that would help sustain my own family in years to come.

"Silver and gold mining in California were still going strong in the early 1900s. St. John's was a thriving community at that time, with new families arriving continuously. There were a lot of unmarried women and girls, and somehow the California miners got word of this." The miners then came to St. John's to look for wives. "These were pretty clever fellows," Margarita recalls, "as they organized a big dance and cookout and invited the whole town. This way they could look over all the girls at one time."

When Margarita was fourteen, her older sister wanted to take her to one of these dances, but they didn't have any nice clothes to wear. "My enterprising mother took some lovely lace curtains, which had come with the family from Spain, and she and my grandmother made two of the prettiest dresses any girls ever had," Margarita tells. "Nobody knew we had holes in the soles of our shoes."

The ploy worked. Her sister married one of the miners, who became quite wealthy. Margarita was seen by a local man who fell in love with her at first sight. Arismen Durand was twenty-five, the son of a French Basque family. "His parents came to see my mother and they worked out arrangements for the marriage," Margarita says. "I still hadn't seen the man." Margarita recalls how she fell in love with him the first time she saw him, when he came to visit her riding a big white horse. "My family teased me, saying I fell in love with his horse," she relates. "We were married on July 28, 1904, and it lasted fifty-five happy years."

Adding some historical detail, Margarita continues her recollections

☙ *Margarita Padilla Duran at 101, making tortillas.*
Photo courtesy of the Duran family. Photograph by Mark Duran.

of those early years in the Arizona Territory. "It was about this time that a boy cousin was stolen by the Indians in the area and it took more than a year to get him back. When the soldiers found him, he didn't want to leave his Indian mother.

"Those early years of marriage were busy times," she says. "Soon the babies began to come, twelve in all. The first four died. To help support our family, I began making and selling tamales as my mother had done. When Mexican nationals were brought in to build a schoolhouse, I was asked to cook for them. My husband's brother was an Apache county sheriff and he had four prisoners on hand, so he asked me to cook for them, too." With the help of her children she stayed very busy. Margarita also made quilts and sometimes traded with Indians the tamales for meat.

"When the lumber mill was established in McNary, not far away, we moved there and I opened a boarding house, which I ran for ten years. All the land in that area belonged to the Apache tribe and individuals couldn't buy land, so when the mill closed we moved to Pinetop, Arizona, in the White Mountains. Here we bought land and built a house and restaurant and bar." Many present-day residents in the area recall Duran's Cafe (the last "d" having been dropped at some point), her daughter adds. At the age of 101, Margarita is still making tamales.

The ever-changing variety of individuals and experiences continues with other centenarians who have traveled the globe at a time when travel was truly an adventure.

❧

ADVENTURERS

Emma Dorsey lives in Delaware, Ohio, the town where she was born 102 years ago. For many years, Emma traveled and "lived an exciting life," she says, first as a teacher in Japan and then as an entertainer, traveling with vaudeville shows and musical companies. "We took culture on the road to many rural areas of the Midwest before the advent of television.

"Playing the organ was my first love, and always will be," says this 1911 graduate of Ohio Wesleyan University. "Singing was second and piano last. I've had many years of hard work, doing all three, but many years of pleasure and memories, too. One early memory was being awarded a prize in music at college. I got a check for one hundred dollars. I continued postgraduate work on the organ while completing my vocal course." In 1914, she married, and the couple spent three years in Kobe, Japan. Her husband, Floyd, taught English for the government and Emma taught voice and piano at Kobe Girl's College, as well as teaching piano and voice privately. "Those are memorable days," she exclaims. "I appeared in many recitals locally and in other Japanese cities. We left Kobe for the USA in April 1917, when World War I was declared. We moved to Cleveland and then to Valparaiso, Indiana, for my husband's work."

On a lark, she auditioned in Chicago for the May Valentine Opera Company's production of *Robin Hood*. "To my surprise I won the role of Alan-a-Dale and toured the entire United States in about six months. We had our own railroad car, scenery, stage hands, and orchestra," she tells. "After that, I formed a quartet called the Song Birds and toured for another season." Upon conclusion of that tour, Emma and her husband were hired by the Chautauqua Company. "We traveled several years to many small towns, in almost every state, before settling down again in my old hometown."

⁊

For a different reason, the Reverend Joseph Penn was also an adventurer. Born in 1886 in Charles County, Maryland, he worked as a pastor traveling around New England for several years. A graduate of Trevecca Nazarene College in Nashville, Tennessee, Reverend Penn explains that he was "called by the Church of the Nazarene to go as a missionary to Africa in 1919." He remained in Africa until shortly before the outbreak of World War II with his wife Susan. It was there they raised a family of four children. "My wife, a nurse, was able to put her training to good use helping the native people," Reverend Penn says.

Reverend Penn pastored in three African nations, including Swaziland. There he helped establish schools, a hospital, and a mission station. He learned several tribal languages and preached in Zulu. "At first, we lived in mud huts, with no inside plumbing or water. Later, more substantial houses were built." The couple had cows, hogs, chickens, and a garden, and things were very much like they were in this country in a rural setting, he says. One thing that stands out in Reverend Penn's mind from those days is that African children were taught to highly respect their elders.

Life was not always serene, though, he tells. "As a missionary, I also worked at the compounds of the gold mines. These mines employed hundreds of thousands of people. A compound consisted of two thousand to twelve thousand men living in dormitories or barracks; many were right out of the jungle. They worked six months under their contract, then went back home for another six months." Reverend Penn recalls how he went to seventy-five or more of these camps. Once each year, he and all his family traveled to a very remote camp. They went as far as they could by train, then took a wagon, for another seventy-five miles. Two or three Africans accompanied them on the journey, which required several overnight stops. "We would build a big fire and sleep in the wagon, under the wagon and in tents. Sometimes we could hear a lion in the distance, but we were never bothered."

After returning to the United States in 1938, Reverend Penn pastored and lectured in various parts of the country, settling for a time in Idaho. At age eight-five, he remarried and nine years later moved to Arizona, where he continued to pastor at several nursing homes. Nearing his centennial year, he retired to devote more time to helping care for his ailing wife.

Ҏ

Fred Steeves, 102, also had a "long career in the mission field. The first twenty-one years of my life were spent on a homestead farm in North Dakota," he tells. "Then in 1910, my whole family moved to Alberta, Canada. My father helped me get a farm of my own, but after four years I decided to quit farming and get an education. It took me six years. I had only gone to school to the fifth grade but graduated president of my class from the Alberta Industrial Academy. After that, I went to Walla Walla, Washington, for a year at the Seventh-Day Adventist Ministerial College.

"During my seven years of schooling, I sold religious books door-to-door. Because of my experience, I got a call to go to Colombia, South America, to sell off a large shipment of books, *Heralds of the Morning*, that had been left molding at the customs house at Burranquilla, Colombia, a small town at the mouth of the great Magdalena River. The man who had been handling them got malaria and literally had to be carried out on a stretcher. This was 1922. After a slow start, learning the language, and many trips by train, steamer, mule, and any other transportation I could get, to Bogata and to many towns and villages all over Colombia, the venture was a success. Eventually, I was made the publishing secretary to promote the sale for the Bibles and religious books in the large territory of Colombia and Venezuela. For fourteen years I traveled up and down from Panama to Guatemala, holding sales institutes, and teaching hundreds of the nations' young people to sell books. The great need and the lure of the frontier fascinated me.

"After being out of the country for three years, I sent for my fiancée, a schoolteacher back in Walla Walla, and we were married on the Isthmus of Panama. We had two children, but neither lived. Later we adopted a boy and a girl. In all, I spent thirty years selling books and preaching. When we returned to the United States in the 1950s, we settled for a time in San Antonio and later moved on to St. Helena, California, where I now live with my second wife of eighteen years. I remarried when I was eighty-four. Interestingly, her husband and I had been friends since 1917. Beatrice was a nurse, and she takes good care of me," he says with a lively sparkle in his eye. "Although I am returned and retired, I am still interested in all the happenings in Inter-America," Fred concludes.

℘

IMMIGRANTS

The kaleidoscope of stories continues, bringing the life experiences of foreign born centenarians into view. According to United States Census Bureau estimates, approximately 18 percent of today's centenarians were born outside the United States. The majority of them came to America either as young children during the last decade of the nineteenth century or as young adults in the first decade of this century.

At first, many settled in the urban areas of the East; some later traveled west to seek their fortunes. Centenarians recall the concern at the time, on the part of more established American families (some only first- or second-generation Americans themselves), that these "aliens" would damage the fabric of American life and culture. As a result, immigrants coming to America found both fulfillment and disappointment. Some recall that their first experiences were unpleasant, frightening or disconcerting. But for others, life in America was so superior to their previous circumstances that they immediately felt this was indeed the promised land, in spite of the obstacles.

Frank Diana, 104, of Lancaster, New York, traveled from Sicily with his mother and brother and sisters before the turn of the century. "My mother's family came around the same time, from Italy," his daughter, Marie, tells. "Both fathers had come to the United States a few years before and worked as laborers to earn passage for their families, a typical scenario. We grew up hearing stories of their journeys and early days here."

The following story is one of Marie's favorites. At the train station in Buffalo, where Marie's grandfathers met their families, there was a fruit stand on the platform. The children looked at it in awe and with longing. Her grandfather told each of the children to choose one piece of fruit, but their mother said "No!" that they could not afford such luxuries. "Both my parents recall their fathers' promise that food in America was not the luxury it was in the old country and that their families would never be hungry again. 'We are in God's country,' Frank remembers being told, again and again.

"That's something we lived by, too," Marie says. "My parents have always been grateful to live in America, and they taught us that to love this country is central to our lives. Frank's father worked hard to give his family a better life than he had experienced, and Frank in turn strove to give his children an education."

Like many centenarians, he succeeded. Marie became a history teacher and at age seventy-four was still on the faculty of the local high school. Frank lives with her, and she takes loving care of her father, who has been so good to his family. Marie says, "Sure, there was prejudice because our parents were Italian immigrants, but my father overlooked it, telling us, 'It's better to be dead in America than alive in Sicily.' That's how strongly he felt about the conditions he left behind. It's understandable that Americans who had been here for a few generations would be worried about the effect such huge influxes of immigrants would make on the culture. Hindsight is perfect, remember. But at that time, they had no idea that what these people could contribute would add to the richness of the cultures, and they were concerned that the values already in place would be eroded."

⚘

Centenarian Mary Gleason of Columbia, South Carolina, also recalls an encounter with fruit when she arrived at Ellis Island. It was 1911 and she had just gotten off the boat from Ireland. Offered a banana, and having never seen one before, she didn't know it had to be peeled and began eating it skin and all. "People laughed at me," she remembers with good humor, "but I learned."

Born on a farm in County Tipperary in 1889, Mary came alone to America at the age of twenty-two in search of a better life. Leaving behind her parents and most of her family, she went at first to live with an aunt on Madison Avenue in New York. Mary met her future husband, also from Tipperary, on the boat coming over. "There were a total

✺ *Mary Gleason, 1911. Photo courtesy of the Gleason family.*

of fifteen passengers in steerage class from Tipperary, and we stayed together," she tells. Her mother later told her that at the dock the two sets of parents said they hoped their children would get to know each other, so they could look out for one another on the journey. For Mary, it wasn't very hard to notice her future husband—his surname was "Gleeson" also, though they weren't related. When they arrived at Ellis Island, the immigration officer misspelled both names with an "ea" instead of "ee" and they just left it that way, she says.

Like many immigrants, Isidor Zeitz also had his name changed at Ellis Island when he arrived there in 1906 with his grandmother. Born in Odessa, Russia, he carried the family name of Zayatz. "The immigration officials couldn't spell it, so they wrote Zeitz, making it sound like a German name. I fled Russia to escape being taken into the army."

Because he entered this country without any evidence of his birth or true name, Isidor was kept at Ellis Island for two days until he could establish his age. "It was a tense time," he recalls. "I was afraid I would be sent back." He remembered he had his bar mitzvah four years before; the immigration department put down that he arrived at age seventeen. As Isidor explains, "According to my grandmother's figures, I was born in 1888, but we had no proof—and so it was only in September 1989 that I became officially 100 years old."

Isidor lived on the Lower East Side of New York, starting work in a factory that made stuffed toys and earning three dollars a week. The Hebrew Immigrant Aid Society offered free schooling and he studied to become an electrician. Later, he became a part of twentieth-century technologic history by working on the lighting in the subway tunnel connecting Manhattan to Brooklyn, which was finished in 1918.

Later still, after becoming an electrical contractor, he moved in 1920 to Lakewood, New Jersey, and belonged to a progressive group called the Workmen's Circle. "We organized a school to teach our children Yiddish and Jewish education," Isidor tells. "I'm proud all three of my children attended."

Isidor is also very proud of his adopted country, and two United States presidents have touched his life, although he has lived through the administrations of more than ten. "My favorite president was Franklin D. Roosevelt. I admired him for his remarkable human response to the suffering of the people who lived through the Depression, and for his ability to relieve the desperate situation many of us were in by instituting measures to create work for the unemployed."

At the family party in Montclair, New Jersey, given to mark his centennial, Isidor was surprised and very pleased by the postal delivery of a letter from then President George Bush congratulating him on his milestone birthday. "Imagine me, a poor Russian immigrant, receiving birthday congratulations from the President of the United States!" he exclaimed.

·୬

Frank Kleminski's earliest memory is of the day in 1894 when his family left Vilnius, Lithuania. "The excitement, all the crying, saying good-bye forever—and it was forever," Frank remembers. "I never saw or heard from my grandparents again, and I don't remember anything of Lithuania. I best remember Ellis Island as the place where I had my first shower."

The family settled in a coal mining town in Pennsylvania where Frank's father found work. The elder Mr. Kleminski didn't read, write, drink, or smoke. "He seemed only to work in the mines," Frank recalls. "It was a poor living. In the mines, people from the old country were called 'Hunkeys.' Your name was how other people spelled it. From our Lithuanian name 'Klemonskis' it became 'Kleminski,' as it is now. There was a lot of prejudice. Life was hard."

Hard, indeed. His first job, in a pipe mill at age fourteen, paid just nine cents an hour. But Frank was a good athlete and he believes it saved him from a life of poverty. "I played a lot of baseball and even played professionally one year," he tells. He was more accepted than some of the other immigrants, he believes, because he played this "American game." "It brought me into contact with other people— Americans. I was able to travel and see more of the country. I had more opportunities because of this."

Frank decided to leave the mill and learn a trade. He apprenticed himself to a carpenter, working for four years for twenty cents an hour. "My father thought I was crazy," he recalls, "but within six years, I started building and selling modern homes for four thousand dollars, including the lot. I was doing so well I was able to sell homes for a small down payment and give the mortgage myself. It helped a lot of people who would not have been able to buy a home."

By 1929, he was a successful homebuilder/seller in the steel mill boomtown of Gary, Indiana. Then the stock market crashed, people stopped paying, mortgage foreclosures came, his own home was in danger, and there was no work anywhere. "I had two children to support, bills galore, and my wife was dying with lingering cancer. I lost her in 1932. I don't know how I made it. All I had left was my pickup truck. Little by little, I started to get back on my feet, and I vowed to myself that when I did, I was going to change my life."

Part of Frank's wish came true in 1941, when he spent a month in Wisconsin looking for that "better life." He found a one-room building on a lake fifty miles south of Duluth, Minnesota, where he could live off the land, have a garden, fish, hunt, and trap. After that, he stayed there seven months out of the year until retirement. Frank has spent the last twenty-five winters in Tucson, Arizona, where his daughter lives, and recently he moved there permanently because of the climate. His son uses the cabin in Wisconsin, and Frank spends every summer with him. Frank, at 102, a veteran of poverty and personal tragedy, still remains fascinated with and optimistic about America: "So many choices, so many things to do, places to go, places to live. Only in America—'land of opportunity' is right, as they say."

For Richard Johnson of Natick, Massachusetts, immigrating to America was not as great a transition as it was for Frank, since Richard began life in Canada. Born in Toronto in 1889, he moved with his family to Bermuda in 1908. His father built the famous Elbow Beach Hotel and operated it for many years. "It is still there," says Richard, pleased. "Pictures of my family in the early days line some of the hallways. The beach-changing cubicles I helped build all those years ago are still there, too." The family had a party at the hotel in 1989 for his sister's birthday. While there, he checked the bathhouses. "They were still standing. I'll check them again when I go back to celebrate her next birthday."

Richard's life in Bermuda prior to moving to the United States was tranquil compared to the career changes and relocating he would do for many years to come. He recounts: "The move to Bermuda was good for me. I met my wife there. We were married April 28, 1913, when I was twenty-four and she was just twenty. We left Bermuda the next day by ship and landed in New York City on May first for the start of our wedding trip. After three days in New York, we set out for St. John, New Brunswick, and lived there for three years near my brother. But my wife didn't like it and wanted to move to Natick, Massachusetts, where she had relatives. In 1916, we left by boat for Boston and then drove to Natick, about an hour's drive in those days. We settled here.

I still live in the large Victorian house we bought shortly after we moved here—the second time, that is, in 1925.

"Between times I decided I wanted to see more of the country and perhaps try my luck in California. A lot of people were beginning to move there. In 1923, I bought a secondhand, seven-passenger Buick, and my wife and I set out for Los Angeles with our small children, three boys and one girl. The first part of our journey was over pretty fair roads, paved with stone, but after we left St. Louis, it became dicey. The gravel roads were, at times, as slick as an icy road, and often we would slide off. We were following the Jefferson Highway in Missouri when we came to the Hackberry River. We had to be ferried across. In the middle of the river, the ferry ran out of gas, and we had to siphon gas out of my car to get the ferry across.

"We stopped in campgrounds along the way. People traveling west to east told me to turn back—there was nothing in California to see. But I kept going. When I make up my mind with something, I don't turn around. We followed the Santa Fe Trail from Independence, Missouri, across Kansas, and then to Santa Fe. It was almost 800 miles. The signposts were painted red, white and blue, but the roads—you would think they were paths compared to the highways today—were not well marked and many times we became lost. I had one really bad breakdown, other than just bent wheel rims and small things. We were miles away from anything, and I didn't know what I was going to do. Suddenly, out of nowhere, a car came along. The driver stopped, assessed the problem with the engine, got out his tools, and fixed it on the spot. He even gave me a spare part—and wouldn't take any money for his time or trouble. That's the way people were back then in rural areas; people helped each other, knowing their reward would be help from someone else when they needed it.

"It took a month to get to Los Angeles. We found a very small cottage and planned to stay. We lasted two years. I couldn't find enough work to support my family. Some people were living very well, but for those who weren't, it was a tough place. The Hollywood Bowl had opened the year before, and the Beverly Hills Hotel was already popular. Some people were having a very good time. Films were being made. It was an extravaganza. There was a lot of money in some areas. All we got to see was the Rose Parade.

"I remember about the time we left for California by car the first non-stop, transcontinental flight took off from Long Island. I heard later that they arrived in San Diego in twenty-seven hours, about one hour traveling time for each day we drove. And to think now you can fly coast to coast in a mere five hours. I like to travel. In fact, I drove across the country in the 1940s just to see it again. That time it only took me two weeks and the roads were much improved.

"When we got back to Natick in 1925, I worked for a while at the Framingham Foundry before starting my own house painting business a few years later. Over the years, I have painted most of the town's public buildings and many of the houses in town. I retired at seventy-eight and started a summertime bed-and-breakfast inn in Auburn, New Hampshire. We didn't make any money, but we had a lot of fun. I was the innkeeper, the groundskeeper, you name it. We kept that up for several years until my wife decided it was time to stop. I liked it; I guess I had the hotel business in my mind from my young days helping my father at the Elbow Beach. I enjoyed meeting guests from different parts of the country who came to stay with us in New Hampshire. It's interesting. No two people are ever the same."

Today Richard keeps himself busy maintaining his turn-of-the-century large Victorian home. He has converted the second and third floors into apartments, which he rents. On the wall of his living room over a large antique curio chest, which he bought when it was new, are three small, crossed flags depicting the three allegiances of his life: a Canadian flag, the British flag of Bermuda, and the American flag. In evidence through the glass panels of the chest are scrapbooks and a collection of memorabilia of his experiences and travels. Outside, from sunup to sundown, he flies the American flag proudly from a large flagpole encircled by a bed of rocks and bright flowers. He enjoys driving around Natick and goes out every morning to the post office, the grocery store, and around town. He still likes to travel but prefers to fly, saying, "My long-distance driving days are over. And, besides, it's so much faster to fly."

✦

As these brief snapshots suggest, centenarians were not only crisscrossing America, they were also crisscrossing the globe.

Mary Ogburn picks up the theme, telling of her travels, "Not as a jet-setter, though," she says in her down-to-earth manner.

Mary was born an only child of a gold miner in Brinkin, Scotland, in 1885. While she was still a teenager, her father left for the Yukon Territory of Canada, to join in the gold mining business there. In 1906, twenty-one-year-old Mary left Scotland by boat to join her father in Dawson, Yukon. "It took a very long time," she recalls, "and the boat was terrible." She then traveled across Canada by train, alone. Once there, she traveled around the Northwest Territories, "sometimes by train, often by sleigh, pulled by a team of horses.

"I married a gold miner, like my father, in 1912. In 1926 he had a job offer in Fairbanks, Alaska, and so we moved. Our children grew up in Alaska and went to high school there. We began to vacation each year in Arizona—do I need to tell you why? Eventually, we moved there permanently." Mary became a citizen in 1935 and now lives with her daughter, Ruth, in Mesa, Arizona.

✖

Like Mary, other centenarians also came to the United States at a later stage in their lives. Dr. Ernest Windesheim, 101, did not leave his native Germany until he was almost fifty years old, and then not as a matter of choice but to flee, with his wife and two children, the Nazi regime in 1937. He left behind almost everything else—relatives, possessions, and life savings.

A graduate of medical school in Munich in 1912, he says, "I sat at the feet of Wilheim Roentgen, who discovered the X ray."

Dr. Windesheim vividly recalls the inception and expanding array of remarkable lifesaving drugs and new technologies during his years as a student and later as a physician. Of them all, though, he believes the greatest and most important discovery of this century was that of sulfa drugs, followed by antibiotics in the early 1940s. In fact, he recalls his first use of the new lifesaving drug, sulfa. An elderly woman was dying from an infection and he could do nothing for her. Fortunately, he had a sample of this new drug, which a representative from a pharmaceutical company had left for him. Dr. Windesheim gave it to his patient and, three days later, she recovered. "It was like a miracle," he tells.

After practicing internal medicine in his native town of Erfurt, Germany, for about thirty-five years, Dr. Windesheim began a new life and practice in the San Francisco Bay area. He was affiliated with the Alta Bates-Herrick Hospital and is well known in the medical community as a compassionate and experienced physician. "I wanted to be a doctor since I was a young boy," he tells, "because I wanted to help people. My mother was opposed; she was afraid I would catch an infection or a disease from a patient and lose my own life. I overcame her objections, practiced until I was almost 100—and I'm so glad I did."

Dr. Windesheim was forced to give up his practice following hip surgery, and a subsequent fall down the staircase at his office. "I worked until November 3, 1987. That day was the end of my medical career. It was awful. I had treated some patients for forty years. I miss being a physician. I miss my patients and they miss me. I still keep up with the medical literature and my medical license is still current."

His sorrow over the end of his practice is nonetheless bolstered by Dr. Windesheim's philosophical view: "But on the whole, I've had a very good life. I am blessed with a close family—my wife of seventy-three years and many grandchildren and great-grandchildren nearby. And I am grateful, and proud, to be a citizen of the United States."

.৯৯

Meanwhile, centenarian Brullio Valle tells a fascinating tale from his past and of the events that led to his family's move from Mexico. On February 1, 1895, when he was eight years old, Brullio was kidnapped near the ranch where he was born in northern Mexico. His father's ranch was near the town of Villaldama, about fifty miles northwest of Monterrey, he tells. "Four men rode up on horses and told me if I went with them, they would give me a goat for my father." So Brullio got up on the back of a horse with one of the "banditos." "I didn't realize that I was being kidnapped at first until they rode far up into the hills to their campsite. There were other young boys there, too. The banditos never stayed in one place very long, always moving from campsite to campsite. I was abused a lot and beaten when I tried to escape."

At this time, seventeen-year-old Doroteo Arango, the young man who would become the infamous rebel leader Pancho Villa, was also in trouble. A year before, he shot and killed a man who had molested his sister. "Arango was on the run, hiding in the mountains, and making occasional risky visits to see his family," Brullio explains. He took the assumed name by combining the first name of his uncle, Pancho, with the last name of his grandfather, Villa.

"I don't know how this came about, but my father befriended Pancho Villa and gave him guns and shelter for a few days," Brullio continues. "He also paid him to find and rescue me. One day, he rode into the banditos' camp with an extra horse. He told me to get on the horse, that he had come to take me back to my father. I was afraid. I had been beaten several times for trying to escape. They told me if I tried again, they would kill me. I remember saying to this man, 'You are only one. How can you rescue me?'

"Apparently Pancho Villa had convinced the group of fourteen bandits that he could lead them to where they could kill some cows for meat, as fresh meat was always in short supply. Somehow he tricked them and doubled back to the camp to get me.

"I can hear him say to me, 'Hurry up! We have to go.' Then he told me my parents names and I believed him. I got on the horse and he took me to my home. He left immediately, fearing he was being followed. It was on the same day that I was first taken, February first, three years later."

In 1910, Brullio's family had another close escape, this time from the revolution in which Pancho Villa figured prominently. "We came to Texas, leaving all our land and belongings behind," he tells. Brullio worked as a cowboy/ranch hand and enjoyed the life; he recalls many evenings playing the guitar for the other cowboys. Eventually, he settled in LaPryor, Texas. He and his wife of sixty-nine years were married in 1920 and had seventeen children, nine of whom survived.

At 100, he lives alone, refusing to live with any of his children. He takes care of himself now after nursing his wife through her last illness for several years. Brullio says his hopes for America in the future are for more research into longevity and more medical inventions so that more people can live as long as he has.

This extraordinary personal remembrance of Pancho Villa is an example of oral history. Preserving these memories by audiotape or videotape recording of interviews with people about their life experiences offers the human element behind the factual material of history. To be sure, there will be some discrepancies in dates, but these can be easily corrected. As Brullio's granddaughter says, "I checked his entire story as part of a college project, and it all proves out." She adds: "It's interesting to do it [corroborating an oral history]. I learned a lot."

✌

Centenarian Ola Canion had it right when she remarked during an oral history taping, "Why, heck, I don't remember exactly—it was around 1905." Ola was being questioned about what year an historical event occurred. And then she went on to chide the interviewer, "That was eighty-five years ago. I'll bet you can't remember the exact dates of some things that happened twenty-five years ago. Besides, it's

❧ *Ola Canion at 100, in her mother's dress, shawl and bonnet*
from 1905. Photo courtesy of the Dorothy Garske Center, Phoenix, AZ.
Photograph by Don B. Stevenson.

not important—you can go look that up. What I'm telling you is the
background of what went on at that time, and that I do remember. And
that's what you can't find in a history book."

Ola adds flavor to her account of the family's migration from one
state to another by telling how she and her family traveled from Texas
to southern Arizona in a covered wagon in the early years of this century. "We children, and the women, had to walk most of the way," she
says, "to make room for our possessions and to save on the horses.
But whenever we went through a town, my father told us to get in
the wagon so the townsfolk wouldn't think badly of him for making
us walk. I was mad at this, though, because I had my mind set that I
was walking all the way from Texas to Arizona. Since I was the oldest,

I refused to get in with the others, and so today I can say that I walked all the way. No, I don't recall the year exactly—it was around 1905," she quips.

On special occasions, Ola wears her mother's dress and bonnet worn on that journey.

What centenarians and others of advanced age have to say makes history dynamic by preserving personal insights of events, people, and places. Their recollections make the past come alive, as alive as the person speaking. In the process, it creates a more memorable piece of history. Centenarians are able to push recollections of history back at least another generation by relating stories they heard, firsthand, from their parents, uncles, and aunts. Sometimes their recollections go back even further to their grandparents' experiences in the mid-nineteenth century, from stories they enjoyed as youngsters and remember still.

As Isabel Clark James, 100, of Wilmington, North Carolina, who grew up in Tarboro, North Carolina, tells us: "I loved to hear my father talk about interesting experiences in his life and to hear my mother and aunt tell stories of the Civil War. They were only in their early teens at the time, but they clearly remembered when the Yankees came and took their mother and father's lovely new home right on the river in Washington, North Carolina, near Cape Hatteras. My grandfather [their father] was killed during the Civil War and my grandmother also died during that war. Thus, I never knew my grandparents, only my precious two old aunts, who had loads of stories to tell."

❧

HISTORIC PRESERVATION

Centenarian Billy Earley of Florence, Arizona, was an early advocate of preserving local history in her adopted state. "I came to Arizona in 1929 because I wanted to see it," she says. "I stayed because I liked it." Billy recognized the potential and the importance of individual contributions in keeping history alive, having lived the first part of her life in several eastern states, which are so steeped in American history and concerned with its preservation.

Beginning in the forties, Billy and her husband, Lynn, traveled around Arizona speaking to civic groups and individuals, encouraging the preservation of historic heritage and memories of earlier times. "Billy is not a nickname," she explains. "I'm named after my father." She has also been a leader and outspoken advocate for many histori-

   🌺 *Billy Earley around 1930, Florence, AZ.*
Photo courtesy of Billy Earley.

cal projects. One, which started many years ago, continues to require her attention from time to time. "I knew the cowboy actor Tom Mix, who made many movies in Arizona in the 1930s. After his death in 1940, in a car accident on State Highway 89 near Florence, I lobbied the legislature to provide a marker at the spot," she tells. A small metal statue of Tom Mix on "Tony, The Wonder Horse," his favorite steed, was eventually installed there. The handsome statue has been stolen a few times over the years, and each time Billy has fought successfully to have it replaced, most recently in February 1994.

In 1988, in her centennial year, Billy received the Governor's Award for Historic Preservation. Since then she has received numerous other state and local awards and recognition for her continued work on historical projects.

✑

Grace Sumner Northrup of Northfield, Minnesota, the centenarian introduced in the Prelude, is another who participated in projects for her local historical societies. In 1975, after she had moved to Sun City, Arizona, Grace was contacted by the St. Paul, Minnesota, Historical Society. One of their oral historians came to interview her in connection with their centennial commemoration of the most colorful event in Northfield's past—the day the Jesse James gang rode into town and attempted to rob the local bank. Grace's father, the town photographer at that time, had been called upon to take pictures of the dead members of the gang.

Grace remembered and repeated the entire story of the attempted robbery for the interviewer, relating it just as her father had told her many times. Summarizing its importance for that area of Minnesota, she said, "This was more than just an ordinary bank robbery attempt. My father told me that the townspeople took pride in thinking that their thwarting the robbery attempt, capturing several members of the notorious James gang, bringing them to justice, and killing three more members of the gang, marked the beginning of the end for Jesse James. He was never able to recover from this defeat. Only he and his brother Frank escaped."

The pictures her father took of the dead gang members were later in great demand, Grace recalled. Before she moved from Northfield, Grace went through all of her father's photographs and donated the important ones to the St. Paul Historical Society and the local historical society. In the spring of 1990, the Minnesota Historical Society in St. Paul exhibited Mr. Sumner's photographs, and the Northfield Historical Society held a Sumner family exhibit in 1989. Without Grace's contribution, these documents from the past would not have been made available, and a vibrant picture of history would have been lost.

ఎ

Interviewing Cape Cod centenarians prompted Randi Cherchiglia of the Dennis, Massachusetts, Council on Aging to conclude: "I doubt if the world will ever meet such a fine generation of folks. They are a proud and loyal generation; they really love this country. It is a pleasure to know them. Their memories are a special contribution to families, to communities, and to society."

ఎ

❧ 5 ❧

Legacy of Values and Beliefs

THE PAST AS PROLOGUE

❧IN addition to witnessing great cultural, social, economic, and technological changes over the course of their lives, today's centenarians grew up with and supported over many decades the basic values and beliefs shaping America's culture, including: the love of family, belief in God and the importance of religion, respect for traditions, the importance of intergenerational relationships and an interest in others; the value of education; the value of personal autonomy, integrity, and dignity; the belief in the ability to improve one's circumstances, particularly through hard work, frugality, and ingenuity; ethical behavior and faith and perseverance during difficult times; patriotism and morality; community service; love of nature; and finding pleasure in everyday life. Overall, centenarians' lives bespeak the possibility of making life joyful and meaningful. Through the course of their daily lives, in rearing their children, involvement in community life, their work and avocations, our eldest citizens have embodied these values and beliefs.

Over many decades, they have seen these values and beliefs embraced by society, rejected or discarded, and now revived again in the 1990s, with the return to traditionalism. Centenarians tell us that what they liked about life during earlier days in America was having the time for family and friends, relaxation and recreation, helping others, and spirituality. These, they say, are the pleasures that ultimately make life worthwhile. Centenarians urge younger generations to focus on living life with deeper meaning, living in the present, enjoying life each day, while deemphasizing materialism, commercialism, greed, and self-centeredness. From having seen it all over the course of this century, they advise us to turn toward simpler pleasures and traditional values and to live with integrity and self-determination.

This wisdom strikes a contemporary note, as many begin to recognize, after a few decades of trial and error, that the same values and beliefs espoused by our eldest citizens—old-fashioned values—really do work best for most people and for society.

These traditional values are exemplified by the story of Ida May Gilland Fox. Ida was born in Wyoming in 1886, four years before it became a state, into a pioneer family that had migrated from the East and that can trace its ancestry in North America back to the mid-1600s. Ida's multigenerational story reflects the important values and beliefs held dear by most centenarians and others of advanced age, in all parts of the country and from varied ethnic backgrounds.

❧

THE LEGACY: FROM THE DIARIES
OF IDA MAY GILLAND FOX

Family Background

"Grandma, Auntie, and Mama revered their heritage—which they could trace to the 1630s—and we girls were taught that our ancestry was a thing to be proud of and lived up to. Before Mama passed her diary on to me, she added this preface, which she titled 'A Bit of Family History by Way of Background':

> From the early 1870s to the first decade of the present century, much of my life was spent on the UC Ranch. And it was there that our children spent their early years, a period to them so happy and colorful that, at their request, I decided to convey to the written page, following my diaries and my Aunt's, as well as my memories, a picture of those early times and the years immediately following for them to preserve. Since every picture needs a background, the lives of their parents were painted in, and their grandparents.

The perspective reaches to their maternal ancestor, Stephen Thurston IV, who was at West Point, and still further back to Governor Simon Bradstreet and his wife, Anne Dudley, our grandparents ten and eleven generations removed, who came over from England with the Massachusetts Company in 1629-30. He served for many years as one of the first commissioners of the United Colonies of England and also as Governor of Massachusetts and New Hampshire under the Union of Provinces. His wife, daughter of Governor Thomas and Dorothy Dudley, possessed much literary ability.

From these early pioneer ancestors, traits of courage, endurance, and sterling integrity can be traced down through the generations that have left their stamp on the communities they helped to build. May the family tradition of striving to "treasure the sunshine" continue.

Ida's Story

"In 1873, thirteen years before my birth, my maternal grandparents, Alonzo Martin and Amanda Phelps Martin, left Rockford, Illinois, to travel west with their nearly grown children, Cora Belle (my mother) and Hobart, her younger brother. My grandmother's unmarried sister, Caroline, or "Auntie," as she was always called, came west, too. Auntie had lost her fiancé in the Civil War and, romantically, remained true to his memory all her life; he was her only love outside of us, her family. My great-grandfather also came and Auntie cared for him until his death a few years later.

"This little extended family traveled by train to Cheyenne, Wyoming, in two days and three nights; rail service to Wyoming had begun a scant six years before. Cheyenne was just emerging from the roughest of its early experiences as a frontier town and the unsavory reputation it held in the East prompted Grandma's query, 'Will it be safe for us to stay overnight?' Their intention had been to continue to Denver and to settle there, but their plans were diverted by old friends from Rockford who persuaded the family to stay. Grandma later said, 'We found as fine a class of people in Cheyenne as a whole as one could wish to meet. We were invited to tea by our friends and served angel food cake and ice cream—far from what we expected way out here on the ragged edge of civilization.'

"In 1874, Grandfather bought ranch land on the prairie in Laramie County (near the Nebraska border) on Muddy Creek, two and one-half miles from the closest town of Egbert (just a railroad stop, really) and thirty miles east of Cheyenne. Although he had been a dairy

❧ *Gilland Family Photo, circa 1915. Photo courtesy of the Gilland family.*

farmer in Illinois, never a rancher, Grandfather was always interested in new challenges. With two hired men, he built a small grout house where, with additions, the family lived for thirty-five years. The house was built of thick boards. Spaces in between the boards were filled with the grout, a rough cement, and plastered on the outside—thus, the name. Grandmother set about with her unfailing optimism to give the prairie home a cozy atmosphere, and well she succeeded.

"Aunt Caroline took up a homestead on the north branch of Muddy Creek, one and one-half miles from the home ranch. She intended to live there only long enough to 'prove up' on it. Instead, this little two-room, tar-paper-covered house became her home for over twenty years. She loved flowers and nature and she collected stones; through the years she collected hundreds of pounds of rocks from the hills to border her walks and flower beds. I can see her now in my mind's eye, sunbonnet-covered head, stick in her hand for snakes, and a big kitchen apron filled with stones, wandering over the hills. She grew sunflowers and other hearty plants in profusion, carrying water for them from the spring.

"Although I loved and respected Mama, Papa, and Grandma, I adored Auntie. Blessed Auntie was the 'extra hand.' She helped to bring to maturity three generations: her own younger brothers and sisters when her mother died, Grandma's children, and Mama's. She was always there to take her share of the hard work on the ranch in the early days. She was also always ready as entertainer, mentor, confidante, nurse, and loving friend. She helped nurse Grandma through her illnesses and her grief when Grandpa died, took me to Cheyenne and cared for me day and night when I was three years old and very ill, and she cared for my sister Vera and me whenever Mama had to leave us. In her later years, she said she regretted her decision not to marry and have children of her own.

"Someone from the ranch went to visit Auntie nearly every day. We took her milk and cream, butter, eggs, vegetables and her mail, papers, and magazines. We girls were regular Saturday visitors. I still remember the good things she cooked for us, dishes not usual in hearty ranch fare. She always served lunch on a damask linen tablecloth and used her best china. Weather permitting, we spent part of the day rock hunting. I loved that. My lifelong interest in rock collecting was born there.

"In 1877, at the age of twenty-one, George Gilland, my father, came west from his native Vermont on an emigrant train (the least expensive way to travel). He chose Wyoming because a Vermont neighbor had a cattle ranch and he was hoping to get a job. When he arrived, however, there was no work for him and the man sent him to Grandfather's nearby ranch. Inexperienced as a ranch hand, he went to work for Grandfather. He was well-suited to ranch life and learned the ropes quickly, eventually rising from ranch hand to foreman. In 1885, he and Mother married. Two years later, at Grandfather's request, he took over management of the ranch and my grandparents moved to Cheyenne.

"My first remembrance is of my grandfather. From what Mother wrote in her diary, he must have been a gentleman, for he saw so much beauty in things around him. He was 'a seeker after the spirit of things,' she said. I don't think he fit in that materialistic frontier environment. His teachings and the memory of his companionship meant as much to Mother as my memories of Aunt Caroline have to me. Grandfather died when I was three years old.

"My next recollection is of going to Mother's bedroom and being shown my sister, a tiny redhead, Helen, named for Grandma and Auntie's oldest sister. Helen was born on October 22, 1890, when I was four.

"There were just three of us girls for a long while. Brother George Jr. did not arrive until 1902, much to everyone's surprise! For years Mama was unwell, sometimes with two or three sick headaches (migraines) in succession. Very early I was made to feel my responsibility for my younger sisters. I felt very important with Vera and Helen to care for. I remember sitting by Mama's bedside—in summer, the room as hot as an oven—and feeling so sorry for her.

"Winters were a real trial for Mother when we were very young. Cooped up in such a small space, how the grown-ups managed I do not know. Each morning when it was not actually storming, Mother put on our wraps—overshoes, leggings, and coats—and wrapped our heads in little 'fascinators,' hoods with tails to wrap around our necks. (Those and our mittens were knitted by the loving hands of Grandma and Mama.) Out we would go to play with our sleds in the snow until half-frozen fingers and toes drove us in. Then all wraps came off to be hung on the backs of chairs as near as possible around the wood stove to dry. Twice a day, all winter, Mother went through that routine. How about using a button hook on three pairs of leggings at least twice a day and the pungent smell of drying wool in a small room?

"Through times of sickness, financial crisis, and other trouble, family members demonstrated again and again their deep love for each other. From my Mother's diary I read: 'On the nineteenth of August 1886, Ida May was born; she did not thrive and after several discouraging weeks we engaged a wet nurse for her during the day and a goat to furnish milk during the night. She rallied slowly and in three months showed encouraging improvement.' In January 1889, I became seriously ill again. Because Mother was busy caring for Vera, Auntie took me to Cheyenne for medical treatment and stayed there for several anxious weeks. From her diary, my mother continues: 'Auntie nursed her day and night, resting only while Ida May slept.'

"Four years later I had yet another serious illness. I have flashes of memory of this bout with chicken pox, which turned into pneumonia in the winter of 1893. I recall at that time a blizzard which drove snow onto my bed that had been set up in Grandmother's room. I also remember being in a folding bed behind the stove in the living room and seeing anxious faces bent over me with hushed voices. A doctor in Cheyenne sent medicines by the train, which went back and forth each day to Egbert. Each day my family would send a message to him as to my condition, and he would send back instructions and medications, which necessitated two two-and-a-half-mile trips to the train. Dr. Marston had sent me powders in folded papers all in a little box— typical drugstore procedure in those days. After I began to get better, he stopped sending the medicine. But I continued to demand it. Good psychologist that Mama was, she browned flour, put the right amount in the papers, put them in a box, and pretended that the men had brought them with the mail.

"Mama was a creative, enthusiastic, and exemplary mother. Although she helped everyone in the family whenever she was able, there was never a doubt in anyone's mind that her children were her first priority.

"Throughout our younger lives, Mama made each daughter's birthday a special day and baked a sponge cake in her honor. Baking in those days was a far cry from today's ease of whipping up a cake mix and popping it into the oven or microwave. Not even cake flour existed. To lighten the flour, corn starch had to be added and the mixture sifted three times. Oven thermostats were not available either, so each cook had to learn how hot her oven was by putting her hand in and feeling the air. Of my fifth birthday, my mother writes: 'She helped bake her cake and frosted it too.' We enjoyed birthdays and holidays, especially Christmas, which provided a chance to bring other unexpected refinements to the frontier.

"Christmas was a time of great excitement for us. Early in December, Grandmother and Mother would shut themselves in Grandmother's bedroom to make new wardrobes for our dolls. I remember that one year (1891) mine appeared as a Bloomer girl in a stylish green suit, a new style for bicycle riding and other sports. Our dolls had china heads and bodies made of cloth stuffed with sawdust.

"Usually at Christmastime we just hung up our stockings. But one year Father made the ten-mile-trip to Pine Bluffs and brought home a small pine tree. The afternoon of Christmas Eve we were told to stay in the dining room. Father, Mother, Auntie, and Grandma were busy in the living room. We had supper. Then, wonder of wonders, we heard sleigh bells and a commotion outside, followed by loud talk and laughter and the sound of someone rushing off, bells ringing. The living room door opened on the most wonderful sight, a Christmas tree ablaze with fragrant lighted candles and decorated with strings of popcorn and cranberries. Our dolls in their new outfits and lovely packages were all around it. Even now the fragrance of burning candles will bring back the memory of that time.

"At times the effort of maintaining refinement and manners on the ranch became frustrating for Mama and Grandma, yet ultimately they succeeded. They were always training us to be ladies and made sure we learned to knit, crochet, and sew. I was a trial to them, more so than my sisters, because I much preferred to be around the barns or corrals while the other girls were happily busy in the house. Perhaps I was a tomboy because I was the oldest.

"And then, Papa expected us to be responsible for things outdoors when no hired men were around. He liked to have us ride with him, and we were proud when he invited us to go on some of his rounds on the pastures or to grease the windmills. By the time we were teenagers, he said we saw more and knew how to handle horses and cattle better than any but his most experienced men. Papa's expectations were often at odds with those of Mama and Grandma. For instance, he expected us to be good riders, but Mama and Grandma insisted that we wear divided skirts rather than more comfortable clothing. There was much discussion at that time as to the propriety of wearing divided skirts for horseback riding. What heavy, cumbersome things they were. It took a mighty swing to get those yards of material over the saddle and to fall gracefully on the opposite side of the horse, but off we would go and along late in the afternoon we would drag home, sunburned, saddlesore, and weary but always eager to go again.

"Another rule of propriety we were taught was never to call a bull a 'bull' because that wasn't a ladylike expression. A bull, Grandma and Mama told us, was to be referred to as a 'banner.' Stallions were also never to be mentioned. And we were not permitted to learn to swim. But with the new century, Victorian beliefs in the practice of extreme modesty were changing.

"One early lesson, though, in which Grandma imparted her sense of propriety affected me for years following, for Grandma could be very stern and would allow no deviation from what she considered good taste and manners. One day when I was with her in the buggy as we passed one of the men who must have tipped his hat or perhaps waved, I met with Grandmother's disapprobation when I waved and smiled back. Grandma said, 'Ida May, you must never smile at a man. He will think you are flirting with him.' I was crushed, and for years

I felt frozen-faced in the presence of people.

"Despite her stern propriety, my sisters and I loved and respected Grandma. In the winter of 1892, Grandma was invited to visit friends in Pueblo, Colorado. How excited we were, watching the making of her clothes for the trip. When she returned, all of us wanted to hear over and over about the fine house the family lived in, the parties, and the clothes they wore. Grandma told us that her friend and her two daughters were prominent socially. Those were the days of 'calls'—even in Colorado! Grandma's friend had her regular day, as did the other socialites, when the ladies were taken from house to house in their carriages. Tea was served with the 'ne plus ultra' of delicacy—beaten biscuits, so light and flaky and nongreasy that a lady could eat them without soiling her white gloves. Mama learned to make them, as eventually we all did. We often entertained at teas at home on the ranch and later when we moved to Cheyenne, which was very social at that time. Five o'clock teas were the style and Mama loved to entertain. The teas were almost a full meal. There were always many flowers and decorations, sometimes around a theme, such as Valentine's Day.

"Our family had many friends in Cheyenne, and it seemed we always had company, especially in haying time. I remember one visit vividly. A certain family in Cheyenne had visitors from the East who were anxious to see a bit of ranch life, so they were invited over for a weekend. They arrived late in the week, evidently dressed in their oldest clothes (prepared to blend in the frontier style, I presume) and were quite superior in their attitude. Sunday came and they made no effort to better their appearance, but their discomfiture became quite evident when one by one all our family appeared: Father shaved and suited, and Grandmother, Mother, and we girls in our Sunday best—as was always our custom.

"At the turn of the century in 1900, when I was fourteen years old, Mother noted in her diary:

Gone were the days of the open range and cattle roundups in the Cheyenne area. Ranchers were putting up fences to contain their herds and continuing the battle to keep out the sheep men and "Sunday on the Ranch" was less often observed as a day of rest than as one of the exchange of social calls impossible to make during the busy week, for a new order of things was coming and already life was speeding up. A Sunday without guests was rare and food seemed never to give out for always there were emergency supplies from the storeroom. This was typical of the majority of the ranches.

"How meaningful for me to be able to relive my own memories of childhood and my own diary entries by reading from Mother's and Auntie's diaries, revealing interpretations of these same events. For instance, in 1900 Mother took us to Cheyenne to meet Colonel Theodore Roosevelt as his campaign train was scheduled to stop there. He was running for Vice President at the time. After his platform speech, Mother explains in her diary, she took us up to him, saying, 'Colonel Roosevelt, these three little girls have driven thirty miles to see you.' His reply was, 'Oh, it wasn't worth all that trouble, was it.' To Mother, it clearly was, and it is an experience I never forgot. In the following years, we took every opportunity to see him after he became President whenever he traveled through our part of the country. In 1903, Father, who had been elected to the State Legislature in 1902, rode with him from Laramie to Cheyenne as part of the Governor's party.

"There was much sociability up and down the Muddy and even as far as Pine Bluffs. By 1901, our Sunday guests included younger people from the ranches around Egbert instead of mostly friends of Mama and Papa. I was keeping a diary of my own by then, and we girls were becoming interested in staging our own social events. On July Fourth, I noted in my diary that July 'started out with a bang and it kept up all month.' To celebrate the Fourth, we had a big picnic at Pine Bluffs east of the ranch. 'I had the most glorious time I ever had,' which included roaming over the bluffs in the forenoon and enjoying a delicious dinner. The picnic lasted all day.

"Such celebrations and socializing were fun, but they also meant more hard work. There was a strong belief in our family—indeed, in families throughout the frontier and across America—that hard work was not only a necessity to getting ahead in life but also a virtue in itself. That 'hard work never hurt anyone' my generation learned from our parents and grandparents and passed on to our own children. Both men and women, young and old, displayed a commitment to it.

"For example, housework on a ranch was never really finished. Churning butter and baking bread and pies were common tasks. Even breakfast had to be a big meal. The men worked hard and had to be fed. When they were bailing hay for cattle, there were sometimes sixteen men for dinner and fifteen for supper, the evening meal. I remember Mother often scrubbing the kitchen floor at midnight and then getting up at five in the morning to start breakfast.

"On January 19, 1901, I recorded, 'Baking seven pies, six loaves of bread, cookies, and two cakes. Grandma and Helen churned butter. Vera and I went to the station and to Auntie's.' On February 14, 1901, I wrote, 'Grandma got up at 2:30 a.m. to get the fires going and to have breakfast ready. The rest of us arose at 4:30. A hired hand took Papa, Mama, and Helen to Egbert to catch the train to Cheyenne. I did the work in the main part of the house, cleaned the lamps and swept the bunkhouse. Grandma and Vera did the dining room and kitchen work, baked three pies; at 10:30 they went for Auntie.' By now, Auntie and Grandma were in their sixties and still working hard.

"In August 1901, I wrote, 'I had to get up at 4:30 a.m. to get the men's breakfasts. Grandma washed all forenoon and helped with the kitchen work. Mama got the men's dinner. We took it to them, then had to go back with a jug of water. In the afternoon, Mama finished my pink waist and put a circular flounce on my dress. Later we washed the dinner dishes, watered the horses, and ironed some. This we did in the darkened dining room (darkened to keep out the sun). Of course, we had to keep a hot fire in the kitchen range to heat those big, heavy irons. Then it was time for one girl to go for the cows, the other to help get supper.'

"We also had to make clothes for school. Grandmother and Mother were expert seamstresses and taught us to sew. In fact, even all through college, I almost never had a store-bought dress. All wornout articles were saved and put to good use, even cast-off clothing of the men. All was washed and ripped up and used either for patches for quilts for the bunkhouse or for rag carpets. Sheets, dishcloths, and blankets no longer fit for any other uses were dyed bright colors and reused. Material used for quilts (we called them comforters) was usually cut in three-inch squares. We had our early sewing lessons on these. We were taught to match the corners very precisely and sew the edges together over and over. We combined the individual squares into blocks until the piece grew too large for small hands and an adult had to finish it. When the quilt finally reached bed size, a day was chosen when no men would be home for the noon meal and the quilting frames were set up across the dining room table. The lining was stretched on the frames, the cotton batting laid on carefully and evenly, the pieced top put on and pinned in many places, and the tying begun. That done, the comforter was removed from the frames and the edges were turned and then buttonhole stitched. Sometimes Mama bought bright cotton yarn, which made the comforters more fun to tie. In later years, we could buy wool batts to use, making warm, light coverings.

"Twice a day, in the morning and in the evening, one of the ranch hands would bring two big foamy pails of milk to the house. I loved it, so I was always on hand for a drink. Then Grandma strained the milk into large ten-quart pans and set them on racks in the small room on the north side where an open window kept them cool. The rack for the pans was covered with cheesecloth to keep the flies out. Each morning she skimmed off the cream, setting some aside for use in the kitchen and for Auntie, which we took along with some milk when we went to her house. The rest of the cream went into the churn for butter. Part of the milk was used for cooking and drinking. The rest was fed to the cats and any calves that might be in the barn. Grandma also did the churning and the butter making. Naturally, as children we three girls were Grandma's shadows and learned her thorough way of doing things. Thus, when she was no longer with us, we were well trained to take over.

"There was a firm belief in our family that there existed a 'right way' to do certain things. There was a 'right way' to use the wash bowl (i.e., wipe it out when finished); a 'right way' to sit (i.e., feet flat on the floor, hands folded in lap); and a 'right way' to sew a quilt (i.e., match the corners very precisely and sew the edges over and over); and a 'right way' to iron (i.e., each piece of linen starched and perfectly done, corners of handkerchiefs exactly square). There was also a 'right way' to dress, to comport oneself, to greet people; to saddle a horse, and to put away all tools or utensils in their right place after using them.

"Though ranch life was strenuous and hard work ever present, Mother seized every opportunity to add educational experience to the daily routine of her children. She started with the basics, just reading books to us, then teaching us to read.

"All in the family enjoyed reading and the house always contained books and magazines. A day was lost if someone did not go for the mail in Egbert to get the *Chicago Herald Tribune*. The *Ladies Home Journal* came regularly. As children, we enjoyed the paper dolls and clothes to cut out and play with that the magazine included. In one issue, sister Helen's picture appeared when she was four. Her photograph, taken along with the family Christmas photograph in 1894, was so good that a local photographer submitted it in a contest and won a prize.

"Our family also took an interest in special events whether near or far. For instance, in 1898, when I was twelve, Buffalo Bill and his Wild

West Show were in Cheyenne and all the family went to see it.

"We were very interested, too, in current and world events. In my diary, I duly chronicled not only daily happenings but also world news. For example, in 1900, I recorded for months the progress of the Boxer Rebellion and Queen Victoria's death in England on January 24, 1901.

"Evenings were given over to reading. Each with a book, we would gather around the living room table, a big Rochester lamp our light. Nine o'clock was bedtime and after we were tucked in, Mother would read aloud to Father. I tried to keep the bedroom door open a crack to hear, so I knew all about *Stanley in Africa*. I still have that book. We also had the twelve-volume set of *Little Masterpieces* that Uncle Hobart sent us from Chicago. Mother read and reread them to us until we were old enough to read them ourselves. We had that set for many years. We also had all of the Louisa May Alcott books, which were read and cried over. *The Jungle Books* were my special favorites, as were those of Ernest Thompson Seton.

"The hard work of frontier life was also softened by the spirit of neighborliness and community cohesion. Mother expressed this eloquently in her diary:

> *'In times of stress as well as pleasure, friends were loyal. In sickness, women depended upon each other, and never did a neighbor fail to give freely of time, sympathy, and skill while ofttimes men exchanged work or willingly helped a brother ranchman at much inconvenience to themselves. All honor to those sturdy men who worked so hard and endured so much and to those pioneer women whose patience, courage, and endurance often surpassed a tale of fiction.'*

"Not all community relations were of a friendly nature, however. During my childhood, both physical and political battles erupted between cattle ranchers and sheepherders. Writing about an event during one such period of conflict, I noted in my diary: 'How Mama hated for Papa to start out anywhere! Mr. Wilkinson, the sheep man, had offered any of his men ten dollars if one could give that George Gilland a good beating. As long as the feud lasted, Papa never left the ranch without his rifle. After they settled their differences, Mr. Wilkinson and Papa learned to respect each other and eventually became friends.

"Above all else, Mama prized the value of a good education, and she fought to have her daughters educated at a time when many considered education for girls beyond grade school both a waste of time and money. Aunt Caroline, who was well educated for her day, served as a model. Auntie had taught school in Wisconsin in the 1860s and later graduated in 1872 from the Rockford (Illinois) Commercial Institute, where she had taken courses in bookkeeping and commercial law. Before she moved to the west, Aunt Caroline had acquired the enormous sum of $1,000.

"The greatest disappointment in Mother's life was not having received a college education herself. She had been accepted at Oberlin College in Ohio when Grandmother became ill. Grandma's long convalescence made it imperative that Mother remain home to nurse her and help with the other work. Later she set about educating herself and taught school for several terms.

"After her children were born, Mother also taught us at home until I was eight and a half years old because there was no school nearby. Then Uncle Hobart accepted a teaching position at the Spring Creek School for two terms to make money to defray expenses at Northwestern School of Law. He drove nine miles each way daily, and the last term he took my sister or me with him, alternating weeks, since the cart would accommodate only two people. That little, two-wheeled vehicle had just a seat with no backrest, and our feet could not touch the floor. We always got tired.

"In June 1895, a school opened in Egbert just two and a half miles from home. At first my sister and I were taken by Mother or Grandmother in the morning and called for at four in the afternoon. But within a year, we were considered big enough to go by ourselves since by that time I could get a bridle on the horse without standing on the water trough. In the morning, the teacher would build a fire and get ready for the day's classes. Always at noon, I had to feed and water the horse and hitch up at the end of the day.

"Because school was in session only eight months of the year, during January, February, and March, Mother taught us. (Wyoming's schools closed during the cold, snowy winter months and ran though the summer instead.) From nine o'clock until twelve o'clock each weekday, we labored at our desks, which Father had made for us. Mother wrote that the hours spent teaching us were among the happiest of her recollections. Mother loved music and was an accomplished pianist. Musical instruments were few on the prairie. (My grandparents had ordered the piano for her through a catalogue after Grandmother's ill-ness, perhaps as some compensation for her sacrifice in foregoing a college education.) Everyone loved to hear Mother play. Whenever people came to Sunday dinners, we had music.

"Mama was adamant that we girls receive both a high school and college education. But Papa did not believe in higher education for women. Mother fought hard for the right to educate her daughters, partially because it was a right she herself had been denied. Mother eventually prevailed over Father, but it caused a great deal of tension, the first real rift in our family. She paid a price for her victory in more hard work, self-sacrifice of personal possessions, and loss of marital harmony. She was determined to provide a better life and more oppor-tunities for her children than she had had. Father, on the other hand, would have liked me to go right to work after high school. In his family, all the children had to go to work at early ages and were expected to be totally self-supporting by the age of fifteen.

"In 1901, when I reached the junior year in high school, Mama decided it was time for the family to move to Cheyenne so we girls could continue our education in the town school and prepare for col-lege. This, of course, was over Papa's objection, but she argued and fought with him and finally got her way. Papa stayed behind on the ranch, and we visited on school holidays and vacations.

"Our hearts nearly broke, however, at leaving the ranch life we loved. I have been homesick many times in later years, but I have never had the feeling of utter desolation that I had then. For the next six years, we went to the ranch only during the summertime. Even when I was away at college in Colorado, the day after I arrived in Cheyenne would find me taking the train for Egbert and the ranch, not to leave until the last possible hour. Those busy days of summer vacation passed all too quickly. I vividly recall that on the first evening of our return Papa would be apt to say, 'Well, girls, want to ride with me in the morning?' We always were up and dressed in our divided skirts and big Mexican-style straw hats, anxious to go.

"My appreciation for the sacrifices Mother made for my education had much to do with my own enthusiasm for learning. I have always felt that my high school graduation was the most important day of my life because it opened the door for me to go on from there to college and beyond.

"In addition to the academics learned during my high school years, I learned something of the harsh realities of life. These were lessons that would serve me well in directing my own affairs. I noted in my memoirs that I felt the lack of adequate funds was one of Mother's most serious problems:

> Many times I have seen her [Mama] put her arms around Papa's neck, asking him for money. How degrading, I thought, that any-one who had given so much of her life to Papa and worked so hard would have to beg for a share of the profit. Our second year in Cheyenne, Mama was forced to rent the two upstairs rooms to two men. Papa did not like the idea at all, but Mama simply had to have the money and Papa did not see the necessity of giving her more. Right then and there I decided I would not be suppliant to any man; if I could not share in the bank account, the man was not for me.

"I am convinced that the several untoward monetary experiences I witnessed in early life—a bank failure when I was seven in which each member of the family, including Aunt Caroline, lost all money on deposit during the panic of 1893; before that, Grandpa's mismanagement of his business and the struggle Grandma, Auntie, and Uncle Hobart had because of it; and finally, Mama begging for money—all gave me a horror of finding myself in a similar situation. Grandma and Uncle Hobart, too, had denied themselves for years trying, as far as possible, to repay Grandpa's creditors. Grandma took in roomers and boarders and did sewing for people while she and Grandpa lived in town. Aunt Caroline lost the entire $1,000 she had saved and was left with only her home, her 160 acres of land, and a few cattle. She had no means of livelihood, so for years she did the family washing and often the washing for the men in the bunkhouse in order to earn money. Washing was not too bad in the summer when she could have the tubs out of doors. Of course, she had to carry all the water from the spring and heat it in the big boiler in the kitchen—stifling in summer—rub the clothes on the washboard, boil the whites, rinse them, and hang them on the lines. In winter, she had to chop a hole in the ice to get water and hang out the clothes no matter how freezing the weather. Worse was the ironing. With a fire going in the kitchen to heat the big irons, the heat was terrific. Often I had seen Auntie, near exhaustion, with a wet towel around her head, ironing hour after hour, each piece of linen, each starched petticoat perfectly done.

*Ida May Gilland in High School Graduation Dress, 1903.
Photo courtesy of the Gilland family.*

"In the beginning of 1904, after my high school graduation, Papa was hard-pressed financially on account of purchasing additional land which he had leased for many years. I knew the time was not right for me to ask for money for college. With baby George needing so much care, I decided to stay home for a year, hoping plans could be worked out for me to attend college a year later.

"Papa would have been content for me to take a teacher's examination and get a teaching assignment somewhere, but Mama had other ideas. The daughter of one of her friends was a student at Colorado College in Colorado Springs. She recommended the school as being a good, quiet one where the girls were well supervised. Mama obtained Papa's reluctant consent to my application. She told me later that I never could realize how near I came to having my hopes dashed. The night before we left the ranch for town on the way to college, Papa said he did not have the money to send me. Mama got her dander up, like a tiger fighting for her young, and told him I was going and he could just go to the bank and borrow the money, as he did not hesitate to do for other things. I think each year—at least for the sophomore year and maybe the junior year as well—she fought the same battle. By the time I was a senior and doing well at working in the laboratory to pay my tuition, he became quite proud of having a daughter in college. However, in order to do this, I had to drop the music lessons which I had taken in the first two years. I was sorry to disappoint Mama because she hoped to have a musician in the family. I had also hoped to take geology in college so that I could pass on to Auntie what I had learned, but girls did not study that subject at the time and the geology professor did not want us in his classes. I did get fine instruction in botany, though.

"Because of my father's disapproval, Mama was among those silent ranks of women who must be credited with pushing the obstacles to equality of the sexes a little further aside. In contrast, my Aunt Ida (my father's brother's wife) would not stand up to her husband when he refused to allow my cousin Edith to go to college. (She went to business school instead.)

"While I was away at college, Papa was making plans to sell the ranch, unbeknownst to us girls. The decision to sell must have been a hard one for Papa to make, but times were changing. Since 1896, Swedish immigrants had taken up farming in the area. At first, the old ranchers made fun of them and predicted that they would not succeed as farmers. They were poor and had to work part-time on the ranches. Through their trustworthiness and hard work, over the years they gradually gained the respect of the ranchmen, who were glad enough to hire them. Other neighbors had already sold their land to a land company that was buying up large tracts of land to subdivide and sell to farmers. Also, Mama seemed happier in town, and Papa was beginning to feel the physical effects of many years of hard work.

"The summer between my junior and senior years of college was the last we would spend at the ranch. Before another one came, Papa sold the ranch and moved the family to Cheyenne. That was the end of an era for all of us. Mama recorded in her diary on May 2, 1907:

'George, Georgie and I went to Cheyenne, severing our connection with the UC Ranch—a few days more than thirty years after George's arrival there in April 1877.'

"One of my fondest memories from those times is how in the evening after supper, when the last dish was done, we would put on our divided skirts, saddle our horses, and ride over to Auntie's or just over the hills in the cool evening air. We would come home late, singing at the top of our lungs. Some nights we put the gramophone on the horse block in front of the house and played cylinders (records) such as 'Bill Bailey, Won't You Please Come Home,' and similar popular tunes.

"In 1908, after I had graduated from Colorado College and the ranch had been sold and the entire family moved to our small house in Cheyenne, I had hoped to borrow money from Papa to take a special course to qualify as a laboratory technician. But my father asked me to stay home instead. The house was in turmoil. Mama was ill and away for treatment. Grandma and Aunt Caroline were living with us. There were three generations living in the same house, which was inadequate at best for so many people. My youngest sister Helen was in high school, and George was just starting grade school. These circumstances in my family kept me from pursuing the work I wanted as a laboratory technician. Ironically, my own experience was turning out to be like Mama's, but at least I had gone to college.

"By the next summer, conditions were better. Mama was well, Papa had bought a larger house in town and the family had room to spread out. There were fewer tensions, and Papa had interesting things to do. He pursued his activities in community events and politics that extended back to 1890, when I was four years old and he had served as a delegate to the State Republican Convention the year Wyoming received statehood. (He had also served in the state legislature when I was in high school.)

"During those years on the ranch, I developed many beliefs that would sustain me throughout my life, but few had more impact than the advice given by my father during our last summer there. I was complaining to him about something one of the ranch hands had not done for me and he said, 'Ida, you've got to learn to carry your own freight in this world.' It is a philosophy I've always tried to follow to this day. This advice, coupled with my determination not to be disadvantaged by marriage, formed the basis for many life choices that followed.

"In 1909, at the age of twenty-three, I married Dr. Galen Fox. When I became engaged, it was a stipulation of our agreement that we share the bank account. He went into private practice in Cheyenne with Dr. Amos Barber (later governor of Wyoming) and was also a physician for the Union Pacific Railroad. We had a new house built in 1916, which served as our home in Cheyenne until Galen's retirement. While our house was being built, we rented some upstairs rooms in Mama and Papa's house. During this time, Grandmother suffered a series of strokes and passed away. (Aunt Caroline, who also lived with Mama and Papa and Grandma after selling her homestead when we all moved to town, had passed away three years before.) Mama tried to care for Grandma by herself at first but then had to call in trained nurses for weeks and then hire a practical nurse on a twenty-hour shift. It was fortunate that I was living in the same house since I could take over during the time the nurse needed rest and help Mama in other ways.

"After we moved into our new house, Mother Fox (Galen's mother) came to stay with us and took over in our house when I needed to help Mama. Grandma was well cared for in her old age, as had been Aunt Caroline. Grandma died peacefully, Mama and I by her side, near midnight on December 16, 1916. Mercifully, Mama was asleep at the time. For Grandma, a long and useful life was ended. For Mama, a faithful and loving vigil was over.

"In 1918, during World War I when Galen was overseas as a captain in the Medical Corps, I went to Buffalo, New York, to perfect myself in YWCA methods. Instead, I was induced to assist in the necessary and interesting work of the Travelers' Aid, a branch of the war service dealing with the safety and comfort of all women and children traveling by train. Mama, Papa, and George drove out for a visit, stopping along the way to see Helen, who had also married a doctor and was living in Indiana.

"It was our fondest wish to have children of our own to love in the same way we had been loved and cherished in our own families, but we found ourselves still childless a decade after our marriage. Therefore, when the opportunity to adopt a child occurred in December 1919, we did adopt four-year-old Kathryn, whose natural mother had died during the flu epidemic of 1918, leaving four young children. It was her dying wish that her children be adopted by loving families, and we were happy to be a part of making her wish come true. All the love and closeness of our family members continued, and now embraced Kathryn as well.

"Mama and Papa led a pleasant and busy life through the next decade, often taking trips by car to Yellowstone Park with friends and longer trips with Georgie to Oregon and California. Papa loved driving even though the trips were often made over primitive roads. Mama was often uncomfortable and frightened and would have preferred to have taken the train, but she endured the road travel for his sake.

"Life changed abruptly for them when Papa lost all his money in a bank failure at the very beginning of the Depression, a fate that befell many other people in the nation. After this calamity, Papa tried hard to earn money. For a number of years he was an appraiser for the State Land Commission. Eventually, it became unsafe for him to drive and I took over. Those were very hard trips, especially when we took the big touring car. But I was happy to do it; the employment helped him to maintain a bit of his pride. I have been thankful that I could be near and share the last of his life with him.

"In 1930, another tragedy struck our family. In August, Vera was diagnosed with terminal cancer. All efforts, including surgery, failed to save her or prolong her life. She died in early December and is buried in the family plot in Cheyenne.

"After Vera's death, Mama, who had been in failing health, again gathered her forces, took command, and never again relinquished it. She was strong and steadfast all the following three years of Papa's decline in health and mentality. When he died in 1933, she shed no tear. I was with her, and Galen came soon after. She told us to go home and carry on our own lives. One chapter of hers was finished; she was starting another, and wanted to be able to live it as she pleased.

"We respected her wishes. She managed her own affairs in a most businesslike manner for ten years, about the happiest of her life, she said, because for the first time she was her own boss. She kept her upstairs rooms filled with teachers (roomers), who were most kind to her. Galen was very proud of the way she managed, especially since by then she was almost totally deaf. (Her incurable deafness, the result of scarlet fever as a child, worsened as she grew older.) She learned to read lips and remained a good conversationalist. She made trips to visit family and friends in other parts of the country and kept very active. She took many Sunday dinners with us but never would stay long, saying she always had 'letters to write.'

"It took me many years to realize that Mama never really belonged to this western country in its early days. Her interests were so foreign to ranch life that she would have been much more at home in the East as the wife of a professor or businessman. But how graciously and uncomplainingly she met each situation and how hard she tried to bring up her children to have some of the social graces.

"Eventually, keeping her large house became too much for her. When she was offered a good price for it, Galen and I urged her to sell and come live with us, which she did. She spent much of her last years writing a number of papers and articles for presentations at various church meetings and clubs, including the Pioneer Club. She also compiled a history of the Pioneer Club, which is now one of its most treasured possessions. All of these papers, along with her diary, are on file in the state archives. Many people have told me that they have found Mother's writings 'of the greatest assistance in the preparation of historical papers.' Mama would like that.

"After Galen retired, we sold our home in Cheyenne and moved to Florida. We found a house that provided a nice room for Mama, but she went instead to live with Helen and her husband, Bob, in Indiana, where she was not quite as homesick as she would have been in Florida. Helen took excellent care of Mama, Bob was always thoughtful of her welfare, and their friends were very kind. George and his wife were nearby and could visit often. Mother died in Helen and Bob's home in 1954; she had remained an intimate part of our lives for ninety-one years.

"Galen and I moved to Clearwater, Florida, in 1950; Galen died in 1961. I remained there for three years, working on my reminiscences and consolidating our family history of the lives and activities of a

✂ *Ida May Gilland Fox, age 100. At age 108 (1994) she still lives in Wyoming.*
Photograph reprinted with permission of The Wyoming Tribune-Eagle.
Photo courtesy of the Wyoming Division on Aging.

pioneer family, from Mother's, Auntie's, and my diaries. In doing so,
I relived those wonderful years. Often I felt the presence of those dear,
departed ones, as I wrote of them. They were honest, wonderful
people, each fighting his or her battle of life, meeting the problems of
each day uncomplainingly, doing well the tasks to be done. Sometimes
I cried as I remembered; more often I laughed. It has been fun to record
and retell. In September 1964 I came 'home' and have lived in Wyoming
ever since.

Afterword

At 103, Ida is Wyoming's oldest native. Her daughter, Kathryn McNabb, says that even at this great age, her mother is very much a lady and has always been organized, self-possessed, and realistic. As the years went on, she has given up gracefully the things she could no longer do. Ida also gave away or donated the possessions she cherished but no longer needed, such as family antiques and her most prized possession, her rock collection. Kathryn tells that of her many activities throughout her long and productive life, Ida's most consuming interest was rock collecting. So much so that "In the forties, Mother organized the Cheyenne Gem and Mineral Club," Kathryn tells, "of which she is now an honorary lifetime member."

In the four decades of her married life in Cheyenne, Ida was active in the community and held office in many civic projects over the years, including presidency of the Red Cross during World War I; presidency of the College Club, which she organized and that later became a chapter of the American Association of University Women; and St. John's Hospital Auxiliary and Nursing School. She was also president of the Women's Club, the American Legion Auxiliary, and the Ladies Aid of the Congregational Church. Following the family tradition, her home was always open to meetings, gatherings, and events.

In later years, Ida made contributions to the community by writing the histories of many organizations and institutions, such as the nursing school. Again, following her mother's interest in the Cheyenne Pioneer Club, Ida made substantial contributions to the preservation of the history of that corner of the state—history that was part of her family's daily life.

⁂

THE TREASURE OF PERSONAL JOURNALS AND DIARIES

Ida's family demonstrates the value of keeping personal journals and of preserving personal records and diaries. From such diaries, the wealth of information about her family's early years was drawn when Ida, at age eighty-five, wrote her remembrances of pioneer life on the prairie. *UC Memories*, titled after her family's cattle brand, is now archived in both state and university libraries in Wyoming, along with Ida's mother's and great-aunt's diaries. Through this contribution, her family has transmitted what was once its own personal story into another piece of our collective recorded past.

Not only can a written legacy such as this show how values and beliefs are passed on, and preserve the history of an area, but it can correct mistaken impressions of the past, too. For example, in reading Ida's chronicle of life on the frontier, some people find it surprising that refined social manners existed there. Her family diaries record a constant struggle to preserve decorum, instill manners, and maintain culture. "Many have the impression that pioneer women were or became rough-mannered 'Annie Oakley' types," Kathryn says. "This impression, while colorful, is contrary to fact." In families such as Ida's, pioneer women brought culture with them, successfully passing it along to their daughters and granddaughters and sharing it with the community.

In addition, as the diaries also relate, pioneer women, such as Ida's grandmother and great-aunt, took with them on the journey west as many refinements of life as they could transport, especially their good china and linens, which they frequently used. Others tried taking large items of furniture, even pianos, but these larger pieces were often left behind as too costly to ship by train and too heavy to take over land. "It was the pianos that were most often left by the wayside," Ida's grandmother wrote. Later, these luxuries could be ordered from catalogues, as Ida's mother's family did, and they eventually became a part of frontier life.

Pioneer women also pursued the fashions of the times, to the best of their ability, Ida tells. If they did not completely succeed in emulating their Eastern cousins, it was not for want of trying but, rather, because of their geographic handicap. To be sure, there were glaring differences; Ida remembers a trip her mother took to Chicago around the turn of the century to visit her brother, Hobart: "Mama had made what she thought was an adequate wardrobe to take with her. But when she came back, she said she would never again take a trip without a larger wardrobe because 'What seemed fine on the ranch certainly was not fine in Chicago.' At times, she felt very ill-dressed."

Without the ongoing efforts of frontier women, such as these in the Martin-Gilland-Fox family, the social and cultural traditions they brought to the West with them would not have survived. As part of the effort, Western women worked hard to develop schools and other community institutions. And in preserving manners and culture, they made the frontier life of the American West more livable.

Thanks to this treasured set of family diaries, and to Ida Gilland Fox and her family, we are privileged to glimpse her daily life in the late nineteenth century and the first decade of this century.

MEMORIES

Remaining true to her father's advice to always "carry your own freight in this world," Ida now lives in a nursing home in Cheyenne. "It was her own decision to go to a nursing home in November of 1983," Kathryn says. "We had hoped she would make her home with us, but she always said she would never live with me, and she really meant it. It is sad that Mother is too old now to have any former friends left to visit her. Always a great reader, her failing eyesight is a severe hardship and her declining hearing is also a concern. It makes conversation difficult, but she still enjoys my visits. I go every day and spend an hour with her each afternoon. I take her treats, sometimes for tea, sometimes for cocktail hour. She looks forward to that, to partaking of daily customs she long enjoyed."

Like many of her peers, Ida Fox's activities are limited. Today, she has only her faithful daughter's visits and her memories for companionship. Most often, she sits alone in her room at the nursing home, twenty miles west of the Muddy Creek and the ranch she loved so dearly. Facing her windows, which look south and east toward the ranch, she tells, "I often think of what I wrote at the close of my *UC Memories*":

> Many evenings, as I have watched the day fade, my mind has gone back and back to those winter afternoons riding between Egbert and the ranch. Topping the hill out of the Pole Creek Valley, there, spread before us, was the vast expanse of snow-covered prairie, the line broken only by the Pine Bluffs, on the east, the faint shadow of the Colorado Rockies to the south, and, over all, the great dome of the sky with the gorgeous colors of sunset. Then, at the brow of the Muddy Creek hill, we looked down at the ranch buildings, our home—the stockyards, the creek, the fields where in summer it was green with alfalfa and hay, the horses and the cattle. Such a feeling of exaltation and thanksgiving welled up within us. Then, at the corral gate, Daisy and Shep running to meet us. They had heard us coming, singing, possibly. Coming home—I have never felt the same toward any other place.

≥ *Part II* ≤

The Challenges of Living to be 100

Introduction

The Centenarian Wish List

EVEN with all the medical advances and improved living conditions during this century, for most, longevity in the United States still holds more pitfalls than promises. In Part II, the focus shifts from the past lives of centenarians to the present. The physical, mental, spiritual, social, and financial challenges of aging are presented. Centenarians tell of their problems and their triumphs, providing insight into what it is like to actually achieve the longevity that so fascinates Americans.

As a society, we now have more older members than ever before, a trend that is here to stay. Although much has been written about aging in general, until recently, little has been directed at aging in advanced years—eighty, eighty-five, and over. For many, including doctors, policymakers, caregivers, and old people themselves, the changes that come with old age are perplexing and the challenges daunting.

What is becoming clear is that many of the changes that accompany old age are not the natural partners of growing old, but rather are due to disease and the way we've lived our lives in earlier years. "It's rather like a health bank account," as centenarian Oscar Wilmeth puts it. "We get out of it what we put into it, plus some interest in the form of added years. If you want to live to be 100 you have to work at it—by eating right, exercising, and avoiding the things that will ruin your health. And then, of course, you need to have the resources to be able to afford it all, and to fix the things that go wrong along the way—like making up a deficit in an overdrawn bank account."

All too often, when relating to older people, the tendency of others is to impose conditions and make decisions without asking what they think, believe, and need to improve their quality of life. Here centenarians themselves describe some of the challenges encountered in advanced age and give their opinions on what would make life better for those who do live long. Their ideas are expressed in the Centenarian Wish List and are explored in the following chapters. This compilation of needs and suggested solutions comes from the vantage point of the very old rather than from the perspective of others, who, however well-meaning, lack the personal experience of living long. This Wish List emanates from real-life experience. The experts are the centenarians themselves.

CENTENARIAN WISH LIST

I wish I could have more vision. I used to love to read. Loss of sight has bothered me a great deal.

—Elizabeth Abbott
Brewster, Massachusetts

I wish I would hear better; I've lost so much contact with the world without it.

—Anna Clark
Grand Junction, Colorado

I wish I could be more independent and be able to walk.

—J. Penn Douglas
Lubbock, Texas

I wish I could do more.

—Nellie Hutchins
Lincoln, Nebraska

I wish I weren't so forgetful. . .sometimes I can't recall what I did yesterday.

(Name withheld upon request)

I wish for a good doctor and someone to take care of old people and not put them in a home. Stay in your own home.

—Mann Allen
Columbia, Louisiana

I wish for better home care.

> —Mary Harvet
> *Chippewa Falls, Wisconsin*

❧

I wish for more home-care programs to help people stay in their own homes.

> —Bertha Bliven
> *Salem, Oregon*

❧

I wish for others that their families would care for them.

> —Lettie Johnson
> *Bertrand, Nebraska*

❧

I wish grown children would be kind to their parents—they need you.

> —Oscar Paisley
> *Coeur d'Alene, Idaho*

❧

I wish for better awareness of the elderly.

> —Margery Sheperd
> *Silverton, Oregon*

❧

I wish for less expensive medicine and medical services.

> —Maude Jones
> *Santa Maria, California*

❧

I wish for good healthcare for old people and visitors when they are incapacitated.

> —Dr. Ernest Windesheim
> *Kensington, California*

❧

I wish for improved understanding by the medical profession of problems of the elderly.

—Frederick Pohl, Ph.D.
Westfield, Massachusetts

৯৯

I wish for a better medical and social system that we can afford and that pays more attention to the needs of the elderly.

—Georgina Santarre
Fitchburg, Massachusetts

৯৯

I wish there were some way I could attend church.

—Mary Hettinger
West Carrollton, Ohio

৯৯

I wish I could live at home with my family and not in a nursing home.

—Lena Collins
Amarillo, Texas

৯৯

I wish that older people could have the feeling of financial security today.

—Fannie Stevens
Medicine Lodge, Kansas

৯৯

I wish for better communication between generations. I wish we were not relegated to the background.

—Margery Hawkins
Sweet Home, Oregon

৯৯

I wish people would be more thoughtful of the loneliness old age brings. Finding more things to be included in would improve our aging years.

—Mary Whiting
Mapleton, Utah

%

I wish to feel needed and wanted and not to be treated as no longer intelligent.

—Myrtle Kyzor
Brownwood, Texas

%

I wish our families would love and accept us as we are.

—Maria Ozelia Lambert
Pierre Part, Louisiana

%

I wish for someone to talk to.

—L. W. Parcel
Montrose, Colorado

%

. . . for more people to drop in for a visit.

—Besie Rusley
Minot, North Dakota

%

. . . for the phone to ring more often.

—Johnsie McSwain
Chestertown, Maryland

%

The lives of contemporary centenarians illustrate both the positive and problematic aspects of surviving to very old age. There are common problems and some uncommon possibilities inherent in living long. Drawing upon the practical experience of centenarians and their families, the information here is supplemented by current thinking from the fields of medicine and religion. Moreover, the stories centenarians tell call into question many of the stereotypes and assumptions about the aging process and about those who are experiencing it.

Some centenarians, such as Billy Earley, Ted Gibson, Helen Cope, Clyde Ice, and Hedvig Peterson, have met the challenges and have gone on to achieve a good quality of life for themselves. These are the few. More prevalent are those such as Ida Fox, for whom life used to be good but who are now severely limited by blindness, deafness, and physical mobility problems. When lack of money, lack of companionship, and a sense of being forgotten by society are added, these challenges create real hardships.

Centenarians seek solutions to meeting the challenges of daily life for themselves and voice concern for others of advanced age. Further, they believe that if some of the losses they have experienced could be avoided or ameliorated, it would lead the way for a better quality of life in old age for others who will follow along the path of longevity. Challenges, hardships, and the difficult circumstances of many centenarians notwithstanding, their singular *spirit* as they persevere is exemplary and is, in itself, a lesson in living long.

✤

✵ 6 ✵

The Will to Live
The Courage to Grow Old

We should not drag our feet
When time commands, "March on";
We should step out briskly,
Within our hearts, a song.
Our memory is a mirror
Through which we view the past
With melancholy pleasure
But such moments cannot last.
We have to face the future
With joys and griefs unknown;
Let spiritual growth continue
So we do not walk alone.

—Mary Edwards Renaker, 100
Lexington, Kentucky

EVEN at their great age, a large number of centenarians continue to have and to demonstrate a strong desire to live. Despite the unquestionable losses, often adverse changes in circumstances, and the many problems inherent in growing very old, their will and courage remain intact. They continue to exhibit both a *joie de vivre* and self-determination that argue against the stereotype of advanced age as necessarily a time of decrepitude and apathy. As centenarians tell us, it is not easy to be very old, especially in our youth-obsessed culture; the realities of their everyday life are often harsh. Yet they manage to sustain the will to live even when this will is not supported by others. Perhaps the title of Art Linkletter's book sums it up best: *Old Age Is Not for Sissies*.

Of course, for many of advanced age, such as those who suffer from Alzheimer's disease and forms of dementia, self-determination no longer exists. Others, whose physical decline is devastating and insurmountable, find that life has become a burden. Still others, however, who are in relatively good health, acknowledge the difficulties and overcome or cope with the obstacles of advanced age, maintaining a positive attitude toward life. Those in this last group, whose ranks are growing daily, are able to renegotiate life at every turn, whether anticipated or unexpected, and carry on. They do not give up. They say: "Life is worth living." They continue to live, to enjoy life, and to do as much as they can.

Amazingly, there are people 100 and over who continue to live alone, caring for themselves, usually with some assistance. An informed estimate is that one-quarter of the centenarian population lives independently. Of the remainder, a larger number live with a family member than live in nursing homes. Even for those centenarians who do not live alone, many still actively take part in their own care and in family and social activities. As John Langham, a resident at the Arizona Pioneers Home in Prescott, put it on his 105th birthday, "I'm still able to care for myself. I can dress and groom myself, get around under my own steam with the aid of a walker now, get to the dining room for my meals, and join in some of the activities and events. I enjoy listening to baseball on the radio and to news programs—and I still enjoy the company of pretty women."

Thus, from centenarians and their families and friends, we learn about the will to live at an advanced age, and the courage it takes to grow old. Attributes that seem to be especially important in sustaining this will and to continue to enjoy living are: a sense of purpose, love and relationships, and a positive attitude. In addition, most centenarians stress the importance of religious belief and faith in God.

∾

SENSE OF PURPOSE

It is stating the obvious to say that as people grow very old their opportunities for "usefulness" or productivity, as we currently define it in America, are limited. Such limitations make the challenges of maintaining a sense of purpose in later years more difficult. This is a particularly vulnerable area because, in addition to societal limitations, there are also physical limitations that come with age. It takes a concerted effort for an old person to participate in a culture with a de facto ethic that says if you cannot produce or contribute something directly useful you are no longer of value.

In fact, many centenarians who would like to be involved say they lack the opportunity. Some say it takes a real commitment to self-preservation to attempt to stay involved when one knows one is at best tolerated. Others say they are doing it anyway and hope for a more charitable response. As the Reverend Roy Miller, a centenarian Mennonite minister, who was honored by his church as the oldest of its clergy, explains, "We never outgrow our need to be needed, to participate, to contribute, to belong to the world."

He continues: "I don't know why I have lived so long, or why other centenarians have lived so long, but I thank God every day for the extra years of life. Perhaps God's plan is for us to teach others how to be old; perhaps we are the examples. I try to live up to that each day—to be a shining example to others of how to manage with the problems and how to continue to enjoy life and living and loving.

"When I retired, I moved to Glendale, Arizona, from my home in Rocky Ford, Colorado. When I was almost 100, in order to make it easier on my family because there was friction, I moved into a retirement center. I didn't want to be here, and I was very unhappy. But then I thought that this must be a part of His plan, and so I dedicated myself to helping others.

"God rewarded me with an unexpected loving relationship. Here at the care center, I met a beautiful woman who was immobilized due to tragic circumstances. My interest in her enriches her days, and her affection for me enriches mine.

"I also talk with people who are depressed and lonely, encouraging them to participate in the activities and social events. And I try to get older people to understand the importance of exercise. I say to people twenty or thirty years younger, 'Come on, get up, walk, exercise. If I can do it, you can.'

Perhaps, as Roy suggests, like the Preacher in Ecclesiastes, the eldest in our communities are here to instruct and to teach through the examples of their lives.

To the Reverend David Moore, 100, of Roswell, New Mexico, the Baptist ministry he learned long ago and has dedicated his life to still helps him fulfill his vision of his life: "My first pastorate was in 1911 in Great Bend, Kansas, at the age of twenty-three. I continued my education and pastored until 1955 and then served as an interim pastor. From there I served as a visitation minister. As I grew older, I adjusted my work in keeping with my age. I didn't try to continue to do the work of a young man, but I know I can still make a contribution, and so I have done what's appropriate. I live on my own and am still involved in doing the Lord's work. I make about thirty visits per week at nursing homes and at the hospital bringing comfort and fellowship to those who are less fortunate. That's something you never get too old to do.

"The visits I make now do me about as much good as they do the patients. It is joyous time spent in each place. Often I am called back evenings and on my days off, and I go gladly, with love."

For Anne Passmore, 101, of Boulder City, Nevada, a long labor of love volunteering with St. Jude's Ranch for Children continues to provide a sense of purpose. "The ranch was started in 1966," she tells, "to provide a home and education for abused children.

"I have been helping with the children since the ranch opened, and I am still involved. I visit the children in their classrooms often. I stay as active as I can, going out for dinner and shopping and traveling to California several times a year to visit my family. I do get tired, so I just pace myself. I stay current with news and world events, so I always have good conversation, and I go to the library every week. I have my hair done every week and try to keep my appearance up, so that I am presentable and appealing to others."

Anne is proud to be the "honorary grandmother" to hundreds of children at St. Jude's Ranch whose lives have been and continue to be touched by her love and caring.

A sense of purpose is expressed in ways as diverse as our eldest citizens themselves. For some, continuing a hobby or special interest or volunteer service provides a sense of purpose; for others, it's compiling their family history to pass on to younger generations. Handmade crafts to donate to charities, such as quilts and knitted items, are a contribution centenarians enjoy making. Some care for pets. Others, such as Clema Aucoin of Delcambre, Louisiana, help rear the children. He lives now with his daughter, Mauray Baudoin, who says of her father, "Since my mother's death twenty-eight years ago, he has turned to his descendants for companionship and his main interest has been in the youngsters. Religion has always been very important to him and he is imparting this to the younger generations. He sets a good example. A priest comes every month to give him Communion." Mr. Aucoin does not speak English, only Cajun French. He has helped teach the young generations in his large family his native language and the Cajun traditions.

❧ *Clema Acouin with his great-great-grandson Luke.*
Photo courtesy of the Acouin family.

A few centenarians, mostly men, continue working, usually part-time. Edward Hanau, 100, of St. Louis, is still working at a manufacturing plant and is proud of his record of never having missed a day's work in his adult life. Many other centenarians, women especially, who have made their families paramount in their lives for decades, say their continued involvement with family on many different levels provides a rewarding sense of purpose. To Carmella Arneli of Jamestown, New York, her role as matriarch of her large family gives her not only a continuing sense of purpose but pride as well.

Others, however, long for greater stimulation and increased opportunities for contact with the community and with their families;

and they long for new friends, activities, and interests. As Tillie Essenmacher, 100, of Edgewater, Florida, says ruefully, "There must be something worthwhile we can do." The feeling of being "all washed up" is depressing, centenarians report.

As they indicate, sustaining a sense of purpose in advanced age takes more than desire. It also takes opportunity, creativity, and sometimes downright ingenuity. Hattie Allen of Palmer, Alaska, tells: "It was hard to give up my home and car and move to the Pioneers Home. It was also hard to adjust to living in one room. So I did one of the things I knew I could still do—grow things. I plant a garden each year and my tomatoes and strawberries are some of the largest around. I share my vegetables and flowers with the other residents. It gives me an interest, and them too."

One of the preeminent psychiatrists of the twentieth century, Austrian Viktor Frankl, author of the renowned work, *Man's Search for Meaning*, teaches that life is unconditionally meaningful and that one's sense of purpose is adaptable. Now of advanced age himself, he explains, "We create meaning through choices and actions as we move through life. Meaning unfolds along with the changes in the life cycle. . . in fact, just as life remains potentially meaningful under any conditions, even the most miserable, so too does the value of each and every person stay with him or her, because it is based on values that he or she has realized in the past, and is not contingent on the usefulness that he or she may or may not retain in the present."

In addressing an American Society on Aging Conference in Washington, D.C., Dr. Frankl acknowledged that, indeed, maintaining a sense of purpose or meaning in life is one of the greatest challenges in living to be old. We are social creatures, he said, and at times a sense of purpose is intrinsically bound with our relationships to others. Yet there can be times and circumstances in our lives—and old age is one of them—when we must revise our definition of sense of purpose and accept that merely being alive, and having lived, is enough to imbue a person's life with meaning and value; and, that this inner knowledge must be enough to sustain us.

Dr. Frankl developed his theory of logotherapy ("logo" means "meaning") while a prisoner in a Nazi concentration camp. He attributes his survival to the mental and emotional discipline he developed by using memories of events past and by imagining pleasurable and good events in the future. As he explained, "They could hurt my body but they could not hurt me, who lived inside this body. I realized then that there is one thing that no one can take from me, and that is my freedom to choose how I will react to what happens to me." This mental attitude gives us the freedom within ourselves to choose our own response to life's challenges, and is particularly relevant to people of advanced age. "Moreover, life can be meaningful by being an example to others," Dr. Frankl believes.

In lay person's terms, the internal thoughts expressed by Dr. Frankl as essential to maintaining meaning for oneself, can be heard in this poem contributed by a centenarian:

You Tell Me I Am Getting Old

✆

You tell me I am getting old:
I tell you that's not so!
The ''house'' I live in's wearing out
and that, of course, I know.
It's been in use a long, long while;
it's weathered many a gale;
I'm really not surprised you think
it's getting somewhat frail.

The color's changing on the roof,
the windows—getting dim;
The wall's a bit transparent
and looking rather thin;
The foundation's not so steady
as once it used to be;
My ''house'' is getting shaky,
but my ''house'' isn't me!

The dweller in my little ''house''
is young and bright and gay,
Just starting on a life to last
throughout eternal day.
You only see the outside,
which is all that most folks see.
You tell me I am getting old?
You've mixed my ''house'' with me!

—Anonymous

LOVE AND RELATIONSHIPS

Centenarians maintain that one never outgrows the need for love and relationships and that having someone who cares keeps life interesting. They give witness to the undeniable desire to remain connected with others, either intimately or socially through contact with the community, organizations, and friends.

The Centenarian Wish List continues with Viva Johnson, 100, of Corning, Iowa, who says, "I wish older people had more love in their lives." Like many of her contemporaries, Viva says it is important to her how she is regarded by family, friends, and her community, where she has been a long-time resident. "I want people to like me," she tells. Viva lives with her daughter in a loving and welcoming environment, surrounded by her extended family, who visit her often. She plays the piano for entertainment at family gatherings, a talent she first displayed as an accompanist in the local movie theater for silent movies. Viva typifies the feelings of many centenarians and others of advanced age. People who throughout their lives have been open and receptive and interested in others, want friends, acquaintances, as well as relatives, to remain central in their lives.

Despite this wish and the related desire, an older person's actual relationships often change dramatically, leading a number of centenarians to say that the hardest thing about being old is the loneliness. Many centenarians and others of advanced age have outlived not only their spouses but also some, or all, of their children. The majority of centenarians, especially women, have been widowed for decades. Some have been alone for almost as long a time as they were married; some for longer, such as Vita Hancock, 101, of Homeland, Florida, who has lived alone for forty-five years since her husband died. A much smaller percentage of centenarians have never married. Of those who have remarried late in life, most are men.

Many centenarians without spouses have developed close relationships with their children, usually daughters, or with other family members, such as a sister or grandchild. These bonds help fortify them in their later years. Others, such as Hedvig Peterson, who has been a widow for almost thirty years and with no children, have developed close relationships with friends through church and community organizations. As her cousin observed, "Heddy has the ability to make friends among all generations. She is interested in them and keeps up with current trends and events that are important in the lives of younger people. After her husband died, Heddy set about making friends and built a support network which has sustained her through these many years. She has actively reached out to others and has made them important in her life. She is loved and admired. Heddy continues to do everything she can for herself. But if she does need help, there are a dozen people close by who would come immediately to her aid. People in the community think of her as an inspiration and an asset to the neighborhood."

This bond with others is very important. Whether one lives alone, with family members, or in a care center, the need for social involvement and community is apparent. People can help support the will to live and interest in life in our eldest citizens and help alleviate some of the loneliness by giving them just a little time and attention and by creating opportunities for our eldest citizens to remain connected to a community. James Lee Moss of Lewisburg, Tennessee, verbalized what a lot of his peers feel: "I like attention and to be noticed. As of 103, I'm proud to be here."

Mary Ogburn, 105, of Mesa, Arizona, illustrates how socialization and relationships with others can improve life and strengthen one's will. "Mother has lived with me for many years," says Ruth Silides. "She has always been a cheerful, outgoing person, never complains, and is nice and friendly with everyone. She always enjoyed being with people. But as she grew very old, the opportunities for social activities got less. Most of her friends died, and there were fewer places I could take her out to enjoy because her hearing got bad and so did her eyesight. We have always been very close, but I work during the day, and she was alone for a lot of hours. Last year, at 104, she began to decline; her spirits dropped, and she seemed to be losing interest in the world around her for the first time since I've known her. She would sit home alone most of the day and watch television or sleep. She was always tired. I finally convinced her to go to the day care center, which is part of the senior center, two days a week. At first she didn't want to go and when I took her, she said she didn't like being there. But within two weeks, I began to see a difference. She was brighter, more interested in everything, more like herself. Then I learned she had made two new friends, both women in their eighties. Now, six months later, she looks forward to going to be with her friends and enjoys the activities at the center. She is much improved over a year ago."

Mary celebrated her 105th birthday with a large party at the day-care center. She gave sprigs of heather to each guest to wear, a reminder of her native Scotland. A local doctor took time from his busy schedule to play several of her favorite songs on the bagpipes. When the pipes skirled "Happy Birthday," tears filled Mary's eyes. They were tears of remembrance for times past, and they were tears of joy and of appreciation for the present camaraderie of family and friends gathered in celebration of her life.

Gertrude Skerston, 100, of Dennisport, Massachusetts, basks in the warmth and love she receives from her daughter. She tells that her daughter's presence nearby gives her peace of mind and happiness. Gertrude lives alone in her own home and has a homemaker come two hours each day. Her daughter and son-in-law live in the house behind her. "My daughter sees to it that I get to bed every night," she says contentedly. "A hug from someone who cares at bedtime is better than a sleeping pill."

Centenarians are also coming up with creative living arrangements and developing new relationships to help meet their needs and yet preserve their autonomy. One enterprising centenarian of Salt Lake City has worked out a successful living arrangement that allows her to stay in her own home. For many years, she has invited a married couple each year from nearby Brigham Young University to live with her. "It works out just fine," she says. "The students have a place to live and enough room and privacy to study, and I have help with what I need. We share the cooking and take our meals together frequently. I enjoy the lively conversation. It's nice having young people around, and it keeps me in touch and up-to-date." Her family also lives nearby and visits often.

For centenarians Agnes Tappe, 105, and Lillian Heller, 106, of Freeport, Illinois, neither of whom ever married, the answer to companionship in their later years came in sharing those years together. They were girlhood friends who lived within blocks of each other. Their friendship continued, and their lives became more entwined when Lillian's brother married Agnes's sister. They began to help raise the nieces, nephews, great-nieces and great-nephews who followed. Sixteen years ago, they entered St. Joseph's Home as roommates.

Other centenarians have found the answer to companionship in their later years by remarrying. Louis Kelly was eighty and a widower for three years when he met Dorothy, seventy-one. "We met in the

✌ *Frank Rowels with his wife Virginia on her 100th birthday.*
Photo courtesy of the Houston Newspapers, Houston, Missouri, and the Rowels family.

spring and were married in the fall," he says. Louis and Dorothy recently celebrated their twenty-third anniversary.

The Reverend Joseph Penn was eighty-five when he married for the second time; he and his wife celebrated seventeen years together. Centenarian Frank Rowels of Houston, Missouri, was in his mid-eighties also the second time around: "I married for the first time at twenty-nine and was married for forty-six years. We had eight children. After my wife died in 1965, I met Virginia, who is a year younger than I am. We married five years later, when I was eighty and she was seventy-nine. We have been married for twenty-one years and holding. We have grown old together. A few years ago, we came to live with my daughter. Recently Virginia's health began to fail, and she now lives at a nursing home nearby where she can get the care she needs. I go to visit with her every day. My daughter takes me, even though it isn't her mother, because she knows it is important to me. I feel it is my duty to be with my wife, and, besides, I want to be. She celebrated my 100th birthday with me in 1988 and I celebrated with her in 1989. That's pretty remarkable, isn't it? When we married, we thought we'd have only a few years together. It's important to us to be together as much as we can. It's hard to be separated now. Just because men and women grow old doesn't mean they stop loving or caring or wanting to be together."

For centenarian couple Ben and Gladys Pruitt, the years of caring and commitment span not only their old age and their centennials but their youth and middle age, as well. They are one of the very few centenarian couples to reach a diamond (seventy-fifth) anniversary and beyond. In May 1991, they celebrated their seventy-eight wedding anniversary.

For many years, the Pruitts lived alone in Springfield, Oregon, in an old farmhouse they purchased when they retired. They developed hobbies and pastimes and interests that they did together, such as oil painting, and other interests that they pursued individually. "I think it's the ideal way to get along and to spend so many years together," Ben tells. When poor health required that Gladys move to a nursing home, Ben moved in, too, because he didn't want to be without her.

❧

A POSITIVE ATTITUDE

Centenarians say that a positive attitude combining hope, faith, love, and optimism develops in earlier years and is then available to serve one well later on. This positive attitude and the ability to adapt are crucial in helping to combat the very real losses of aging and the life changes that occur as we grow older.

In their individual, often quiet ways, many centenarians' lives are validations of their positive outlooks, even in the face of serious illness and hardship.

Mary Gleason is one such centenarian. At the age of ninety-eight, she had a leg amputated because of poor circulation and the onset of gangrene. At the age of ninety-nine, she lost the other leg. "She suffered a great deal of pain and required a lot of care, which was hard for her to tolerate," her daughter, Eileen Matonak, says. Then at 100, she began attending a day-care center in Columbia, South Carolina, to give her daughter some time to herself during the day. A van picks her up each morning and takes her home in the afternoon. "Her lively Irish sense of humor has remained intact," her daughter says. "She doesn't dwell on what she has lost. She is thankful for what she has."

"When I get to feeling sad about things," Mary says, "I start to count my blessings. I came to this country to make a better life for myself, and I have. I had a long marriage to a handsome man I loved, and we had two beautiful children. Even though I have had to give up my home, my daughter has taken me into her home and takes very good care of me. I'm thankful I don't need more care and to have to be in a nursing home."

The late Dr. Norman Vincent Peale, author of *The Power of Positive Thinking, The Tough-Minded Optimist*, and many other best-sellers, was a lifelong symbol of the importance of a positive attitude. "[To] overcome, to achieve victory, to go forward," he wrote, requires a will to "continue hopefully and cheerfully to expect the good no matter what the situation." Optimism, he asserted, "is not . . .the super-cheery, the ultra-bright or the fortuitous. . .but rather [an ability] to see the worst in complete realism, but still to believe in the best."

Centenarian Mabel Correa of Oakland, California, lives this philosophy. Mabel still attends Mass every Sunday in the same church where she went to Catholic school, made her first Holy Communion, was confirmed, and later married. It is also the same church that held the funerals of her husband, who died more than two decades ago, and her twin sons, who both died during World War II. Mabel's deep faith has sustained her through adversity and sorrow for many years and continues to infuse her daily life with hope and a sense of goodness.

"I lived through both of the big earthquakes and many smaller ones," she says matter-of-factly. In 1906, I was still living at home with my family when it hit. I didn't know what it was. My father grabbed my hand and we ran out of the house while he shouted to my mother and the others to get out, too. We stood in the street. Later we watched the fires across the bay and listened to the talk of neighbors about the hundreds of homes destroyed and the hundreds of people killed. But during this last quake (1989) I was alone. I said to myself, 'Here we go again.' This time, I just stayed in bed and prayed. I prayed for all those people who were outside and in more danger than I was. I prayed that so many wouldn't lose their lives like the last time. It was much closer this time, and I was afraid. But there was nothing I could do but pray to the Blessed Mother to protect us."

Mabel attends the St. Mary's Senior Services program at her church, which offers meals and social activities two days a week. On the other five days, she attends programs at a senior center farther away from her inner-city home. "It once was a nice neighborhood," she tells. Her only means of transportation is the public bus. "It's not too bad coming to St. Mary's," she says, "but on the other days I have to transfer and take two buses each way." On her way to the bus stop, three blocks from her home, she passes drug users, pushers, pimps, and prostitutes. "I try not to look at them hoping they will leave me alone. Sometimes they do. Sometimes they don't." Sometimes money is taken from her. Occasionally she is physically abused. "I'm always afraid," Mabel admits.

Yet she arrives at the church, though sometimes shaken, with a smile of gratitude on her face, enthused to be with others, all of younger generations, who are her friends; to pray in the quiet of the small church that is home to her; to light a candle in thanksgiving for the privilege of being alive and to pray for others who are less fortunate than she.

Looking at her life objectively, one could say that Mabel is among the less fortunate. Her circumstances are far from atypical, however. Thousands more of advanced age share with Mabel similar living conditions. Her once neat home is in desperate need of repair. Her worn clothing bears the unmistakable stamp of styles many years outdated. She is small and frail and vulnerable and alone. Her home has been broken into three times in the last few months. The last time she was awakened when a large man sat down on her bed (having broken in through a bedroom window during the night). "He was rocking back and forth, sitting on the bed. He kept saying, 'Give me money, give me money.' I knew he was on drugs. I told him all the money I had was some change in my purse and turned on the light so he could take it. He grabbed my purse and turned it upside down, shaking it hard. A few coins fell out—it was all I had. He got mad and began pulling things apart—drawers, clothing—looking for more money. I told him I didn't have any more. Then he started hitting me. I thought I was finished. Suddenly, he ran out of the house through the front door, taking the television set with him and leaving the front door wide open. I was just glad to be alive," she says with a sad smile.

Sister Vicki of the St. Mary's Senior Center comments on Mabel's continued cheerfulness and positive attitude. "She never complains.

When she arrives at the center, she takes her usual seat along the first row of tables, near the windows. She greets everyone she passes on the way in with a smile and a compliment or some commiseration for how they're feeling. She eats her meal, plays cards, or visits with her friends, always supportive and cheering them up. Then she stops in the church to say a prayer and light a candle. We see her little figure trudging off again, to take the bus back home, in mid-afternoon.

"She never tells us what has happened to her since the previous time she was here. Even when she has a cold, she comes, smiling, blowing her nose. We only find out what has befallen her from others who hear about it in the neighborhood. We marvel that she can keep going like this—and not be defeated by the circumstances of her life. She's just so happy to be alive."

In today's psychological literature much is being written about the importance of a positive attitude to physical and mental well-being. Active centenarians not only support this view, they attest to it. See the sunny side of life, they counsel; see the glass as half full rather than half empty. This philosophy makes life much more enjoyable, makes relationships better, and contributes to the feeling, as Mabel Correa believes, that life is worthwhile and precious at almost any cost.

⁓

ADAPTABILITY

In sustaining the will to live, adaptability also seems to play a key role. It doesn't make life worthwhile in itself; rather, it is a tool that enables one to continue meeting challenges and coping with adversity. Some people are highly adaptable and always have been. Others are less so. But centenarians, whether through an inborn characteristic they have enjoyed all their lives or a behavior learned through many years of life experience, rank high in this attribute. A bit of common wisdom holds that what you become accustomed to do in your youth, you do in your old age. As people age, they may lose certain physical and mental abilities and one part of their personality may become dominant, but habits tend to remain constant. Whatever we developed in our youth—or gain through experience—we fall back on in our maturity.

Centenarians counsel on the importance of developing this trait over the years. If we are adaptable in our younger years, we tend to be adaptable when we are old, many believe. Paul Arley's life is illustrative of the advantages of successfully developing this quality.

Paul Arley

" 'Paul's unusual,' my father always used to say, trying to explain my behavior to family and neighbors in Rotterdam, Holland, where I was born." Every day Paul would carry his father's lunch pail to the railroad yard, where his father worked. He recalls coworkers saying, 'One of these days your son will be working here beside you,' but his father would reply, 'Not Paul. Paul will never work here.' My father was right. I was always curious about things, about the world and about other people."

Around the turn of the century, when electric streetcars were being introduced, Paul's father, friends, and other family members would gather at night and discuss the coming of electricity. They predicted that houses would burn down because the wires would get so hot. The electric streetcar, which was to be introduced soon in The Hague, the capital city, was the special target of ridicule. Not only Paul's father but newspaper editorials, too, were against the change, predicting that people would be electrocuted when they touched the brass rails of the car and that birds perched on the wires would be fried when the electric current went through them.

As the day approached when the streetcars would run for the first time, the speculation of calamity grew stronger and wilder. "I didn't believe it, so I decided to see for myself," Paul says. "I walked the twenty miles or so from Rotterdam, stealing away early in the morning because my mother would never have let me go. When I reached the city, I sat on the grass and watched streetcars running clickity-click up and down the track, and people getting off and on, smiling, holding onto the brass railings. The birds would perch on the wires and then fly away. I was so pleased—I stayed there quite a while, just watching. It was the first time I ever had the feeling that I was right in my thinking, that I could trust my thinking, and not have to believe as others did about things."

These happy thoughts occupied Paul on the long walk home and helped keep his mind off being tired and hungry. He arrived after dark, to his mother's relief and his father's wrath. "Funny, isn't it," he ruminates, "how something like that long ago can make such a difference in your life. From then on, I never stopped believing in myself, and in my own thoughts, and what I could do with what God had given me. I just did the best I knew I could do, whatever the circumstances."

Paul's motivation as a teenager was to earn as much money as possible to help his mother. At only 5′2″, Paul was very short but unusually strong for his size and very muscular. His brother suggested he be a boxer, so at the age of fourteen he left school and gave it an unsuccessful try. Later, after a few months of compulsory service in the army, he joined a theater, singing in the chorus in Amsterdam "because they paid a lot of money," he explains, which he sent home to his mother. Although he liked singing he felt he wasn't using his natural gift of strength. Paul had seen acrobats in the theater and seen picture advertisements of the stunts they performed. "I studied what they did and believed I could do better," he says. Paul left the theater and went back to his home where, with two other men, he began to practice stunts in his father's barn. "I imitated what I saw acrobats do," he tells. "Also, I would lie in bed at night, picturing stunts in my mind—I could see just how they would look. Soon I began thinking up new ones and imagining how good they would look when I performed them." Interestingly, what Paul discovered on his own so many years ago is now the popular technique of visualization used in many fields but particularly in athletic training.

One day while working out on the hand rings, an accident happened that would eventually change the course of his life. "I fell, head first, and hit the ground," Paul remembers. "My injury limited the movement in my arm, at the elbow. The local doctor said I would never be able to use my arm again and it would have to be amputated. I wasn't ready to give up my arm so quickly, and so I refused the operation. I remember thinking about his advice, that there was nothing that could be done, much the same way I thought about my father saying that the electricity would kill people on the streetcars and the birds on the wires."

Even though the injury was very painful, Paul decided to try and fix it himself, figuring that if a head-first fall caused the problem, then a feet-first fall should put it back in place. Holding onto the rings, he jumped off a high stack of boxes. "The weight of my body pulled hard on my arm—it really hurt—snapping something and straightening my elbow. Miraculously, it healed, and I didn't lose my arm."

At that time, Paul was still concerned with his immediate goal of earning enough money to ease his mother's hard life. She, in turn, was worried that he would become like the gypsy acrobats performing in the street for money. Paul assured her he intended to be part of the best circus, and, in time, he was. Just to be on the safe side, though, and to save his mother from any embarrassment, he used a different name when he joined the circus, changing from the family name of Olaff to Arley.

By 1908, Paul had become a star performer with the European circus doing a daring routine he developed for what was called the perch act. "The Arley Troupe was the only act in Europe that could successfully do this stunt," he tells. "I would climb a thirty-foot pole, balanced on my partner's forehead usually, but sometimes on his shoulder or the top of his head. I would stand on my head on the top. I also did other stunts at the top of the pole—sometimes as many as three of us would go up the pole and perform different stunts, me on top and two others from an apparatus attached to the sides of the pole. Every time I went up the pole I said, 'God be with me,' and He was—I never fell. The audiences loved it. When we played Rotterdam, I invited my parents to ringside seats—I wanted to show them that I was successful and popular and not just a gypsy acrobat—but each time I glanced at them, my mother had her face covered—she couldn't watch."

Then Paul decided he wanted to go to America. He read as much as he could about the country and was impressed by its size and especially by the cowboys. "I made the act more and more daring, hoping to attract the attention of a scout, and it worked," Paul continues. "I was asked by Ringling Brothers to come to America, to perform in their three-ring circus, instead of only one ring in Europe. It was 1914, and I had a two-year contract. I was bursting with happiness to be taken to America by the greatest circus people on earth and to live in the greatest country on earth."

At that time, Ringling Brothers had already purchased the Barnum & Bailey circus, but they toured as two separate troupes keeping the original names; later, the two circuses were combined. "The new show combining the two troupes became a super circus," Paul says with excitement. "It opened in Madison Square Garden in March of 1919. That is how I became part of 'The Greatest Show on Earth!'"

Paul stayed with the circus for twenty years, traveling all over the country. In the off-seasons, the Arley Troupe played in vaudeville. "I got to see everything," he says. "I loved it."

In 1922, Paul met and married his wife. She was part of the same circus, a stunt rider—"a cute little girl on a white horse," he recalls with a smile. "She wanted to join my act—she said she could do what I did, stunts at the top of the pole. My partner thought it was too dangerous for a woman to do our act, so he quit when I said I would give her a try. I said I would train her. Even circus people were very skeptical, but we did it and were married a few months later."

All this while, Paul was using his natural ability to heal peoples' injuries as he had cured his own many years before. Ever curious, Paul made it a goal to figure out how he was able to do so.

One day in 1933, in Bridgeport, Connecticut, a doctor of chiropractic and owner of the Eastern School of Chiropractic in New York paid Paul a visit. He had heard that this circus had the lowest rate of people on sick leave from injuries and wanted to meet "the guy that fixed everything," Paul says proudly. "He said he came to see me because I was an unusual person. We talked. He asked me what it was I did to help people. I told him. He said, 'Do you know what it is you are doing with your hands?' 'No,' I replied. 'Do you?'"

Paul was told he was a natural chiropractor and was invited to attend the school. "It was like a miracle to me," Paul says seriously. "Suddenly, here was someone offering to teach me what I wanted to learn most. But I felt I couldn't afford to leave the circus because I had two children to support, and I could not pay for chiropractic schooling. However, he said he would teach me himself and it would not cost me a thing. We had enough money saved up so we could just manage to live while I studied chiropractic. And so, at the age of forty, I left the circus and began a new career. In 1936, I opened my office on Fifth Avenue in New York and practiced there for twenty-five years."

During these years Paul was very happy helping people feel better. There was a lot of prejudice against the new field of chiropractic, but he ignored it. His fondest wish was granted when his two children became chiropractors also. "I am very proud of them," he says. "They were good kids and good chiropractors. My daughter is still practicing in Old Greenwich, Connecticut. I told them never to listen to negative people—just think your own thoughts and do what you know you can do."

The one tragedy of Paul's life was the death of his son, in his early thirties, of leukemia. "I felt so helpless watching him suffer," Paul says, "there was nothing anyone could do for him—his illness was beyond the help of medicine at that time. It was the darkest time of my life. I felt I did not want to go on any longer, but after a time, I began to think that my son would not have wanted me to give up helping other people just because I could not help him. He knew that chiropractic can be very helpful sometimes, but not always and that medicine can do miraculous cures sometimes, but not always. So I accepted his fate and went on trying to help other people. I retired in 1961. My wife died in 1979, and after that I moved to Connecticut to live with my daughter."

For Paul Arley, one of the greatest tests of his optimistic and adaptive nature came when he moved into a nursing home. "I lived for several years with my daughter in her home," he tells. "In my ninety-seventh year, I had a stroke which left my leg muscles weak and I was susceptible to falls. She was afraid to leave me alone after that. Funny, isn't it? After all those years in the circus as an acrobat, me falling. But it happened. I couldn't seem to stop it. My legs would just give out under me, so I had to use a wheelchair. I push it with my feet and get around by myself, but there are a lot of stairs in my daughter's house. Finally, it just got too much for her. She didn't have the strength to take care of me and earn a living too; she had to find another place for me to live nearby. I know she checked carefully and found the best nursing home for me, but when she took me there I said to her, 'Are you taking me here to die?' I felt so sad, I cried. 'No,' she answered, 'I'm taking you here to live.' 'But until I die?' I said. 'Yes,' she answered. And she cried too.

"I had a very difficult time for a long while. Even though I have a large cheerful room to myself and everyone is very nice to me, I felt sorry for myself to have ended up like this after all these years of accomplishment. But then, approaching my 100th birthday, I began to pull out of it and to try and look on the bright side. Other people were being so nice to me, and the staff was making such a big effort for my 100th birthday party. The administrator tried hard to involve others in the community in the celebration so I would have a lively event. And it was. My 100th party was the best ever. I gave a birthday address saying how I fitted in at the home, and I thanked the staff and fellow residents for being so friendly and accommodating. And then I told stories of the circus and made people laugh. I read a poem I had written many years ago, giving my philosophy on life—called "All the World's a Circus, So On with the Show." When the party was over, I thought I'd better start taking some of my own advice.

"A nice thing happened to me shortly after that. I received the kind of recognition that has meant the most throughout my life. I received a letter addressed only to Dr. Paul Arley, Greenwich, CT 06830. On the outside was written: 'Postmaster, he was mentioned on the "Today Show" on July 14th as being 100 years old today. Hope you can find him. I knew him years ago. I feel it's worth the try.' Just four days later, the postman delivered it to me at the Nathaniel Witherrell Home. Amazing, isn't it? The letter came from a lady in Massachusetts who said I had helped her mother in the early years of my chiropractic practice in New York City. She sent me birthday congratulations and said, 'I have fond memories of all you did for mother and I loved the stories about the circus.'

"That letter reminded me how I always wanted to help people and how helping makes me happy. So I began to look at being here as living here, not as dying here. Every day now I talk with other people and try to cheer them up. I tell them stories of the circus sometimes—everyone loves the circus. And everyone wishes they could be somewhere else, but for some of us, there is no other choice. We can either be miserable until we die or try to be happy till we die. All the world's a circus, and you are with the show. This is the way I'm living each day now."

⊰ *Paul Arley arriving for his 100th birthday celebration. Photo courtesy of his daughter Constance and the Nathaniel Witherell Home, Greenwich, CT.*

As spiritual leader for one of the largest long-term care facilities in the country, Rabbi Samuel R. Seicol is familiar with the adjustments older people must make. "The losses, and the grief accompanying the losses of aging, are very real," says Rabbi Seicol, Chaplain at the Hebrew Rehabilitation Center for the Aged in Boston and chairman elect of the American Society on Aging Forum on Religion, Spirituality and Aging. "What is often labeled as depression in the elderly actually is very legitimate grief. But we as a society don't accept grief as an appropriate response to having to give up one's home or one's car— in essence, one's independence—and move into a nursing home or retirement home or with family, for example. We only understand grief when it is associated with a death, but there is grief associated with all kinds of losses, including the loss of one's health, one's strength, mobility, vision, and hearing. It is legitimate for elderly people to grieve for the parts of themselves they have lost and the life they had which they can never live again, and it is our challenge to help them deal with their grief and to comfort them and support them in the process of accepting their changed circumstances. Some people cope better than others. They are the survivors. We need to help and encourage those who are struggling with this grief."

He explains that while there's no formula for every person experiencing grief, the first step is to recognize and to accept the fact. For instance, if a person can no longer live independently, the first step requires that this be confronted and recognized, as Paul Arley and his daughter did. The next step in the grief process is to find answers for questions such as: How can I create meaning from the loss? How can I grow through it? How can I find the gain and develop it? If the loss is the death of a loved one, the path forward is paved by shared love and the remaining memory of the loved one. The final step is adapting to the changed circumstances. This provides for a sense of new life and new hope, which develop out of the recommitment to oneself and to the future.

Yet, as we all understand, no one can be infinitely adaptable.

ॐ

RELIGIOUS FAITH AND SPIRITUALITY

Religion and spirituality are central to most centenarians' lives. As Tempa Robinson, 101, of Lenoir City, Tennessee, explains, "Spirituality, to me, is the feeling a person has of not being alone in the world." Trust in God, believing it is His will that they have lived this long, and that they will be called "home" when He is ready, are common themes among centenarians. Belief in an afterlife, they say, strengthens their resolve to live. Through faith, they find the strength to carry out God's purpose, whatever they perceive that to be.

The religious faith of our eldest citizens is long-standing. Most centenarians were raised in religious families. Cora Alice Clark of Salem, Oregon, at 102, writes of her childhood: "Every morning before leaving the breakfast table, my father read from the Bible, stories fitting out age and understanding. My mother also did not go about her work but sat still and listened and then we all knelt while he prayed before our day's chores or beginning our daily activity."

For the Reverend Sidney Powell, 100, of Stuart, Florida, "Religion has been everything to me. My Sunday school teacher got me interested in religion at the age of ten. At eighteen, I went to Bible College. I served as vice president of the Northern Baptist Churches. I preached and spoke over the entire country and Canada. In the 1920s I conducted services on the earliest radio station in Newark, New Jersey. I stayed in New Jersey for thirty-five years and was pastor of the Frenchtown, Sussex, Arlington, and Newark churches.

"I had a desire to reach as many people as possible. After thirty-five years, I resigned as a pastor and became an evangelist until I was seventy-five. I took the Lord's word to the Bowery of New York, and I took a job as Chaplain at Fort Dix. I knew Billy Sunday, the famous evangelist, in the early years; perhaps I modeled myself after him. I tried to be inspiring in my own oratory. I also wrote six books on different religious subjects."

Some came to embrace their particular religion in early adulthood. Both men and women centenarians report that they have been very involved in church work and volunteer organizations for most of their lives. Attendance at church is very important to them; those who are physically able to do so attend church regularly.

Don Nafe, 100, of Ypsilanti, Michigan, reads the Bible every day and never misses church on Sunday. For many years, he was chairman of the deacons at Calvary Baptist Church, taught Sunday school, sang in the church choir until he was ninety-six, and traveled with the choir to perform in many states. "Doc," who lives alone, says he's very appreciative that his daughter or son-in-law drive him each week. "I still attend church every Wednesday evening and Sundays, morning and evening." Louis Kelly now hires someone to drive him and his wife to church each Sunday because his failing eyesight prevents him from driving. Others, including Mabel Dudley, 100, of Florence, Colorado, and William Sutton, 100, of Stockdale, Texas, are also proud to say, "I still attend church each Sunday." In New York City, 104-year-old Marie Minnies laboriously climbs up and down three flights of stairs from her apartment, assisted by a family member, "almost every Sunday" to attend church.

Those who are physically unable to attend church because of health or mobility problems or lack of transportation say they wish they could participate in Sunday service and church activities. Many say they would be happier to be more active in the church like they used to be. For others, who live in retirement or nursing homes, Sabbath and holiday services may be provided in the facility. An important part of Rabbi Siecol's work is "to continue to enhance each resident's involvement in religious services and programs and to ensure spiritual life to the fullest extent possible. But," he adds, "a great many of our elders, who are homebound in the community, belong to churches or synagogues that are letting them down." Rabbi Seicol believes religious groups should be doing more outreach to help the frail elderly. "When people can no longer come to their house of worship, it is necessary for the ministry to go to them. This is not the time to leave them alone, just when they need the comfort and solace of their belief the most.

"If religion has been an important part of a person's life, both spiritually and socially, it forms a part of the personal history, imparting a sense of identification and value to the individual. To have that cut off when a person ages or is not able to physically 'keep up' undermines an intrinsic part of the individual's life experience. We should not leave our old, no matter how 'broken' or 'useless,' behind," Rabbi Seicol continues. "Rather, it is the community, in shared service and responsibility, which must provide religious services and social activities for its oldest members. We will all be richer for doing it," he teaches. "It is the essence of charity and righteous deeds."

Like many of his generation, Angelo Maltas, 102, wants to be remembered as an integral part of his church community. "Thanks be to God that I am still able to be active in my church at my age," he says. "They have made a place for me."

For Angelo, the Holy Trinity Greek Orthodox Church in Bridgeport, Connecticut, has been a mainstay of his life since arriving from Greece in 1913. "The first thing everyone did was go to the church to get acquainted," he tells. "The church community is the center of our religious and social life." Eventually, Angelo became treasurer and served several times as president of the church council. He is pleased to have observed the eightieth anniversary of his membership with the church. "My wife of sixty-three years and I were both dedicated to the church and we raised our three children to be communicants. I still go every Sunday with one of my children."

Over the past several years, Angelo has held a place of honor, standing by the seven-day candles and assisting people to light them. Often he would light candles for those who had sent in requests. "In the Greek Orthodox religion," he explains, "candles play an important role. We light candles for every service, including baptisms, as a blessing or as a sacrifice to whatever we are praying for. We don't do anything without a candle, except for funerals." Angelo draws a comparison of the candle to life. The flame burns brightly at first, the candle straight and tall; then the wax melts and drips down, forming irregularities in the shape and massing at the bottom to form a base; the flame grows dimmer as it burns down; and, finally, the flame burns into the base and is snuffed out. All in its time.

The metaphor of the candle is one that Angelo has lived with for a long time. A newer metaphor occurred to him on the eve of his 100th birthday, captured in the only poem he has ever written:

Leaves of Life

The day was gray
the wind was whipping up the leaves
the trees were bared.
All except for one little leaf left
way up on top of the tree.
I sat and looked at the lonely leaf
struggling in the wind
But it hung on despite it.
A melancholy thought came to me—
it is, I thought, just like myself.
I am now a century old
all my friends and my partner in life
are gone.
But the leaf and I
hang on.

Centenarians also bear witness to the fact that meeting religious and spiritual needs is a lifelong process that does not diminish with age. Religious faith and spirituality sustain them not only in their will to live, but in their acceptance of death. Sometimes a special event, such as approaching the 100-year mark, or a special occasion gives a person an extra motivation to live for a time. As Gertrude Ridinger of Euclid, Ohio, tells, "My dear father, John Lutsch, was determined to reach his 100th birthday. He made it plus twenty-three more days. At his party, he sang 'Let Me Call You Sweetheart' to my mother while I accompanied him on the accordion. (They met at a concert while he was performing with a German men's singing group in 1912.) On his birthday, one would not have suspected that the end was so near."

The staffs of nursing homes say they frequently see a preparation for death played out, with a person's focus changing from trying to stay alive to accepting dying. As one administrator recounted, "We had a resident who was approaching 100. She had been working on crocheting an afghan for the weeks preceding her 100th birthday. After her birthday, I entered her room the next day and she was carefully folding up her yarn and the unfinished afghan. She had already prepared all of the other few possessions, including her clothing, in a similar manner. When asked what she was doing, she answered, 'I am getting ready to die.' I talked with her for a while, and then I said, 'I'm disappointed. I was looking forward to seeing the afghan. I would like to have it.' And then I left her. The next day, she was seated in her rocking chair working on her afghan again, and I was pleased, but each day I noticed she was only wearing her robe and that her clothing remained neatly folded as she had left it the day we talked. One day, she called to me saying the afghan was ready. She handed it to me, went to her bed, and lay down. By the next morning, she was gone."

Others have been known to make calls or send messages to family and friends to say good-bye, foreseeing that they will be leaving soon.

                                    ·ᡧ·

The story of Nannie Cook Moree of Athens, Tennessee, as told by her granddaughter, Sharon Willet, expresses the essential nature of her will to live, the courage to grow old, and her readiness to die. It honors the elder's enormous love and commitment to family, a family that filled Nannie's life with meaning and sustained her to the age of 106.

Born on December 30, 1883, outside the small town of Madisonville,

Tennessee, Nannie had a very hard life but lived by her faith in the Lord, the virtue of honesty, and, most of all, she says, love. The oldest of six children, Nannie took over the household after her mother died when the youngest was born. She left school in the eighth grade to care for the family. She never dated until all of the children were raised and had left home.

In 1917, at age thirty-four, she married and at thirty-five she had her first child. On Sundays, the family went to church by horse-drawn buggy. At thirty-nine, Nannie had her second child. Seven months later her husband died and she soon lost the farm where they lived. Nannie and her children went to live with her father, caring for him until he died. She always took her children to church and lived a strongly religious life, putting her faith and trust in the Lord, knowing He would provide for her.

Eventually, she bought another farm and worked it, along with a job at the local hosiery mill, until her children were grown. Later, she went to live with her daughter, son-in-law, and two young grandchildren in Athens, Tennessee.

Nannie Moree's life and death have left a strong impression on her granddaughter, who says:

"I remember when I was very small, Mamaw, as we called her, taught me the alphabet and numbers before I started school. She would play with me, my brothers, and my cousins and help care for us. When we were sick, she would cook us something special. She was always like a mother to me and my brother. She was always there for us to go to. She always showed us so much love and attention and had a very gentle way about her—you couldn't help but love her. Mamaw taught me so many things while I was growing up. She taught me how to sew and cook and can vegetables and make jams. Everything she ever taught me has helped me in my life. She would read us Bible stories and teach us about Jesus when we were small. She taught us to trust in the Lord. And she always told me not to say I couldn't do something. Everything I can do I owe to her because of that. When I was grown, she helped care for my children so I could work, and she cared for my brother's children, too. All her family loved her dearly. There is nothing we wouldn't have done for her. When she was in her late nineties, she was still cooking and helping clean house.

"Mamaw had more than her share of illness, numerous surgeries, and a heart condition. But she always had an amazingly strong will to live. Often the doctors would tell us she didn't have long to live, but by a couple of weeks, she would surprise them and be just fine. Two days before her 100th birthday, she fell and severely broke her hip. A surprise party had been planned, but, of course, it had to be canceled. The doctors only gave her a 10 percent chance of surviving the surgery because of her age, but she came through it with flying colors. The hospital gave her a small party in intensive care with her family present. She was so happy that day.

"The doctor then said she needed to go to a nursing home so she could get therapy on her leg or she would never walk again. I knew she wouldn't be happy in a nursing home, away from her family, so I found a physical therapist who would come to our home. At home, my brother and I worked with her after she started her therapy, making sure she did her leg exercises. It wasn't long before she was walking again, this time with a little help from a walker, but that didn't matter. We thought it was wonderful she was able to walk at all, and Mamaw gratefully accepted the assistance that the walker provided.

"Around 104, her health began to decline. Her memory started to fail, and she would get very mixed up at times, but she always knew who we were and that she wanted to stay at home. Sometimes I think she would struggle hard to appear all right, just so we would not give up on her and put her in a nursing home. She celebrated her 106th birthday on December 30, 1989, and received a birthday card from President and Mrs. Bush. On the fourth of January 1990, she was taken by ambulance to the hospital and admitted with a severe case of pneumonia. She got to the point where she couldn't eat and she was sleeping most of the day. She kept getting thinner and weaker. Every day, her family was there with her. We all knew the inevitable was coming this time. She was suffering a lot, and there were times when she would stretch her arms up like she was reaching for Heaven.

"It's so hard when you love someone so much to helplessly stand by, unable to help. All you can do is to pray that the Lord will ease their pain. There wasn't a day that went by that I didn't tell her I loved her whether she was awake or not. On February 5, she was awake the whole day, for the first time in almost six weeks. Her voice was very weak and I had to get very close to her to understand what she was saying. That night her doctor didn't think she would make it through the night, but she did. Early the next morning, when I went back, she was awake and started talking to me. 'I am going to Heaven today,' she said.

I began to cry and she put her hand on my face to wipe away my tears. I told her I loved her very much and she said she loved me, too. I leaned over and we gave each other a kiss. I told her that I wouldn't let her die alone and then we both started to cry. I sat by her bed and talked to her and held her hand. Then she told me not to cry or to feel sad. She said she was happy and at peace and she was going home, she was not alone—nor was she afraid.

"Mamaw died a little after ten p.m. I miss her very much. She will always be a part of my life, and I know she is still watching over me."

❧

7

Challenges to Physical Health:
Coping with the Losses of Sight, Hearing, and Mobility

CENTENARIAN Dr. Michael Heidelberger is considered by many to be the father of immunochemistry.

In 1959, he was a world-renowned scientist when he retired after twenty-seven years from Columbia University in New York, with the title of Emeritus Professor of Immunochemistry. A revered educator and pioneer researcher, he had laid the foundation from which all subsequent understanding of immunology has followed and had twice been president of the American Society of Immunologists. One day, Dr. Heidelberger was invited to Cleveland to deliver a lecture at Case Western Reserve Medical School. "My professor dragged me off to hear the lecture," recalls Dr. John Boyer, now Professor of Internal Medicine at the University of Arizona. "I recall that, at the time, it was thought remarkable that Dr. Heidelberger had been publishing on research and biochemistry for at least forty years.

"I anticipated a reminiscing and rambling dissertation on how it was done in the old days, but my thinking was quickly reoriented by a fast-paced presentation of his work in progress and his use of state-of-the-art methodology," Dr. Boyer recounted. "Dr. Heidelberger made no reference whatsoever to his long and distinguished career, which began with fifteen years at the prestigious Rockefeller Institute in New York, or of his pioneering research there. Nor did he mention his substantial contributions to the field of medicine, notably in treatments for African sleeping sickness, for influenza meningitis in infants, and immunization for certain types of pneumonia, all of which had saved countless lives since the early decades of this century. Immunology was a very young science when Dr. Heidelberger entered the field.

"My impression was of a no-nonsense scientist who was interested mainly in the work at hand and the contributions that his research might make to the world of science," Dr. Boyer recalled. "That was thirty years ago. Imagine my surprise when, in 1989, I opened a copy of *The Journal of Immunology* to read a tribute to Dr. Heidelberger, who was still working on research, writing, and lecturing at age 100!"

After retiring from Columbia, Dr. Heidelberger had embarked on a research affiliation with Rutgers University in New Jersey. A few years later, finding the train commute from his home in New York City too time consuming, Dr. Heidelberger had moved his research and teaching to a more convenient location at New York University Medical Center in Manhattan. There, for the past twenty-five years, he had continued to work in his research laboratory, to write, to teach, and to advise students.

What is his personal formula for success, which has allowed him to remain, figuratively speaking, "in the race"? Keeping active is the advice offered by Dr. Heidelberger. He encourages everyone to develop interests outside their work that can fulfill them in their later years and to keep active as they age. An accomplished musician, Dr. Heidelberger enjoys playing the clarinet with amateur chamber music groups and with friends all over the world at every opportunity. He himself adheres to an almost daily exercise regimen, walking around his West Side neighborhood in New York City. He also faithfully does calisthenics ten minutes each morning, "stretching my arms and bending." He stresses the need for exercise in his daily life, saying this is "in order to keep from becoming flabby and soft."

A native New Yorker, Dr. Heidelberger's daily routine also included taking two buses and a brisk walk of several blocks to work, a regime he had kept up since he was seventy-five. His concerned colleagues at New York University Medical Center repeatedly urged him to take taxis as a safer mode of transportation. When he turned 100, he reluctantly agreed, "so they wouldn't worry about me," he added. When

       ɔ *Dr. Michael Heidelberger in his laboratory*
at New York University Medical Center at age 100, 1989.
Photo courtesy of NYU Medical Center. Photograph by John Kennard.

we meet centenarians like Dr. Heidelberger, we must again redefine the concept of aging.

At the beginning of this century, life expectancy was about forty-eight, around the number of years we now think of as middle age. Now, in the last decade of the century, it is not unreasonable for people to expect to live to the age of eighty, or beyond. This increase is in great measure the result of medical advances. The development of penicillin, sulfa drugs and antibiotics substantially increased the chance of survival. Centenarians say that before these life-saving drugs, and the development of disease-specific inoculations, almost everyone expected to lose at least one child in the family. Many centenarians recall the losses of young siblings, often through common diseases such as smallpox, diphtheria, measles, scarlet fever, or infections caused by any number of circumstances. They tell, too, of the prevalence of tuberculosis, and almost all knew of someone who had died in the flu epidemic of 1918.

The increasingly sophisticated arsenal of diagnostic, medical, and surgical techniques, and the development of safer anesthesia, have also contributed dramatically to helping people live longer. Centenarian Peter Engh of Northwood, North Dakota, recalls that when he underwent an appendectomy in 1910, it was done "on the kitchen table". The anesthesia was chloroform. "I'm fortunate I survived," he comments.

Dr. Heidelberger's longevity has been made possible, in part, by striking advances in medical science and technology characteristic of the past half century. However important, though, these advances are but one factor in a complex scenario allowing for a long and productive life.

"The combination of obstinacy, chance, and luck," he says, "which have played a part in most of the events and circumstances of my life, also played a role in saving my life. At age eighty-nine, I was on my way to lecture at the University of California at Davis when I collapsed and passed out in the airport. My weakened aortic valve started leaking badly under the stress of carrying a suitcase and clarinets at the airport. Back in New York, the head of surgery at the University hospital was willing to give me a new valve in spite of my age and, with the help of a skilled anesthetist, I was back in my laboratory in six weeks. At that time, 1977, I was the oldest person ever to have a valve replacement operation. At the age of ninety- eight, I had a pacemaker implanted after a bout with pneumonia. The following year, my life was again saved through medical intervention. I felt ill in the night, put my clothes over my pajamas, and took a taxi across town and down to the NYU Medical Center. They admitted me, did an exploratory operation, and discovered I had pancreatitis. I'm now on a low-fat diet, and I stick to it."

"We are alive at a historic moment when for the first time advanced medical technology has coincided with preventive master planning for the good health necessary to live longer," comments Dr. Walter Bortz II. For as important as the medical and technological advances are, they are but one factor in the complex scenario leading to the healthy and long life. Medical science tells us that lifestyle choices can directly affect our health—for good or ill. We are all aware now of the effects of smoking. In addition, five of the ten leading causes of death—cancer, diabetes, chronic liver disease/cirrhosis, heart disease, and stroke— are thought to be diet related, in some instances, and to some extent. Self-help measures can reduce major risk factors, research reports. Not smoking, preventing obesity and watching one's diet to keep cholesterol under control, controlling high blood pressure, and exercising regularly to maintain good cardiovascular function and muscle strength, combine with preventive medicine and medical technology and prescription drugs to help us live longer than ever before in history. The goal is, additionally, to improve the quality of our added years by staying healthy longer.

Among today's centenarians those who exhibit energy and vitality are so impressive and instructive because they are the exception. And even within this group of the brightest and strongest, the challenges of aging are visible. The lives of many centenarians illustrate not only the will to live but also the challenges to both body and mind that often accompany longevity. As Americans live longer, more and more of us will be faced with these challenges.

❧

When he was eighty-five, Oscar Wilmeth decided he wanted to live to be 100. He had already survived a near-fatal accident in his eightieth year. He was driving on a high mountain road in the Colorado Rockies, on the last leg of a 10,000 mile solo motor trip around the country, when, he recalled, "I blacked out and went off the road and down into a ravine." It was hours before help arrived. "The doctors gave me up for dead and called in my family from California. But I fooled 'em."

After undergoing multiple surgeries to mend his broken bones, he spent several months doing intensive physical therapy because he had to learn to walk again. Once out of the hospital, he bought another car, promising his worried son he'd be careful. "The altitude got me, that's all," he insisted.

At ninety, Oscar suffered a heart attack. Once again, he was not expected to survive, but he did. He was given a pacemaker. He learned about exercising and eating right. In fact, after his heart attack, he changed his diet completely, giving up sugar, chocolate, and fried foods—which he had always loved—in favor of a low-fat diet.

For a while, Oscar lived on his own. He kept active and exercised regularly. Then at the age of ninety-seven, he had a stroke, which left him partially paralyzed on his right side. Physical therapy enabled him to regain much of his former functioning, but he had to make some adjustments, such as giving up driving. Finding it hard to write by hand, he taught himself to type on a portable electric typewriter, which he used to keep up with his correspondence of dozens of letters a month to family and friends. He also began typing his autobiography— in anticipation of his 100th birthday: "Looking back over the years of my life, I would say that maintaining one's health is the most important thing to do with one's life. All too often we put it aside to earn a living or to care for others. I've been lucky. But not everyone can depend on luck or good genes to get them through to a "ripe, old age." I think it's wonderful to see younger people taking such an interest in health and exercise and diet. I'm all for it—for people of all ages. It's never too late to take good care of yourself."

Oscar began planning his centennial celebration when he turned ninety-eight. He booked the ballroom at the local Hilton and invited more than 200 people. At ninety-nine, however, he came down with pneumonia and began to worry if he would reach his goal. So he moved into a small group home, where he had a room of his own and his meals were provided. A nurse's aide was in attendance day and night. Oscar bought an oxygen tank and mask to keep handy in his room when he had difficulty breathing; he also bought two new hearing aids and a hand-held device that increased the volume on the television so he could watch his favorite programs. His eyesight failing, Oscar went from bifocals to trifocals. As he said: "I did everything I could to take care of myself and tried to get information on the latest developments in vitamins, and all those newfangled devices to help

✺ *Oscar Wilmeth achieves his goal of living to be 100.*
Photograph by Laurette Alexander.

with functioning, short of a wheelchair—I draw the line there.

All in all, it's a pretty good time to be old. There are so many medical miracles nowadays that help keep people alive, such as my pacemaker, and so many new ways of diagnosing disease and then being able to cure it early on before it really takes hold. We're never as young as we used to be, but we can stay in pretty good shape for the shape we're in when we're old, if we work at it and take advantage of all the miracles out there. And they are miracles to me because I remember when I was young growing up on a farm and my grandfather came to live with us. He was old and there was nothing anyone could do for him except make him comfortable. He died of old age, the doctor said. Today we don't have to settle for that. We can get a diagnosis and try to fix the ailment a lot of times. But you have to ask for it sometimes. You just can't be complacent. I remember when I was still in my seventies, I complained to my doctor that I had a pain in my leg; he said it was just old age. I told him that my other leg was just as old and asked how come it didn't hurt. I found another doctor who treated me for the arthritis in my leg. That's what you have to do—you have to make sure you get the medical attention and not just let anyone pass it off to 'old age' and give up on you."

On his 100th birthday, Oscar was triumphant. He greeted each of his 200 guests and spoke to them on and off for four hours, giving the highlights of his life. When he cut his birthday cake, he jokingly introduced a woman sixty years his junior, a personal friend whom he called upon to share in this ceremony, as his girlfriend. "That shook things up a bit," he said, chuckling.

Margaret Wine of Covina, California, represents a more typical profile of what often happens to otherwise healthy people of advanced age. Born in 1880, she outlived both her children, who died in their seventies from heart disease. Relatives say she never had a heart attack or serious illness of any kind. Margaret lived by herself until she was ninety-four, when she fell and broke her hip. After that, she was moved to a convalescent hospital. Although she was unable to walk, she remained alert and conversant until her hearing and sight began to fade. When she could no longer hear or see well, it began to affect her memory and her ability to communicate. "She slowly withdrew into herself when she could no longer hear us; she remembers little now," a relative remarked.

As the Centenarian Wish List affirms, the losses of sight, hearing, and mobility are common among people of advanced age. There are others, and everyone has his or her own individual challenges, as well, but these are the most frequently mentioned physical losses that adversely affect the quality of life in advanced age. Yet while such losses are fairly predictable, they are not necessarily immutable in all cases. Often there are steps that can be taken to shore up against the loss, to partially correct it, or to compensate with a wide variety of adaptive devices and strategies.

Physical changes may be the result of a medical condition that is correctable, or the effect of which can at least be minimized. Sometimes the change is the result of medical treatment itself, most commonly a prescription or nonprescription drug. Other changes are simply a result of disuse, especially disuse of the muscles and certain mental faculties, often brought on through lack of stimulation.

Even when the loss is irretrievable, much can be done to lessen the impact; life-style and environments can be altered to enhance a person's range of experience and activity. Our eldest citizens display a remarkable array of creativity and spunk when it comes to inventing methods of adaptation and compensation that work for them. Modern technology holds out many more possibilities for adapting to physical changes. The first step, as Oscar put it, is "to find out what's out there."

҂

VISION

At 108, Henry Hayes of Barnwell County, Georgia, decided he would try to do something about his failing eyesight: "I figured, as long as I was still on this earth, I might as well see what's going on. It bothered me a lot, not being able to see, and the older I got the harder it was. Got so as I couldn't recognize anybody's face. The doctor told me it was cataracts in both eyes. I tried one operation first, and it was like magic. Pretty soon the fog cleared and I could see colors and shapes and recognize faces I hadn't been able to see in years."

A year later Henry had the cataract removed from his other eye. "It worked once," he said. "I figured I'd try it again. Now I can see people coming way up my road." Henry was pleased to be able to enjoy the world around him again after many years of having it dim. "The doctor done me good," he said.

During a routine examination as a part of the medical service provided by her retirement center, Laura Crottogini, 100, of Hayward, California, learned she might have glaucoma. "I was already wearing eyeglasses to help me see better," she said. "I didn't know what to do about it. The doctor told me to see a specialist to have my eyes checked. My friend took me. The specialist said I have glaucoma and prescribed eye drops that I have to remember to take three times a day, regular as clockwork. I'm glad I went to him. I don't want to lose more of my eyesight."

Centenarian Mabel Dudley of Florence, Colorado, also knows what it means to live without adequate clear vision—and to see well again.

Henry Hayes at age 108. At 114 (1994) he continues to live alone, enjoying the benefits of his improved vision. Photograph by Philip Lord, 1989. Reprinted with permission from the Aiken Standard, Aiken, SC. Photo courtesy of the Barnwell County Office on Aging.

In her late nineties, Mabel received a cornea implant. It allowed her to continue to live on her own and to not be entirely dependent on others for her care. "I still live alone, drive myself around town and to church, and take care of myself," she says proudly. "I do my own cooking, dishes, and light housework and lots of other odd jobs around the house. I do my own grocery shopping, get my own medicine, go to the bank, and I enjoy playing cards at the senior center. I also enjoy crocheting and letter writing. Without good eyesight, I wouldn't be able to do these things."

Henry, Laura, and Mabel have three things in common: they are very old, their vision became impaired, and they've done what they could to improve it. Vision change, whether moderate or severe, inevitably accompanies aging, calling for adjustments that range from wearing reading glasses, bifocals, or trifocals to medical treatment and surgery for some diseases of the eye. In fact, 70 percent of the nation's 1.4 million people with low vision or blindness—nearly one million people— are over sixty-five. The good news is that with medical help and vision aids, impaired vision can often be brought back into the range of functional vision.

Older Eyes

As early as childhood, the lens of the eye starts losing elasticity. It continues to stiffen over the years to the point where, by their mid-forties, most people have difficulty focusing on printed material when it is close up or very fine, like the print in the telephone book. In addition, as one ages, the lens tends to become cloudy, and the retina at the back of the eye becomes less able to send messages to the optic nerve that goes to the brain. By age seventy cataracts can become a real problem.

Age-related changes of the eye, called presbyopia, are considered normal because they happen to almost all people. As the years pass:

- Objects, as well as printed material, appear out of focus, making it more difficult to recognize them or do small, detail work;
- The ability to distinguish between close shades of color diminishes; this problem can make it difficult, for instance, to distinguish the sidewalk from the street;
- The pupils become smaller, resulting in a need for brighter light to read, write, or move around one's living space; by age seventy, the need for light increases 50 to 70 percent;

- Eyes require more time to adjust to light changes, as when moving from a brightly lit place to a darker one;
- There is an increased sensitivity to glare from sunlight and bright lights; and
- Opacities, referred to as "floaters," commonly occur.

Loss of vision is usually described in three ways: *visual impairment*, *low vision*, and *blindness*. The American Foundation for the Blind reserves the word "blind" for those with no usable vision and prefers the terms *visually impaired* or *low vision* for persons with some usable vision. Centenarians or others of advanced age are more likely to be visually impaired than to be totally blind. This means that through medical treatment or assistive devices, some can be helped enough so they can regain their ability to watch television, read, or perform routine household chores. "Although glaucoma and cataract formation become more common with age, if treated appropriately, they rarely cause blindness," says Dr. Paul Rousseau, Chief of Geriatrics at the Hayden Veterans Medical Center in Phoenix, Arizona.

Regrettably, many older people either do not receive the regular eye examinations necessary for early diagnosis of eye disease or resist treatment because they (or their caregivers) feel that they are "just too old." It is important for older people to see an ophthalmologist and have regular eye examinations. Eye disease and slow deterioration in vision should be detected as early as possible—the earlier, the better.

Aids for Failing Vision

Regardless of the cause of vision impairment, and in addition to medical treatment, other steps can and should be taken to correct low vision or make it easier to live with. Assistive devices, community services, and home modifications all have a role to play in helping people adjust to and live with low vision. (The cost of some devices may be prohibitive, but in many communities, volunteer organizations and nonprofit agencies can provide help.)

GLASSES: There are many types of special glasses to help people with low vision, such as trifocals. Other types include glasses with a clip-on magnifying lens (called a loupe); a telescopic lens for distance; a telemicroscopic lens for close up; prism lenses that divert light to differ-

❧ *Mary Vandewege at age 100 with the stand-up*
magnifying glass and florescent light she uses when doing "close work."
Photo courtesy of the Vandewege family.

ent (still intact) parts of the retina; wide-angle mobility lenses to help those whose peripheral vision is impaired; and night scopes to help people with night blindness be able to see in low light.

GLARE REDUCTION: Sunglasses can be either prescription or non-prescription. Some eyeglass lenses can also be treated so that the lens darkens in bright light and clears indoors. Wraparound sun shields worn over prescription eyeglasses provide greater protection than clip-on versions; they are inexpensive and can be found at most pharmacies; ophthalmologists often have them for sale at their offices.

MAGNIFYING LENSES: Besides the familiar hand-held magnifying glass, there are "hand-free" magnifiers worn around the neck and supported against the chest by an attached bar. Easier to use is the stand-up magnifying glass, surrounded by a bright, fluorescent light, such as the one Mary Vandewege, 100, of Firth, Nebraska, has. Mary lives in her own home and is able to see well enough to do her own housework and cooking, but she uses her magnifying lens, as well as her glasses, for doing close work and to keep up her favorite pastime, crocheting afghans and sewing her own clothes. "I've only had two store-bought dresses in my life," she says proudly.

Katherine Case, 101, of Glendale, Arizona, lives alone in her own apartment at a retirement center, and, like Mary, does her own cooking and housework wearing just her glasses. She uses a similar magnifying glass and light for keeping up her correspondence and doing paperwork; hers is a desk-top unit. She also uses this device when piecing together the many quilts she donates each year to homeless families.

LARGE-TYPE AND TALKING BOOKS: For those with mild impairment, books, magazines, and newspapers printed in large type are a simple solution to difficulty reading. Reader's Digest is but one example of a periodical available in large type; The *New York Times* publishes a 36 page large-type edition weekly that includes a crossword puzzle.

For those with severe impairment, talking books (that is, books recorded on tape) are available from most libraries. Often the recorders on which the tapes are played are provided free of charge. "Talking letters," such as the cassette tapes Hedvig Peterson's young relatives send her from Sweden, are another use of today's technology that allows a person to maintain contact with friends and relatives without having to read.

It is helpful if friends and others writing to people of advanced age type their letters and use either a special larger type (the kind used for typing speeches) or all capitals. Some typewriters and all computers have a special feature that makes the print **BOLD** as well as bigger. "Big and bold is the easiest to read," says Ted Gibson. Of course, double-spaced typing is even easier to read this way. When hand-writing a letter, it's best to print with a wide-tip felt pen, skipping lines or spaces.

HIGH-TECH READING AIDS: Thanks to computer technology, many new low-vision aids have been developed. A recent catalogue lists more than 100 computerized devices that help visually impaired people read and write. Most of these devices are expensive, but some can be borrowed through libraries or other community service organizations. Such technology affords people of advanced age the pleasure, and mental stimulation, of being able to read once again. Creative means of obtaining these assistive devices may be found through agencies servicing older adults and reference books.

Even more high tech and offering great promise for the future is a machine that uses synthetic speech to "read" ordinary print. At present this device, called the "Kurzweil Reading Machine," is priced beyond individual means and is complicated to use. However, new developments in computer technology may make it both easier to use and more affordable. It is anticipated that by the end of this decade personal hand-held units will be widely available. "For now," says centenarian Billy Earley, who tried a similar device, "I'll settle for a person to read to me."

OTHER ASSISTIVE DEVICES: Large-number timers, clocks, scales, thermometers, and telephones provide other options. For bright lighting, fluorescent bulbs that screw into regular light sockets can be purchased.

HOME ADAPTATIONS: Home adaptations are often inexpensive and simple to make or arrange. For example, a visually impaired person may have trouble finding a white coffee cup on a white tablecloth. Changing either the cup or the tablecloth to a contrasting color can make it easier to see. Glare from a window can reflect off smooth surfaces creating a hazardous walking area. There are many books available that contain ideas and photographs of simple adaptations for the homes and living places of visually impaired older people.

REHABILITATION PROGRAMS: When vision impairment is severe, a low-vision care specialist will often recommend a rehabilitation program that teaches ways to compensate for the losses. Low vision frequently leaves a person feeling isolated and vulnerable. Grace Lyon, 101, of Burbank, California, speaks for most centenarians with vision problems: "My life would be better if I could only see better." Many communities have free services that assist the visually impaired in adapting to low vision and rebuilding their confidence. Counseling for the family or caregivers of the visually impaired is just as necessary; unfortunately it is frequently left undone.

❧

HEARING

Noticeable hearing loss affects 60 percent of Americans over sixty-five, 90 percent of Americans over ninety, and almost all centenarians. For those seventy-five and over, it is the second-most chronic condition after arthritis. Beginning in the mid-teenage years, the ability to hear declines about one decibel a year. This reduction in hearing acuity usually becomes noticeable at around age thirty for men, thirty-seven for women. Age-related hearing loss, called presbycusis, is the most common form of hearing loss and is usually caused by degenerative changes in the inner ear. However, aging is by no means the sole cause of hearing losses.

Among many other causes, drugs and medications that may affect hearing include some of the more common prescriptions and over-the-counter treatments. The severity of a medication-related hearing loss depends on a variety of things, including dosage, peculiarities of individual susceptibility, length of use, and the presence of other drugs in the body.

Hearing Exams and Treatment

Regardless of the origin of the hearing loss or disorder, the first step when a change in hearing is noticed is to see a physician. If the physician cannot cure the loss, a hearing evaluation is the next step. This may be performed by an audiologist, a professional who has earned a master of arts or master of science degree and is trained in the nonmedical diagnosis and treatment of hearing impairment, or by a state-licensed hearing aid distributor.

The hearing evaluation usually results in a treatment program that includes the consideration of a hearing aid or other assistive device, rehabilitation, and, in some cases, counseling. Often overlooked, counseling can be an important part of a hearing loss treatment program. Family members and caregivers of the hearing-impaired person should be included in the counseling so they can develop an understanding of how best to communicate with the person and gain some sense of the frustration and other emotions that people who are hearing-impaired experience. State, country, or city government offices and the National Association for the Deaf can be contacted for information on such programs.

A hearing treatment program may also include a rehabilitation service. Rehabilitation primarily consists of lessons in speech reading, which teach an individual to observe carefully the visual cues of speech, such as lip movement, facial expression, and the physical gestures, and to use these cues to understand and follow conversation. For most people, some degree of speech reading is automatic, but when hearing is severely impaired, it becomes important to learn to use all available cues for understanding what is being said.

It is also important for hearing-impaired persons to let others know what will aid them in hearing, for example, speaking more slowly, placing themselves so that light falls on their faces, and facing the older person so that expressions and lip movements may be read. A common misconception is that hearing-impaired persons will be able to hear better if others simply raise their voices. Increased volume can help, but the *tone* of one's voice is also a factor. It's common when raising one's voice to speak in a higher pitch, which can be more difficult for the older person to hear. Some simple techniques for helping elders follow conversations are to sit close to them; to look into their faces while speaking to them; to speak loudly, slowly, and deliberately, giving them time to assimilate what is being said; and to wait for them to respond. Making this point, centenarian Mark Jones of Eugene, Oregon, adds his wish: "for people to have the time for us to hear, think, and then speak. When questions are asked, we are slower to answer, and we may not hear all that is said. We need more time and patience."

As we age, the distance at which we can clearly understand the speaker's words decreases. By age seventy, for instance, this distance shrinks to fourteen feet (from forty feet at age thirty). Often older people are embarrassed to admit that they cannot hear and younger people often become impatient with their grandparents or parents when they can't keep up with their conversation at a more rapid pace.

By the time they have lived 100 years, most centenarians have overcome their feelings of embarrassment and will tell others that they cannot hear well. Some will even give advice on how others should speak in order to make their words understood. For example, Judge Harry Fisher of Fort Scott, Kansas, who has a telephone with an amplifier, tells the caller right away that he has a problem hearing and then instructs the caller to speak more slowly and in a lower voice so the amplifier will function at its best. "Check with your local telephone company; they could help you," he advises. Still, for many centenarians, it is extremely difficult to hear enough to converse comfortably over the telephone.

Living with Hearing Loss

The inability to hear can make it a very lonely world. Social withdrawal is a real problem, starting early in the process of hearing loss, usually when a person is in a room in which a lot of people are talking. The confusion created by the jumble of sounds is intimidating and produces so much anxiety that some people simply stop attending such gatherings. Because the ability to hear is vital to everyone's connection with the outside world, psychologists consider hearing more socially important than sight.

Since severe hearing loss is prevalent at advanced age, it very often limits or creates a barrier to effective communication and interaction with others. This problem is frustrating for the older person and for those surrounding or coming in contact with him or her, thus contributing to isolation in old age. It should be addressed and compensated for as completely and early as possible. Rather than waiting until a person is in his or her eighties or nineties to acquire a hearing aid or other assistive device, steps should be taken to improve hearing as soon as noticeable loss occurs. Many elders say it is difficult to get used to wearing a hearing aid or using other assistive devices, and it helps to start sooner rather than later. Family and caregivers need to be sensitive to this loss and assist in providing the most appropriate compensatory devices and services possible. As with visual aids, new technology is expanding and improving these means. In general, assistance devices are in five categories: hearing aids, assistive listening devices, telecommunication devices, television decoders, and alerting or signaling devices.

Looking into the future, one can imagine an entire generation of a million or more centenarians of the baby-boom generation communicating through computers. Computers designed to assist people with disabilities are becoming available. Perhaps, for some centenarians, taking advantage of this technology is not beyond the realm of possibility today.

∾

PHYSICAL MOBILITY

It is a curious and disturbing fact that what is probably the most pervasive loss with age is the one people can do the most to control. Some decline in physical stamina, strength, and agility is normal, especially as people pass into their upper decades, and serious loss of physical mobility is sometimes caused by disease, illness, accident, a fall, or surgery. However, much of the loss as one ages is the result of disuse, and much of it can be prevented by regular exercise. As renowned gerontologist Dr. Robert Butler has been saying for years, "If exercise could be packaged in a pill, it would be the most prescribed medicine around."

Centenarians such as George Gillespie follow this prescription. "I'm no couch potato," he says. George, who moved "lock, stock, and barrel," with his wife, Myrtle, to Fort Collins, Colorado, at the age of 100, after living seventy-nine years in Wyoming, "travels" about 100 miles a week on his stationary bike. He and Myrtle also travel by car to visit relatives throughout the Midwest each year. "It takes a little longer—sometimes twice as long," George says, "but we still go."

His hobbies include fishing, hunting, photography, playing pinochle, and baking cakes "from scratch." When asked by a reporter what he does for entertainment, George replied: "We enjoy life. You'd think it would be boring, but it goes fast."

❧ *George and Myrtle Gillespie at home.*
Photo courtesy of George and Myrtle Gillespie.

The physical mobility needed to perform normal daily activities and to stay as active as George Gillespie requires fitness. We are physically fit when we have the heart and lung (aerobic) capacity to pump oxygen to the muscles, sufficient muscle strength to accomplish reasonable tasks, and flexibility in the joints to permit movement. When it comes to maintaining physical mobility, the simple axiom "use it or lose it" says it all.

"It's certainly been true in my life," agrees 101-year-old Hazel Fergus of Juneau, Alaska. She attributes her longevity mainly to good health and having had plenty of exercise during her life as a rancher's wife in Montana and "plenty of time spent outdoors in the clean, fresh air." Hazel keeps fit by attending daily exercise classes (mild aerobics) at the day-care center near her retirement apartment. The classes are led by a ninety-four-year-old doctor who developed the routine to keep himself flexible and now shares it with others of advanced age.

In New York City, former professional dancer Milton Feher has also developed a combination of exercise, relaxation, and dance that he has been teaching for almost fifty years. Milton was forced to retire from the Broadway stage in 1941 due to arthritis in his knees. "It happened all of a sudden," he tells. Milton's very successful career, performing in such popular shows as *Song of Norway* and *I'd Rather be Right* by George M. Cohan, was cut short in its prime by the affliction that limits so many older people. "I then developed a way to cure myself after I gave up on doctors," he explains, "and I've been teaching people of all ages ever since. The concept is to relax into a straight line and to keep the body centered. The problem people have, and the reason so many older people fall, is that people are moving their weight off their feet. The key is to always feel that your body is resting on your feet and not let it get away from you. It sounds simple, but it takes concentration and practice."

Milton's star pupil, Claire Willi, 100, credits his work with her over the last thirty years to getting her to the century mark. "There are two things that older people fear most," she confides, "falling apart and falling down. Exercising regularly, learning how to use one's body correctly, in balance, and using relaxation techniques improve flexibility and coordination and help with both. Exercise keeps you younger, no matter what your chronological age," Clair says with certainty, and from experience.

At age seventy, Claire, who emigrated from Switzerland almost fifty years earlier, felt old. She never exercised, tired easily, and never walked for pleasure because her feet hurt when she did. She was starting to stoop and shuffle her feet when she moved and used a small pillow under her dress to hide her swayed back. A beautiful woman, Claire minded the changes that age was bringing. She had led an exciting life, happily married to one of the largest champagne dealers in New York and was a celebrated hostess. Her career, she says, was helping her husband by entertaining and running their personal life, managing their schedules and their three homes in Florida, Pennsyl-

℘ *Claire Willi at age 100 in the Milton Feher Dance Studio in New York City. Photograph by Theo Westenberger. Photo courtesy of Claire Willi.*

vania, and New York. It bothered her tremendously that at seventy she felt like an old woman and beyond hope.

Quite coincidentally, while in a health food restaurant in her neighborhood near Carnegie Hall, she overheard a waitress tell another customer about the marvelous dance lessons she was taking, which not only invigorated her and improved her posture but also relaxed her. "My ears perked up at this," Claire recalls.

She made her way to the Milton Feher School of Dance and Relaxation on West Fifty-eighth Street, located in an apartment building she could see from her building. There, above the din of city traffic, she began attending classes three times a week plus some individual lessons. Claire has been a regular student ever since. She attributes Milton's training to what now keeps her healthy, beautiful, and graceful at age 100. She wears a leotard and leggings and her body is trim and shapely. Claire and Milton, an octogenarian, have been featured in numerous magazines over this last decade as a true success story, including *Prevention* Magazine (January, 1992) in an article entitled "Dance Away Arthritis Pain."

"Claire has succeeded in staving off the loss of mobility that so often accompanies advanced age. She keeps up with people half her age in the one-hour dance class, and afterward, as has been her practice for these thirty years, she takes a long walk in Central Park," Milton tells. Claire advises, "It's never too late to begin."

Aerobic Fitness

Exercise that speeds up the heart rate, pumps more oxygen throughout the muscles, and stimulates the lungs can offset the decline in mobility that accompanies aging. Some loss of aerobic and breathing capacity is natural as one ages (a fit thirty-year-old can outrun a fit ninety-year-old) but far less than what most people experience. After the age of twenty, lung function for most people declines by about 10 percent every decade because as one ages, the muscles that operate the lungs weaken. However, athletes lose only between 2 and 5 percent per decade. Research has shown that older male athletes have greater aerobic capacity than sedentary men in their thirties. As they have told, many centenarians walk for aerobic exercise or ride stationary exercise bikes. The Reverend David Moore adds his "two cents worth," saying, "I walk fifteen blocks every day and do some gym work."

Muscle Strength

Muscle strength also declines with age, but muscle tissue can be rebuilt at any age.

A recent study conducted by the United States Department of Agriculture (USDA) and the Human Nutrition Research Center on Aging at Tufts University placed frail, elderly participants on a closely supervised, high-intensity weight-training program. The participants were recruited from among the residents of the Hebrew Rehabilitation Center for Aged in Boston. Their average age was ninety, with the oldest ninety-six; they had all been inactive for many years. The results were dramatic. Participants increased their muscle strength threefold to fourfold in just eight weeks and increased their walking speed an average of 48 percent. Some participants who had been using canes were actually able to discard them. "The importance of this study is that it shows that even at very advanced age, physical frailty is treatable," says Evan Hadley, Chief of the Geriatric Branch at the National Institute on Aging. As the researchers conclude,". . .a portion of the muscle weakness attributed to aging may be modifiable through exercise." Maria Fiatarone, M.D., Assistant Professor of Medicine at Harvard Medical School and one of the principal researchers in this landmark study, advises that ". . .strength training provides benefits that are more specific to the muscles themselves—benefits you can't get from just taking a walk." Of course, all people (especially older people) should consult a physician before beginning any exercise program.

In July 1994, Dr. Fiatarone reported, "it's very gratifying to do a study like this." Begun in 1989, the research continues: "Forty of the sixty people who are still alive from the initial group of participants are still exercising with us regularly," including a participant from the original group who is now 101 and "doing very well," she said. Further, she went on to point out an important factor in her work, and in so doing, underscores a theme that is prevalent throughout this book, as articulated by centenarians and others: "You have to not think that it's okay to just warehouse [old] people, but assume that, in fact, there's potential for more improvement and that it is worth doing. Even if you don't make someone live longer, it is worth making people live a little better and making them walk around with more ease. You have to believe this is a worthwhile goal."

At an August 1992 Conference on Successful Aging Through Fitness in Indianapolis, Indiana, William Evans, Ph.D., Chief of the Human Physiology Laboratory, USDA, Human Nutrition Research Center on Aging, stated: "Much of what we call aging is a life-style of inactivity and poor nutrition. Muscle weakness causes an individual to give up doing things, such as household chores, lifting, and walking, and thus promotes the disengagement or active involvement of that individual in their life." Since muscle strength dictates function, the good news is that it is possible to increase both through strength training exercises. Light weight-lifting exercises are one means of maintaining muscle strength. Along with new research findings offering hope for maintaining and reclaiming muscle strength in advanced age, new technology has been developed that may offer an alternative in weight-lifting devices and enable their use by more people. (See resources.)

Flexibility

The third fundamental aspect of fitness as one ages is maintaining flexibility—the ability to reach down easily and pick up something from the floor or to dress oneself, for example. Loss of flexibility detracts from the movement of even the most aerobically fit and muscular person. As with all the other dimensions of fitness, using our bodies, even if the movement is slower or the range of movement limited, is the key to maintenance. As Claire Willi attests, when normal daily activities are not adequate to maintain what health professionals refer to as a "full range of motion," deliberate exercises are essential.

Coordination

Another dimension of mobility that is central to maintaining fitness is the capacity to coordinate the muscle activity needed to do what you want to do. Technically, this is referred to as "motor performance." However, coordination also depends on the state of a person's hearing, vision, and touch and the functioning of the central nervous system. Disruptions to these senses or organs will affect motor performance. Poor coordination and loss of balance are signs of such deterioration. As with the other dimensions of fitness, regular exercise can be of great help in maintaining motor performance skills.

For Abe Goldberg of West Palm Beach, Florida, ballroom dancing has been his mode of exercise, as well as recreation, for more than thirty years. "I took up dancing when I was seventy, after my wife died," he tells, "to help adjust to the change and to the loss." He says dancing has kept him fit and young. At eighty-five, Abe took a trip to Israel and at 100 to California. After hip surgery at the age of ninety, he was told he might never walk again, much less waltz, but he did both. "I danced my way through my eighties, nineties, on my 100th birthday and every year since then," he tells. On his 104th, Abe celebrated at the Jewish Community Center at, what else—a dinner-dance in his honor.

Shoes

After medical attention and regular exercise, the most important factor in maintaining balance is something often overlooked or taken for granted—wearing the right shoes. Shoes with even slightly elevated heels can be a hazard and can cause falls. Athletic shoes and walking shoes may meet the needs of older people and provide better stability. Shoes that offer extra support around the ankles can also help some older people maintain balance. Most people's feet have a tendency either to turn outward or roll inward, throwing them slightly off balance with each step. The right shoes can correct this problem and may give the balance needed to keep a misstep from becoming a fall.

Falls and Their Consequences

The incidence of falls, and the fractures resulting from them, increases with age. Bones become more brittle, and many people of advanced age suffer from broken hips, especially, as a result of falls. For most, hip replacements offer the only way to regain mobility, and the procedure is being continually improved. Nevertheless, as the old adage goes, "An ounce of prevention is worth a pound of cure."

Since lack of balance contributes to falling, regular exercise and proper shoes can really help. Poor eyesight, hazardous home environments, and adverse weather conditions, such as rain, snow, or ice, also contribute to the incidence of falling. Side effects from some medications can cause dizziness that can throw one's balance off and cause a fall. Even a person's disposition can lead to unnecessary falls.

At 102, the Reverend Roy Miller was physically fit. He kept fit by exercising and walking every day. In 1987, he led the annual Governor's Cup Walk in Phoenix, Arizona. A temperate man, having been a minister for most of his life, Roy was in great shape and had no health problems. He was also experienced in what could be called the "art of falling," an art he says he mastered while running his son's roller skating rink in Rocky Ford, Colorado, when his son was drafted into the army during World War II. "I had never skated before, but I learned fast, the hard way," he tells. "Before long, I was giving lessons. I kept up my ministry, too. I even married a couple once on roller skates. After the ceremony, the entire wedding party went around the rink with the colored lights playing off the mirrored ball in the ceiling to the tune of the wedding march."

Roy admits to taking a tumble in the hallway of his retirement home one day when walking with a nurse. He was instructing her in his special method of walking, holding hands with arms crossed, as couples do when skating. "She tripped and pulled me down with her," he says, "but I wasn't hurt because I was paying attention and knew how to fall."

Then one day in his 103rd year, the very active Roy was visiting his son with his granddaughter. Roy became uncharacteristically impatient and wanted to leave. Although she asked him to wait for her, Roy ignored his granddaughter's request. He got up "in a huff" and started out to the car. In his pique, he was not paying attention and tripped on an uneven place in the sidewalk; the fall broke his arm, at the elbow, requiring surgery. While in the hospital, Roy developed pneumonia. Eventually, he returned to the retirement center, this time to the intensive care unit. A once-bright, intelligent, cheerful example of the best we can be at 100, Roy now became disoriented and at times confused. He sometimes failed to recognize family and friends who came to visit. "I blame myself," he said. "I caused this through my own impatience."

Myrtle Howe, 101, of Bradenton, Florida, is another example of the hundreds of thousands of people each year over age eighty-five whose lives are irrevocably changed as a result of a fall. With a note of sadness, she begins her story by explaining that she worked all her life and kept very active, first as a farmer's wife in Michigan and later, when she moved to Florida in 1950, by working in a hotel as a waitress and later still taking care of elderly people in their homes. She never retired and was still caring for others at ninety-five when she fell in a store. A bone specialist determined that she had a compound fracture of her spine: "There was nothing I could do," Myrtle says, "so I just had to live with it. But I couldn't work anymore. My son took me to the doctor. For the past six years I've been taking medication for my back pain. I still live alone, but it's hard for me to walk now and hard to write. And I can't take care of my house or yard, which I used to love to do. I thank God for my good memory and mind and for the family, neighbors, and church folks that help take care of me. If it weren't for that fall, I think I could still be working or at least helping others."

When Prevention Doesn't Prevent

Because of disease or accident, some people eventually experience serious restrictions to physical mobility, usually losing the ability to walk. However, such restrictions to one part of the body do not mean that all other parts must remain inactive or that exercise should be forsaken altogether. Exercises that maintain upper body and limb strength and flexibility can be done in a chair, wheelchair, or bed. As previously mentioned, centenarian Mary Gleason, whose legs were amputated because of poor circulation, attends the Palmetto Senior Care Medical Day Care Program in Columbia, South Carolina, four days a week and has been doing so since she was ninety-nine. She is able to exercise by participating in physical therapy with other attendees (such as tossing a beach ball around the circle of wheelchair users), and she's "so much happier having the companionship of others and enjoys the craft activities, which exercise both her hands and arms and her mind," reports her daughter.

For elders who can't move around on their own, there are also small motorized chairs that make mobility possible. After a stroke made walking difficult, Walter ("Pop") Talbot, at 101, began using a walker. This active Iowan, who winters in Arizona each year, soon found the walker slow and tiresome, so he switched to a motorized scooter. "Now I can get around my apartment, the yard, and the senior center lickety-split," he's pleased to say. "It's really a big help and fun."

Ramps can replace difficult steps in the home, handrails can offer support in many rooms (especially the bathroom), and a raised toilet is much easier to use than the standard one. A seat that fits in the bathtub, nonslip mat, and a hand-held shower attachment can make bathing easier. Windows with easy-to-operate crank mechanisms can replace heavy, old-style sash windows. Remote controls can operate many electrical appliances. Special dogs are even being trained to help disabled people open doors, pick up items, and perform similar tasks.

In many cases, the use of these adaptations and assistive devices, perhaps in combination with enrollment in an adult day-care center, allows a person of advanced age to avoid institutionalization. In short, many activities that have become difficult for an older person to do can be made easier through the use of an assistive device. "It may take some doing to find just what will help make daily life more livable," Oscar Wilmeth reminds us, "and it takes effort to learn new ways of doing things after all these years, but it is worth a try."

❧

ACTIVE AGING

A sedentary lifestyle is showing up as the "culprit," the determinant for many of the ills that accompany aging. Exercise and activity, both physical and mental, are seen as the offset, even for people with some limitations. There seems little excuse, and even less reason, not to exercise in one way or another. Some people, for example, find that canes and walkers can help them continue to exercise as well as just get them from place to place. Also, exercise machines such as stationary bicycles allow people to get exercise in their homes, or wherever they live, in all kinds of weather. Centenarians George Gillespie, Billy Earley, and Ted Gibson prove they're not too old to use them. All three ride their exercise bicycles regularly, racking up "many miles a week," Ted says. "I keep track of my mileage—I'm going to make it around the world."

That older people want to remain as active and independent as possible is a fact borne out by research and simply by listening to what elders themselves have to say.

To "age gracefully," then, takes on a whole new meaning for the 1990s. By learning and practicing the proper exercises, the loss of mobility—including diminished strength, balance, and endurance—can, to some degree, be controlled, minimized, and sometimes reversed. An exercise program of moderate weight-bearing exercise (such as walking), strengthening exercises, and flexibility exercises can become a beneficial part of an individual's lifestyle. Perhaps this will one day reduce the number of people of advanced age labeled as "frail elderly."

In addition, regular exercise has also been credited with improving health by strengthening the heart and improving circulation; controlling weight; lowering harmful blood cholesterol levels and raising beneficial blood cholesterol; improving digestion and elimination; and relieving stress, tension, and depression. What's more, when properly done, exercise can be an essential component of the treatment of certain medical conditions, such as diabetes, arthritis, osteoporosis (bone thinning), high blood pressure, heart disease, and many more. New studies continue to substantiate the additional health benefits of exercise and physical activity in helping prevent heart attacks and osteoporosis and helping to control high blood pressure.

Recent research finds that any amount of exercise is helpful and at any age, even the most advanced. The goal is to make exercise part of your life-style. Centenarians who exercise regularly say they enjoy doing it, that it improves their overall mood for the day and that they have more energy and enthusiasm for other daily activities as a result. This holds true for people of all ages, researchers report. Billy Earley reminds us to "start gradually and use common sense. You can exercise without pain or strain and still get the gain, as they say." Of course, people of all ages are cautioned to see their doctor before beginning any exercise program; for older people, the assistance of a physical therapist or other type of supervised and monitored regime might be recommended and beneficial.

The best news of all may be the proof by centenarians that one is never too old to want to exercise, to have the desire to take good care of their health, and to remain active. Centenarians' collective advice to younger generations is clear: The most important thing you can do with your life is to take care of your health. Along with this, the current thinking from medical science is that the rate of biological change varies as we age, depending on our individual level of physical activity. Thus, for now, exercise and staying active as we age may well be thought of as one part of the formula for a longer and healthier life.

✥

Centenarians such as Dr. Michael Heidelberger, whose story opened this chapter, inspire us all. Martin S. Begun, Associate Dean of the New York University Medical School, says that Dr. Heidelberger's presence there—in his 103rd year—working in the laboratory and as an active student advisor and mentor, are great assets to the medical school. "The sharing of his knowledge and experience, together with what he is accomplishing at an advanced age, is a wonderful example of life's potential for our students," acknowledges Dean Begun. Hopefully, his example will also sensitize these future doctors to the continued viability of older patients. Commenting on his current role, Dr. Heidelberger says: "I do things more slowly now, and I'm grateful for the stimulation of my many colleagues and students. I retired from Columbia University more than thirty years ago when I reached mandatory retirement age; but, you know, you can always do what you want after you retire.

"I'm working on my scientific swan song now, collecting into a single paper former studies on various bacteria, which would have been unsuitable to publish separately. I would like to publish it in the same journal that published my first immunological research. After that, I will not be writing any more scientific papers. I want to spend time instead writing some amusing stories that happened along the way for my grandchildren and great-grandchildren. And I want to organize the pictures I've been taking and collecting since my wedding trip in 1916. I was given an album to put them in several years ago but haven't had time to work on it—the pictures are just stuffed into a desk drawer now."

❧

Centenarians don't hold the secrets to longevity—or do they? They tell us what they've done that has worked for them. They tell us what goes wrong so that medical science can know where to focus its attention. They show us by their examples, both good and bad, whether current research is on the right track.

So do they or don't they hold the secrets to longevity?

In responding, Dr. Heidelberger, reflecting the wisdom of his peers, answered with his favorite quotation from Shakespeare's *Antony and Cleopatra* (act 1, scene 2):

> Charmian: Is't you, sir, that know things?
> Soothsayer: In nature's infinite book of secrecy
> a little I can read.

8

Challenges to the Mind

I wish medical science would come up with a way for people to age with their minds intact.

—Helen Cope, 101
Greenwich, Connecticut

E most fundamental and frightening loss that can be encountered as one ages, elders tell us, is losing the ability to think, remember, and reason. As Mary Gleason, at 101, puts it, "I can live with the loss of my sight, and if my hearing goes, well, so be it—as long as I can keep my marbles—that's the most important thing."

Mildred Reiger would concur. She and her twin sister, Adeline Moran, turned 100 on April 11, 1993. "My eyesight is troublesome," Millie says. "I can hardly see anything on TV anymore. I can take care of myself and I still go to the Senior Citizens Friendship Club and go out as often as I can. But my sister just sits in a chair now; she has slipped a lot since our birthday. We have someone who lives with us to take care of her."

Millie finds it strange that she and her twin should be so different now. With relish, she repeats the family story of their birth: "No one knew our mother was expecting twins, so we were a real surprise. The doctor delivered me and carried me out to the kitchen to hand me over to my aunt. Going back to tend to my mother, at the doorway he exclaimed, 'There's another one!' My sister was already lying on the bed. We are five minutes apart. We have always enjoyed being twins."

Millie continues, "We have had a wonderful life. For the past thirty years, we have lived together in Addie's home in Evanston, Illinois. It's so sad to see Addie like this now. I don't think she even recognizes me anymore."

.⅗

It is indeed puzzling how some people can remain alert and mentally functional for 100 years, and more, while others, even a twin or other sibling, may not. It is generally accepted that some mental slowing and changes do occur as a person ages. Lately, however, it is evident through scientific research and observations of older people themselves that total mental incapacity is not the inevitable companion of old age. Rather, severe mental incapacity is a consequence or result of disease or some other medical problem.

In his book *Aging Well*, Dr. James Fries of Stanford University Medical School notes that most of the time the slowing down in reaction and response times associated with aging is benign and of little practical importance unless one becomes unduly preoccupied with the changes and "dwells on it." That is unnecessary, he contends, and only makes things worse. Our brains are incredibly sophisticated and powerful, and it is foolish to think of them as though they were simply some form of long-life battery that follows a uniform path of decline. In the absence of disease, the capacity to learn new things and new skills and the ability to be creative is always there. So, too, are inspirational examples of centenarians (and others of advanced age) who are proving this to be true.

Demonstrating that one is never too old to learn, Centenarian Selma Plaut made the news when she received a bachelor of arts degree from the University of Toronto. Mrs. Plaut, who fled Nazi Germany, eventually settled in St. Paul, Minnesota. In her seventies, she moved to Toronto to be near her son. At age eighty-eight, she began auditing classes of interest to her in theology, Jewish history, and French. She did so well that she decided to take further classes for credit and to work toward a degree. Although she was short a few credits, the university awarded her the degree in commemoration of her centennial; she graduated in June with the class of 1990—100 years from her birth.

To Eli Finn, as well, a full life at age 100 includes continuing to realize a lifelong dream of receiving a college education. "I am back in college—studying American history. I am mentally occupied, which

❧ *Selma Plaut, age 100, and Sadie Lewis may be separated by 78 years,*
but they joined together in receiving degrees at the University of Toronto.
Photograph by M. Slaughter, used with permission from the Toronto Star.

❧ *100-year-old student Eli Finn at Fairfield University.*
Photo courtesy of Fairfield University, Fairfield, CT. Photograph by Dave DeFusco.

is most important for me," he says. Born in Russia, Mr. Finn came to America in 1907 in search of education. "My father refused to allow me to go to college in Russia; he wanted to educate me in the rabbinate. But that wasn't for me, so I came to America." He attended Springfield YMCA College in Massachusetts and was eligible for a degree in 1917 but was prevented from reaching his goal when the degree was denied by college officials because he was Jewish. "I asked why they accepted me in the first place," he recalls. "They said they hoped I would convert." Seventy-two years later, when Springfield College officials heard of this story, they awarded him an honorary degree.

Eli could have rested on his laurels, content with having finally achieved his goal. After all, he had just retired, at age 100, following several decades working as an appliance salesman in New York City. Yet showing again that one is never too old to learn, in the fall of 1989, he enrolled at Fairfield University in Fairfield, Connecticut, because, as he says, "I am just trying to better myself."

Centenarians such as Eli and Selma, along with Dr. Michael Heidelberger, Hedvig Peterson, Helen Cope, Ted Gibson, and Louis Kelly, to name a few, add to the mounting evidence that impaired mental functioning and loss of memory are not inevitable consequences of longevity. What is necessary, however, is that people pay more attention to mental health as they age, just as they do to their physical health.

Billy Earley is another sterling example of aging without loss of mental acuity. At 105, Billy is still going strong, and her mind is as sharp as ever. Always current on the latest news and·events, as well as developments in the fields of politics and medical science, her particular interests, Billy enjoys traveling as a way of broadening her knowledge, and makes several trips each year with her daughter, Angie. In the spring of 1992, they went to Washington, D.C., from Arizona "because Angie had never been there and I thought it was important that she see and experience the capital. I knew she would never go alone, later, so I took her now. I wanted her to see it at its best, in the spring, with all the azaleas and cherry blossoms in full bloom. We had the most perfect week; it was absolutely beautiful. We did everything—all the monuments, the Capital Building, the Smithsonian, Kennedy Center—we even went up the hill to the National Cathedral when we had an hour to spare. I had never been inside before, not even when I lived in the East, so it was a new experience for me, too. It's the second largest cathedral in the United States and the fifth largest in the world. President Wilson and his wife are entombed there; I didn't know that. Well, you see, Billy is still learning history, too!"

Billy's mental powers are something many younger people would envy. What keeps Billy's mind as agile as someone half her age? "I don't know," she says, "but I wish someone did. If one person can be like this, it should be possible for more to do so, with help from the medical profession and good common sense in caring for themselves." Billy seconds Helen Cope's wish that medical science would address the mental aspects of aging. She and other centenarians and their families stress the devastating effects that diminished mental ability and memory loss bring to elders and those who care for them. Many say the fear of this loss increases as they move through their seventies, eighties, and beyond.

Even when an older person's mind is functioning well, living with the uncertainty of not knowing when that may change and how they will manage then, is a concern. The fear of dependency goes hand in hand with the fear of loss of adequate mental functioning. Often the decline is slow and gradual and the old person is aware of what's happening but powerless to stop the process. Many say there's often no place to turn to for help in the medical profession because of insufficient knowledge in this area; perhaps often because of misperceptions of the patient and the problem; and sometimes because there is little interest in helping them. "It's just old age. There's nothing that can be done about it" is too common a substitute for a thorough look at the underlying cause and a thoughtful and informed recommendation of what *could* be of help; this assessment should include referrals to community resources, where appropriate. All too often, the old person and the caregiver are left to grapple with what can become a monumental problem on their own.

Scientific and medical researchers say that despite all the advances of the last twenty years, because of its complexity, there is still much to learn about the brain and how it functions. Fortunately, there is a great deal of current interest among researchers in understanding the mysteries of the brain, and many scientists who started out working in other areas have moved into research on the nervous system, of which the brain is a part.

Indeed, the challenge is so compelling that 1990 to 2000 has been declared "The Decade of the Brain" by Presidential Proclamation. "The 1970s and 1980s were noteworthy for the major accomplishments in cardiac research. The goal for the 1990s is to achieve in neuroscience strides of the same magnitude as took place in cardiac research in the two prior decades," states the National Foundation for Brain Research in Washington, D.C. "The brain is the last frontier of the human body— the last area to be fully understood."

At this time, among the key determinants for continued mental function in later years (and beginning after age fifty) are thought to be the quality of a person's daily mental activity, the effect or absence of disease, and the ability to compensate for a decline or loss of some function. Medical research offers the potential for new drugs that will help maintain mental function as we age and new drugs for curtailing the devastating effects of some of the diseases, more prominent in later years, that attack the nervous system and the brain. Of interest will be a greater understanding of the role genetics may play in continuing brain function.

"Sharp" and "bright" are the two words most commonly used by centenarians and their families to express the medical term "cognitively alert." Centenarians use these words often to describe themselves or others. They are acutely aware of the significance of these attributions. John Langham, 105, a nursing home resident in Prescott, Arizona, gives this sobering observation of the importance of remaining cognitively alert and how destructive its loss can be: "I see it every day in this place. So many people can't even remember their own name. If I got like that I wouldn't want to live any longer."

Still others who have remained mentally healthy, such as Billy Earley, remind us to use self-help in caring for our mental health and to not take it for granted that we will automatically retain it or lose it as we grow old. Many centenarians offer suggestions and encouragement, saying it is worthwhile to keep doing as much as possible to take good care of our minds and to not give up hope.

֍

HOW THE BRAIN AGES

One premise that is widely accepted about the nervous system is that throughout our life we lose brain cells. These cells, like others in the nervous system, differ from ordinary cells in the body in that they do not regenerate. When nerve cells die, the loss is permanent. Research indicates, however, that this "normal" brain cell loss does not account for any dramatic or sudden decline in mental ability—that is almost always a result of disease or injury. Minor problems—especially with memory—may occur because of this loss of brain cells due to aging.

It is thought that losing brain cells creates breaks in neural pathways through which signals pass (like breaks in telephone cables), causing problems with the way in which thinking, remembering, and reasoning take place. According to the National Institutes of Health, "One of the most fruitful findings in the past several decades has been the discovery that nerve cells secrete special chemicals, neurotransmitters, that convey nerve signals from one nerve cell to another." One neurotransmitter, called acetylcholine, has been identified as vital to mental functioning. Problems might therefore occur either for a lack of such chemicals or from breaks in the brain's circuitry, which might be caused by the death of brain cells, or as the result of a combination of the two. Promisingly, it is now thought that these neurotransmitters might be supplemented or stimulated to improve thought processes. Since nerve cells can form new branches (called dendrites) to reconnect pathways, this new growth might be encouraged. Although perhaps connecting in a different pattern, the new connections might compensate for the loss of brain cells.

Recent studies in this area suggest that being intellectually challenged and physically active can enhance this regrowth. Conversely, it is thought that mental inactivity—when the mind is idle or unstimulated—can actually cause the dendrites to shrink. Neuropsychologist Marion Diamond, Ph.D., at the University of California at Berkeley, who is currently involved in research in this area, says: "You know yourself that if you've been sitting around for a couple of months it takes a while to get back up to speed, physically or mentally. If the dendrites have come down, you've got to work to bring them back again. But the brain's wonderful plasticity remains throughout life."

Lack of sufficient oxygen to the brain is a known cause of brain cell death. As one ages, the amount of oxygen taken in through the lungs declines; this decline is accelerated if people become less active and/or develop arterial diseases, such as atherosclerosis (hardening of the arteries). Medical researchers continue to uncover evidence pointing to the positive influence life-style choices—emphasizing physical and mental exercise—can have in resisting the decline in brain agility. There is now reason to hope that if people work at it, what might have been assumed to be an inevitable slowing of the mind can be arrested, avoided, or compensated for in some way, making possible not only a more active but also a "brighter" and "sharper" old age.

Activity Maintains the Brain

One challenge to centenarians and others of advanced age, then, is to continually stimulate and exercise their minds. Just as it is never too late to start exercising the body, absent disease, it appears that it is also never too late to reengage the inactive mind through mental exercises. There's no need for a special set of mental gymnastics—mental exercise can simply be a part of a person's everyday activities.

Some centenarians say they read the newspaper each day in order to keep their minds from becoming "rusty" from disuse. They do cross-word puzzles and play Scrabble and other word and board games. Playing cards is a popular activity, especially bridge and pinochle. A keen observer of world events, at 102, Lu Lu Doran of Deshler, Nebraska, was able to read the print in *Newsweek* and *Time* magazines, as well as read them "cover to cover" each week. No longer able to see such fine print at 106, she still enjoys the large-print edition of Reader's Digest. "And she's still an excellent card player," her son-in-law says.

Eva Unkel, 101, of Dayton, Texas, offers her illustration of how to keep one's mind active in everyday activities. "Although I retired from piano teaching in my mid-eighties, I continue to handle my own business—rental property, farms, oil and gas, etc." At 100, Frank Andersen drives to his office every day to oversee the business he started several decades ago and continues his philanthropic activities for youngsters in Saginaw, Michigan. Nellie Hutchins, 104, of Lincoln, Nebraska, gives her prescription for staying "bright as a dollar," an expression that reminds us that dollars were once coins. "Don't live in the past," she says. "Move on to new things." Centenarian Jessie Holman of Dodson, Montana, reports that she still does her own book-keeping because "it would be too easy to simply give up and let some-one else take it over."

Hattie Mae Wilson, 100, of Little Rock, Arkansas, boasts a prodi-gious memory. "I can remember everything of my life from age six to 100," she says. With the aid of modern technology, Louis Kelly exercises his remarkable memory by memorizing and reciting poems and orations, such as the Gettysburg Address. No longer able to read, he has a friend read and record the text to be memorized on a tape recorder. He then listens to the recording until he has it memorized. "I often recite at meetings of our boy's club just to show off," he dis-closed. "We have a group of cronies just a decade or two my junior who meet once a week; I show them I can keep up. I can remember almost every detail of many events of my life. Sometimes I record what I can remember on the tape recorder and then listen to it over and over to be sure I don't forget it. Our memories are important to us, they're part of our lives, a part of us. I enjoy doing it. For me, it's easier to record them on tape than it is to write them out or type them, and just as use-ful. Sometimes I like to hear them myself!"

It's much easier to remain mentally active and alert when there are interested and understanding people around. Those who live alone or in unstimulating environments face a more serious challenge. "It can make one want to give up," says centenarian Sarah D. At her 100th birthday celebration, Sarah sat alone, slumped in her wheelchair, where she had been placed near the piano player, who was cheerfully singing and playing show tunes from the "good old days."

Conversation with her didn't reveal much about her except that she was not enjoying her party. "After all, it's my birthday," she said softly but a bit defiantly. "Where are you from?" the interviewer asked. "Georgia," she answered after a long pause. "You're a long way from home," the interviewer offered. "Yes," Sarah agreed.

The visitor interrupted the piano player in the closing strains of "Daisy" and asked him to play "Georgia on My Mind," but Sarah didn't respond. After a few more tunes, Sarah said she wanted to go back to her room. "Why Sarah," said the administrator, "you haven't even heard 'Happy Birthday.'" "I've heard enough," Sarah replied.

The entertainer was then asked to play "Dixie" instead, and as he did so, Sarah's head lifted slowly off her chest. Her chin rose, higher and higher, and tears rolled slowly down her cheeks. The room became silent. When the song ended, she said, "I always cry when I hear that song—it reminds me of home. I wish I could stand up. My Papa and everyone in my family always rose when 'Dixie' was played." She began to talk about her early years, of her family and marriage and of moving far away from her home a few years earlier to live near her son and daughter-in-law. "I think I would be happier if I were still in Georgia," she said, "where people know of my family, instead of here, clear across the continent, where no one knows me."

Sarah went on to enjoy her party, accepting the greetings of the well-wishers and smiling when the gathering sang "Happy Birthday." She talked more about her home and of growing up in the South. "I was a true Southern belle," she said. "Imagine what my mother would think if she could know she produced a child who lived 100 years!"

Later, Sarah told the interviewer, "I have nothing in common with these people. Most of them have lost their minds, poor things. And the staff thinks I have, too. They call me 'Honey,' and 'Dearie,' and I refuse to answer to such silliness. Now that my son is gone, I only have the visits from my daughter-in-law to look forward to."

Sarah's experience is but one small example of what can happen in an environment where there are plenty of people and activities around but no meaningful interaction. What is missing, it seems, is an understanding of the essential need to communicate with people of advanced age as individuals. We also need to *listen* to them and avoid the patronizing that so often overtakes a conversation.

Many centenarians who spend much of their time alone watch television, especially news broadcasts and game shows—a favorite is "Wheel of Fortune"—using them to keep their minds active by guessing the answers out loud. Radio news and talk shows also help to stimulate their thinking. Others, such as Pansy Ragan of Loveland, Colorado, tell that letter writing is a favorite and important form of communication with the outside world; centenarians enjoy having pen pals of all ages, as well as corresponding with relatives. Exchanging cards and letters "sharpens" their wits, "brightens" their lives, and "lifts their spirits," many tell.

๛

MEMORY LOSS

Despite the examples of centenarians whose minds are alert and active, a great many people of advanced age suffer from impaired mental functioning, most frequently from memory loss. As mentioned in chapter 7, other changes associated with aging, such as impaired vision and hearing loss, can lead to difficulties that can be misinterpreted as memory loss or even as mental decline. If an older person appears confused by a conversation or asks later to have something repeated, one shouldn't assume that this indicates a problem with memory. The difficulty could be a loss of hearing or any number of other problems, including immobility following an illness or a fall. Sometimes an older person's behavior after being inactive for a prolonged period of time is suggestive of loss of mental function. Studies have shown, however, that with exercise and resumed activity, patients often regain mental alertness, as well as physical mobility.

Real memory loss, when it does occur, is not always as severe or frightening as might be imagined, and people can still function quite well in most situations. They should not simply be given up on but rather worked with and related to in ways that are appropriate for their time and circumstances in life. This takes patience from younger people, it's true; it also shows empathy and caring.

For the daughter of Roger Warfield, caring has now reached a painful stage. For the past twenty-four years, they have lived together in his home in Tampa, Florida. A native of Barstow, Florida, Roger was born on June 23, 1893, and is in good health, with no physical problems except almost total deafness. A few months before his 100th birthday, he had cataract surgery to improve his vision and enable him to remain mobile and watch TV.

"Until a couple of years ago," daughter Wilma explains, "he was fine; his mind is the problem now. He doesn't recognize most people anymore, and sometimes he doesn't even know who I am. He will sit there and talk about me, not realizing who he's talking to. It hurts me, but I'm accepting it and doing what I can to be supportive of him in what does still give him enjoyment and pleasure, as small as those pleasures are now. I've been lucky all these years because his health was good and he was able to take care of himself."

Over the objections of some family members who felt it was "not worth the bother," Wilma held a large outdoor family reunion in honor of her father's 100th birthday. "We had a big crowd, plenty of good food and beautiful weather, a big cake—it couldn't have been nicer. My father sat in a comfortable chair and greeted everyone and accepted well-wishes and hugs. He had a wonderful time. It's true that he didn't recognize many of his relatives, especially the ones who live far away and whom he only sees once or twice a year, but, all in all, it was a success. He remembered the party for a few days and talked about it, and then the memory was gone. Was it worth doing? I think so. I think it's worth letting him enjoy what there is in his life now and to give others in the family a chance to be with him, if they want to. He knows he's 100 years old, and he's proud of it. He still knows who he is, he just gets forgetful much of the time about the rest of us."

While a condition like Roger's is not uncommon among people of advanced age, it is not indicative of *all* of our country's elders—and yet the stereotype of old age as synonymous with loss of mind endures. With it comes the fear that a little loss of memory signals the beginning of "senility." Interestingly, the word "senile" is derived from the Latin word *senilis* and means simply "to grow old." Somewhere along the way the definition took on a negative connotation of meaning both old and mentally impaired, especially in judgment and in memory. This presumption of "senility" hangs over the older population like the mythological sword of Damocles, with both the old and those who care for them waiting for it to fall.

Memory Theories

In part, this fearful presumption was supported by early theories of brain functioning that allowed for only one type of memory. Today, it is believed that memory exists in more than one form, that is, the brain contains several different systems, or types, of memory, and a decline in one system doesn't necessarily indicate a decline in the others. Most researchers agree that the brain has both a short-term memory and a long-term memory, and a decline in functioning of one does not necessarily correspond to a similar decline in the other. The terms short-term memory and long-term memory are not new and are familiar to most people. What is often confusing to laypeople is that the scientific definitions of the terms, as applied to a person's memory at the moment, are new and are quite different from the definitions used by the general public.

In the scientific field, short-term memory is used to refer to what one is thinking about, or mentally processing, at the present moment; long-term memory is the sum total of what one has learned in the past, be it several minutes or several years ago. Therefore, people can still function in the present on a daily basis, and enjoy that time (as Roger Warfield does), but not be able to recall by the next day what their activities were or what they did or said. As laypeople, we usually think of this as, indeed, short-term rather than as a function of long-term memory. Understanding it as such could encourage our forbearance of this frustrating and often discouraging occurrence.

One promising theory—Tulving's Multiple Memory Systems Theory—includes this distinction between short-term and long-term memory but goes on to propose that within long-term memory the brain has several "systems" of memory (the *episodic*, *semantic*, and *procedural* systems) and that each of these memory "systems" is specialized for different functions. "The good news for older people is that the semantic and procedural memory systems do not decline with normal aging," says David Mitchell, Ph.D., a professor of psychology at Southern Methodist University who is testing Tulving's theory in experiments with various age groups.

EPISODIC MEMORY

Episodic memory, as the word implies, can be described as for remembering temporary or occasional occurrences of a limited duration, such as a conversation or an event. It is for keeping track of things in a person's own experience, such as where the car keys were put or whom one met at the grocery story yesterday. Decline in episodic memory, which most people do experience with aging, possibly beginning in their fifties, may often be compensated for by learning to use external memory strategies, or "memory joggers," such as writing things down or setting out reminders.

It is generally thought that people experience more difficulty with a loss or slowing of episodic memory (become more forgetful) in their seventies. Studies suggest that the decline in episodic memory is related to a degeneration of the brain's frontal lobes, which are used to remember things, such as words or names just heard, or recent events. It is not yet known whether using episodic memory more often, or "stretching" it, as some centenarians say, can slow this decline. The hope is that some of this loss may be simply attributed to changes in life-style that most people undergo in their later years, either as a result of retirement or the loss of a spouse with whom to converse or, in general, a diminishing of an older person's world, all resulting in the mind not being stimulated as much as it once was.

Dr. Robin West, a University of Florida psychology professor, suggests that older people who are bothered by a decline in episodic memory create a "memory place," a designated location for important and often used articles, such as keys and glasses and telephone numbers. "You need to live in an organized environment," she says. "It may take a little while, but once you've established such a routine, you will dramatically reduce your memory load." Adds centenarian Billy Earley, it will reduce your concern about day-to-day forgetfulness as well.

If organization is an asset in memory and mind functioning, then centenarians generally exhibit a characteristic that helps accomplish this: orderliness. A large number of centenarians and their families say that throughout their life, they have shown a penchant for orderliness and organization in their daily lives—not necessarily to the point of being rigid or boring—but rather in a functional sense so they could make the most of their time. In today's jargon, their strategies might be called "stress reduction" or "coping skills." It is encouraging to learn how some centenarians, though aware of a decline in episodic memory over the years, have learned to compensate for it.

Another explanation of episodic memory suggests that every memory begins with an event and therefore as an episodic memory. Repetition of an event, such as putting the keys in the same place or repeating a new person's name frequently, converts this episodic memory into a permanent or semipermanent knowledge base, called semantic memory.

SEMANTIC MEMORY

What is called semantic memory is what would commonly be thought of as knowledge—retained information and facts. Again, as the term implies, semantic memory has to do with our ability to explain and describe in words, to ourselves and to others, the world and people around us. It is thought that semantic memory does not decline in the normal aging process; however, it may be affected by certain types of brain disease often encountered in old age. According to Dr. Mitchell, "Semantic memory is the seat of wisdom. When you make decisions and judgments, you draw on this store of knowledge." In addition to being the most "robust" memory system for an older person, Dr. Mitchell further suggests that "it grows." "In the past few years, data on memory in the elderly began to show clearly that it was semantic memory older people rely on for distant memories, while it is a failing episodic memory that interferes with remembering recent events. The memories from long ago are of stories or emotional moments that people have thought about over and over, storing them in semantic memory."

This would also help to explain the puzzling phenomenon that is generally observed in a great number of people of advanced age—that they can recall with ease events of long ago but have difficulty remembering things that happened recently. Mary Gleason, for one, is troubled with this type of memory problem. "I can recall arriving at Ellis Island; I can recall the crossing (of the ocean); I can remember my Gaelic—but sometimes I can't recall what I did at the day-care center the day before," she says. Some psychologists agree that semantic memory may even improve in old age because people have thought about these events so often over the years that they are better "imprinted" on the brain.

PROCEDURAL MEMORY

Also encouraging is research suggesting that healthy adults generally experience minimal decline with age in procedural memory or implicit memory, which deals with "how to do" things that become almost "automatic" over time, such as performing routine tasks of cooking, driving a car, or getting dressed. Once again, as the definition of the word implies, procedural memory has to do with accomplishing something or acting in a series of learned steps followed in a regular order. Moreover, these steps have become an intrinsic part of a person's function.

Using the example of driving a car, which many centenarians learned to do decades ago, one centenarian who winters in Arizona related that her home state of Montana had refused to renew her driver's license because of her age as she reached her 100th birthday. Suffering the loss of her independence for the time being, she confided: "When I get back home in the spring, the first thing I'm going to do is get in my car and drive all over my spread. I own hundreds of acres and no one will see me, and I'm going to drive all I want." Clearly, for this centenarian, procedural memory was very much intact.

This memory system helps explain, too, how Clyde Ice and other centenarians who were pilots, can fly a plane at age 100 after not being at the controls for many years.

Procedural memory also includes cognitive skills (thinking and reasoning) such as solving jigsaw puzzles, and verbal skills, such as relearning a previously known poem or song. It helps explain why centenarians who had been professional musicians, such as Virginia Billings of Sun City, Arizona, who played piano for the Marx Brothers, will "come alive" when they sit down at the piano and play from memory the songs from that era, and yet have difficulty recalling daily conversations and events. Also it helps us understand how centenarians like Sarah D. can remember and immediately relate to songs learned early in life, even though not heard for many years.

⚭

While some losses in memory and mental agility among older persons can be compensated for through life-style adjustments, the more serious threats to the health of mind and memory include diseases that may permanently and irreversibly destroy the mind. The essential first step toward treatment of either permanent disease or temporary impairment is timely and accurate diagnosis. Clear evidence of memory loss should never be shrugged off as "just aging" or avoided out of fear of discovering an irreversible form of dementia; many types of memory loss are treatable.

If memory loss is a problem, a careful medical examination should be done, which would include consultation with a neurologist, testing using sophisticated new scanning devices, a blood analysis, a thorough cardiovascular examination, and a nutritional evaluation. The patient's alcohol intake and medication should also be reviewed. At many medical centers, magnetic resonance imaging (MRI) is being used to detect not only changes in the brain, such as stroke, but other medical problems in the body that can affect mental capacity.

Poor nutrition can also affect mental functioning and memory, as can some side effects of medication and the combination of certain drugs. Hospitalization can make an older person disoriented; so can anesthesia. Depression and grief can create symptoms similar to those of memory loss and impaired mental functioning. Such considerations should be kept in mind lest people jump to the wrong conclusion about an older person's health of mind. It would be better to think instead, "When in doubt, find out," and to at least give the person of advanced age the benefit of the doubt, accompanied by patience and compassion.

✒

DEMENTIA

In contrast to a tendency to forget recent events or a mere slowing down of the thought process, any extreme and permanent loss of memory and mental ability in old age is the result of a disease or other abnormality. This loss is not simply a natural part of the aging process. Such losses, which affect a disturbingly large number of centenarians and others of advanced age, are categorized as dementia, which means, literally, deprived of mind. (It is important not to confuse dementia with mental illness. Persons suffering from mental illness have a psychiatric disorder while dementia sufferers have a cognitive disorder.)

Medically, dementia is defined as a loss of intellectual functioning (thinking, remembering, and reasoning) severe enough to keep one from successfully completing tasks of daily living. Dementia is not a disease itself but rather is a collection of signs and symptoms. These include memory loss; loss in learning ability, attention, and judgment; disorientation; difficulty with language; personality change; and changes in behavior. This group of symptoms can be caused by a variety of medical conditions, such as Alzheimer's disease, strokes, Parkinson's disease, and Huntington's disease. If the dementia is caused by one of these, it is permanent. Dementia caused by such things as nutritional deficiencies or drug reactions may be cured.

Other physical problems can also bring about dementia. According to the U.S. Department of Health and Human Services, after Alzheimer's, the leading cause of dementia in aging is blood flow obstruction in the brain. This can be caused by a number of factors and can be either intermittent or constant. Hardening of the arteries (atherosclerosis), variations in blood pressure, or a stroke may be the cause. If the heart is not pumping efficiently, if there are disturbances in heart rhythm, malfunctioning heart valves, or other indications of heart disease, the brain may suffer from lack of oxygen. If the lungs are unable to transfer oxygen into the blood vessels (if they are blocked by a blood clot, for instance), this also can starve the brain and lead to symptoms of dementia. It is estimated that 20 percent of dementia may result from disease of the blood vessels.

Most commonly, a blood clot will clog a blood vessel, or a vessel may burst, hemorrhaging into a part of the brain. Such a small stroke may not bring on dementia and may even go unnoticed or it may result in specific symptoms—a slurring of speech, perhaps, or a numbness in one hand. The outcome depends on the region of the brain in which the stroke occurs. *Multi-infarct* dementia is the medical term used for mental deterioration due to extensive blood vessel disease in the brain. People who suffer from multi-infarct dementia often have a history of high blood pressure, heart disease, vascular disease, previous stroke, or other vascular or neurological disorders.

Alzheimer's Disease

The single most common cause of dementia affecting older people is Alzheimer's disease, a degenerative disease that attacks the brain, seriously impairing memory, thinking, and behavior, and eventually leading to death. Although it is a disease that attacks people when they are older, it is *not* part of normal aging.

Unfortunately, for many years the symptoms of Alzheimer's have been commonly thought of as synonymous with old age itself. As Dr. Robert Butler, psychiatrist and eminent gerontologist, Chairman of the Department of Geriatrics and Adult Development at Mt. Sinai Medical Center in New York, has stated, "The 'write-off' of older persons as 'senile' because of problems of memory. . . is being replaced by an awareness of the profound and most common form of what is popularly referred to as 'senility,' namely Alzheimer's disease."

First identified in 1909 by Alois Alzheimer, the German physician after whom the disease was named, both the cause and a cure remain undiscovered. It has only been within the past ten to fifteen years that Alzheimer's has come to public attention. Federal funding for research did not begin until 1976 and remains but a small percentage of that allocated to other nonage-related diseases. Yet Alzheimer's is the fourth leading cause of death among adults in the United States, after heart disease, cancer, and stroke. It is estimated that presently four million people are afflicted. Called the "silent epidemic" by Lewis Thomas, author of *Lives of a Cell*, the National Institute on Aging estimates that "approximately 10 percent of the population over sixty-five years of age is afflicted with Alzheimer's disease." Forty-eight percent of those eighty-five and over are thought to have it. By the end of the decade, it is forecast that six million Americans will be victims of this disease that indiscriminately strikes every social and economic level.

According to the National Institute of Neurological Disorders and Stroke, "Neurologists now agree that over half the dementias occurring among the elderly, disorders called senile dementia, or chronic organic brain syndrome, are actually cases of disease of the Alzheimer type, but beginning at a later stage of life." Alzheimer's disease usually begins gradually, its early symptoms being difficulty recalling recent events and performing routine tasks. As it progresses, nearly all the symptoms of other dementing diseases are present, including a general change in behavior, not finding the right words, or not completing sentences. In time, the illness robs its victim of all cognitive thinking and judgment and, heartbreakingly, often leads to such a severe memory loss that the afflicted person can no longer recognize or relate to his or her own family members. Also heartbreaking is the fact that an Alzheimer's victim may suffer for many years. From the onset of symptoms, the life span of an Alzheimer's patient can range anywhere from three to twenty or more years.

Since most Alzheimer's patients are cared for at home, this disease is devastating for the victims' families as well, thus affecting even larger numbers of the population. Estimates of what Alzheimer's disease costs society range from $40 billion to $80 billion annually, depending on whether the costs of home care and loss of income for caregivers are added to the costs of institutional care. In addition, the majority of nursing home residents are Alzheimer's patients.

Researchers are still uncertain about the cause of Alzheimer's disease. Many possible causes are under investigation. Investigations of environmental toxins, infectious agents, such as slow viruses, and changes in the immune system have not yielded definitive information. More promising are the current efforts to track down the causes of cellular decline and death. Because the disease sometimes strikes more than one member of a family, many researchers suspect there may be a hereditary factor involved, perhaps a defective gene. Recent work in this area is strongly suggestive of this. However, genetics is not the final answer, many believe. Studies of identical twins, who inherit the same genes, have found that one may develop Alzheimer's and the other not at all or much later. If Alzheimer's disease were all genetic, the research concludes, then both twins would develop it at about the same time. Since this is not the case, it is thought that other factors must be involved. What has emerged is that there seems to be a difference between early onset and late onset (after sixty-five) Alzheimer's.

Most drugs that offer relief or that may slow down the process of mental decline are still in the experimental stage. Cognex (tactrine) is the first drug specifically approved by the Federal Drug Administration for use in the treatment of Alzheimer's. Introduced in late 1993, it is not expected to help all Alzheimer's patients (perhaps 30 percent, based on clinical trials.) According to the Alzheimer's Association, many caregiver comments are more encouraging than the scientific data.

JoAnn McConnell, Ph.D., Senior Vice President of Medical and Scientific Affairs at the Alzheimer's Association, tells us, "We are encouraged by all the work currently being done in Alzheimer's disease. Despite the lack of a cure, diagnosis is important to rule out other possible and treatable causes of dementia. Alzheimer's disease remains a diagnosis of exclusion in life—after all other conditions have been excluded. More than sixty conditions mimic Alzheimer's disease; some are treatable and/or reversible." The lack of an accurate method of diagnosis for Alzheimer's disease has long been an impediment to its treatment and cure. "A simple, easily administered diagnostic test for Alzheimer's would help," Dr. McConnell affirms. "With proper diagnosis, families are better able to prepare for the person's eventual care." Various researchers are working to see if brain imaging technologies— such as MRI—may one day provide an easy and quick test.

In the meantime, a greater awareness of Alzheimer's disease by society and on the part of the medical profession is mandatory. To ensure advances in Alzheimer's disease research, more funding is needed. Such a commitment is of great importance to those millions of now middle-aged people who expect to live a long and full life. It is imperative for us to understand that if progress is not made in combating this disease in the near future, the quality of their life in advanced age is at risk. For now, older people and caregivers are urged to see their doctor when changes in mental functioning or acuity are present and to have ruled out various other possible causes before a diagnosis of Alzheimer's disease is considered. Also, those who are interested should contact their local chapter of the Alzheimer's Association to keep informed on the latest developments in treatment and research and for information on support groups and other programs.

Dementias That May Be Reversed

It is often difficult for people to appreciate that the symptoms of dementia in an older person may not be permanent, that they might be caused by something other than progressive brain disease. In fact, dementia, including impaired memory, disorientation, and apathy, can be caused by many other things, such as vitamin deficiencies, anemia, problems with nutrient absorption, infections, thyroid disorders, brain tumors, head injuries, alcoholism, depression, and adverse reactions to prescription drugs (including overmedication and reactions to incompatible combinations of medications).

Severe depression is often accompanied by symptoms that also occur in dementia and can lead to a misdiagnosis of Alzheimer's or some other permanent brain disease. The loss of a spouse or other loved one can lead to distracted behavior and withdrawal or sometimes even the illusion that the deceased person can be spoken to. Grieving people often appear slow, passive, confused, or "dazed." When the person who exhibits such behavior happens to be old, others often too hastily conclude that the person is simply "senile." Loneliness, loss, and disappointment with the quality of one's life-style can also affect an older person more adversely than a younger one and bring on feelings of depression and grief. Depression is an emotional, not a cognitive, disorder. It is certainly treatable and sometimes reversible; it requires altogether different treatment from permanent dementias of Alzheimer's, multi-infarct dementia, and other progressive brain diseases.

Problems with medications—over medication, side effects of medication, and adverse reactions caused by incompatible combinations of medications—are a serious concern for people of advanced age. The consequences of mismedication can affect the mental health, thinking, functioning, and memory, as well as the physical well-being, of an older patient, often to a greater extent than with a younger person. According to a report by the U.S. Department of Health and Human Services, Americans age sixty-five and over use an average of fifteen prescription drugs a year, more than four times that of Americans under the age of sixty-five. They consume 30 percent of the prescribed drugs in this country to treat multiple chronic medical conditions at an estimated cost ranging from $4.5 billion to $9 billion annually.

Richard Kusserow, Inspector General of the U.S. Department of Health and Human Services, reported to the U.S. House Select Committee on Aging in February 1990 that one of the reasons for the high incidence of adverse drug problems among elderly people is that older people, for a variety of reasons, metabolize drugs very differently from younger people; however, most drugs are not tested on elderly people, not even those that will be used primarily by them. Moreover, people over the age of sixty-five are twice as likely as younger people to suffer damaging reactions from medical drugs.

As centenarian Roy Miller points out, "What a lot of medical people don't understand is that many of us have never taken much medication, if any, in our whole lives. On top of that," he adds, "we can't tolerate the same amounts as younger people." Roy's belief is repeated again and again by other centenarians and their families, many of whom have had personal experiences with this problem.

Since medication has the potential for producing reactions that impair an older person's mind and memory, family, friends and caregivers should watch an older person's behavior for signs of change when medications have been prescribed and administered. If the older person appears confused, forgetful, lethargic, or exhibits any other atypical behavior, the first question to ask is: "Could medication be a possible cause?"

Adverse reactions to medication are compounded in nursing homes where people are often prescribed medication to control symptoms, when instead an effort should be made to find out what is causing those symptoms. In some nursing homes, tranquilizers have been used as a routine part of "patient management." Fortunately, this practice is being scrutinized both within the industry and through recent federal regulations aimed at improving the quality of nursing home care. Families or guardians of nursing home residences should check to see what medications the older person is receiving and why. It may be necessary to obtain answers from the doctor, himself, who is responsible for the patient's care, rather than from the nursing staff. All too often family and caregivers are intimidated or afraid to ask these questions. Medication should not be accepted unless the reason for its use has been clearly justified.

The physical changes that can affect an older person are bad enough. Far worse is the prospect of having one's mind—sometimes the only part of the individual that is still intact and functioning adequately—inadvertently altered. It requires a degree of vigilance and advocacy on the part of families, caregivers, and organizations concerned with the well-being of the older population to help remove this additional risk of medication problems from the already long list of obstacles to a good quality of life in old age.

℘

THE IMPORTANCE OF GOOD NUTRITION IN MAINTAINING THE MIND AND BODY

The quality of an older person's nutrition is another important factor affecting the quality of life in later years. The specific nutritional needs of older people, though, have not yet been comprehensively addressed. Even more remains to be learned about the nutritional requirements for keeping the mind healthy as we age. Dr. Irwin Rosenberg, Director of the USDA, Human Nutrition Research Center on Aging at Tufts University, has stated that as many as 5 percent of senile-dementia cases are related to nutrition deficiencies.

It is believed that in old age, the calories needed to function declines, presumably because of a lower activity level. Yet it is unclear if nutrient requirements also change or if they stay at the same level as were needed to maintain good health in younger years. A growing number of experts suspect that nutritional requirements are actually very high for older people and believe that good nutrition in advanced age is essential. Some consider the Recommended Dietary Allowances (U.S. RDA; revised and updated in 1989) not enough to meet the specific needs of the older population. The role of nutrition as part of preventive medicine in maintaining good physical and mental health, and in the treatment of disease, is rapidly developing.

"I've always paid attention to nutrition and eaten good food," Billy Earley tells. " 'You are what you eat,' is an adage that has been around about as long as I have. I don't believe in fads or special diets unless there is a medical reason. Nowadays, I eat a lot of food, but good food, not junk or empty calories. I keep active so I don't gain weight. I pay attention to eating a balanced diet every day. I believe nutrition is very important in old age, but many people let it slip. It's not something you hear a lot about. I'd like to see more publicized about the importance of good nutrition in later years and specifically guidelines for people as they grow older on vitamins, minerals, proteins, and so forth. People either take it for granted that they're eating the right things or they think it's no longer important."

Most active centenarians agree with Billy that good nutrition is important in later years, and say that they pay attention to it. The goal of healthful eating is to eat a variety of foods in moderation with emphasis on those of greater nutritional value and least harmful components such as fat. For many older people, the danger lies in not eating enough food, or living on a diet of mostly empty calorie foods that can be insufficient in vitamins, minerals, and fiber. This can lead to malnutrition and jeopardize good health.

A nutritional assessment should be a part of an older person's basic medical examination and continuing medical evaluation, especially if significant medical problems are present, or if medications are being taken. Medications may affect nutrition in adverse ways, such as causing nausea, and some drugs will cause the body to lose essential nutrients. Malnutrition can also be brought on by certain illnesses that inhibit the processing or absorption of nutrients; in this case, medical intervention may also be needed to counteract the problem. In general, good nutrition helps the body cope with stress and disease. Since older people are more susceptible to disease, it seems reasonable to speculate that a well-balanced, nutrient-rich diet is as important, and may be even more critical to adults in old age than it was earlier in their lives.

Because an older person's diet may be short of the proper nutrients, and because certain health conditions common to old age or medications hinder the absorption of nutrients from the foods selected, some people of advanced age are particularly susceptible to iron-deficiency anemia. This type of anemia is a nutrition-related disease that results in a reduction in a number of red blood cells and a reduction in the amount of hemoglobin they contain. It is the red blood cells that carry oxygen to the brain and other organs; thus, it is especially important for older people to guard against iron-deficiency anemia, which can even further reduce the brain's oxygen supply. The essential nutrients needed for the manufacture of red blood cells are protein, iron, copper, folic acid, vitamin B-12, and vitamin C.

Lean red meats contain heme-iron, the type of iron needed to protect against this form of anemia. Older people who are poor are particularly vulnerable; studies have linked a high incidence of iron-deficiency anemia with elderly people living on low incomes. The suspected cause of anemia in this group is poor nutrition due to the inability to afford iron-rich foods. A deficiency of animal protein (or its equivalent for vegetarians) in a person's diet can result in anemia in a relatively short time. The primary symptom of anemia is fatigue, sometimes reaching exhaustion; in older people, this symptom can occur as a general lethargy.

E. Kresent Thuringer, a registered dietician in the American Dietetic Association and a nationally published columnist on nutrition, says, "The most common type of anemia is iron-deficiency anemia. The first step in treating any anemia symptom is to have a blood test for signs of deficiency. A treatment plan should be developed by a physician and registered dietician. Changes in diet can be prescribed as well as vitamin and mineral supplements, if necessary. But a word of caution here. Self-diagnosis should not be done. For example, the taking of supplemental iron can readily lead to elimination problems and can mask other types of anemias that are disease related.

"In general, older people need to practice good eating habits to guard against malnutrition and specific nutrient deficiencies by:

- Eating foods that maintain a proper level of cholesterol in the body. Although cholesterol and its relationship to heart disease is the most important nutrition-related health concern today, for people of advanced age, not everyone needs to be on a low-fat diet—your doctor should be consulted. For those who do need to be on a low-fat diet, many publications are available to give guidelines and suggestions.

- Eating a proper amount of roughage (now called fiber) to stimulate digestion as foods pass through the small intestine and to promote proper elimination.

- Drinking enough water—at least six to eight glasses per day is a long-standing rule of thumb. It is common for older people not to drink enough water; often their response is, 'I'm not thirsty.' While the sensation of thirst may diminish as a person gets older, the body's need for water does not and great care must be taken to avoid dehydration, which can happen more readily than most people realize. Water is an important nutrient, as essential as any.

- Eating enough protein. Most younger people eat more than enough protein, but people of advanced age may eat too little. People at risk include those who have difficulty chewing and swallowing solid foods, those with digestive problems, and those who cannot afford protein-rich foods.

- Replacing "empty calorie" foods or beverages with those high in nutritional value. Given the smaller portions of food most older people eat, it is important that meals be healthy ones."

Poor nutrition among older people can arise from a number of factors. A decrease in the amount of food eaten and loss of appetite contribute, as can insufficient income. Older people living on limited fixed incomes often simply cannot afford to buy enough food or enough of the right kinds of food that will provide the nutrition they need. People who are taking prescription medications sometimes have to use their food money to cover the expense.

According to Senator David Pryor, Chairman of the Senate Special Committee on Aging, "There are millions of Americans who no longer can pay for their prescription drugs. Five million Americans today have to choose between buying the prescription drugs that their doctor has prescribed for them, or buying food for the table."

Some prescription drug manufacturers are currently making selected, commonly prescribed medications available, in limited quantities, at no cost to patients who qualify and do not have the means to pay for them. The Senate Special Committee on Aging recently conducted a survey of pharmaceutical manufacturers and compiled a directory that provides details on forty-two "indigent patient prescription medication programs," as they are called. (Contact your local area Agency on Aging for information on who qualifies and how to apply for this assistance.)

Citing the need of older persons for such assistance, the Senate Special Committee on Aging reports that prescription drug price increases have tripled the rate of general inflation increases since 1980;

these increases have far outpaced increases in the income of the average older American.

Finally, living alone can also be a factor in poor nutrition. People who do, particularly those who are in ill health, are less motivated to prepare food or even to eat a meal prepared by others. Studies have shown that mild nutritional deficiencies exist in perhaps as many as half of those older Americans who live alone. Health problems and living alone can also lead people to eat more "convenience" (prepared) and processed foods, which may be high in fat and salt and low in nutritional value.

Centenarian Hints for Maintaining Good Nutrition

Some centenarians offer examples to others of advanced age on how to take care of their nutritional needs.

Ray Paul Nieto, 101, of Yuba City, California, says, "There are lots of good ways to feed yourself if you just pay some attention to doing it. You can't always wait for someone to do it for you. We've had a lot of experience eating in our lifetimes! If you think of the foods you ate as a youngster, the ones your mother fed you, you'll come up with some nourishing food that's easy to eat and not too costly—and that you'll really enjoy."

Ray Paul is proud of the vegetables he grows in his garden and recommends them as staples of healthy and inexpensive eating. Potatoes, especially sweet potatoes, top his list. (The Center for Science in the Public Interest corroborates his choice in rating a skinned sweet potato as the healthiest vegetable based on its percentage of U.S. Recommended Daily Allowances (RDA) for fiber and vitamins A, C, calcium, iron, folates, and copper. Raw carrots ranked second, followed by collard greens, red peppers, kale, dandelion greens, spinach, and broccoli.) "Everyone knows that vegetables are good for you—otherwise mothers would not have made such a fuss over our eating them," he continues.

Raw fruits and vegetables are often difficult for a person of advanced age to chew. Now, however, thanks to modern-day juice extractors and blenders, people can "drink" homemade fresh fruits and vegetables.

This liquefying method of consuming nutrition-rich, fresh foods, can be applied to a wide variety of food groups. Meat and poultry are also difficult to chew and swallow for many older people. Chopped, finely ground, or pureed in a blender (follow the instruction booklet; some liquid usually needs to be added), a cooked piece of meat, poultry, or fish is a delicious and nutritious way to provide protein in an easy-to-eat consistency yet with the taste of "real food." Along with semiliquid mashed potatoes and perhaps that timeless favorite of the centenarians' generation—gravy, and a pureed vegetable, it's a complete meal.

"Don't forget eggs," Ray Paul adds. "They're an inexpensive way to get protein. My mother used to give them to me as a youngster, with cheese mixed in—in those days, it was fresh-made cheese, remember that?"

"I like tuna fish for 'brain power'," says Billy Earley. "It's quick and easy to prepare, and easy to chew," this active centenarian reminds us. Billy says she also enjoys a tuna salad as her evening meal.

Setrak Boyatian, 105, of Los Angeles, swears by his yogurt. He makes a gallon of it each week, using an Armenian family recipe. Even if it's purchased from a grocery store, yogurt has a lot of nutrients, especially calcium, and is easy and convenient to eat.

Mary Gleason adds a footnote to these home remedies for good nutrition. "Bananas were called 'old people's food' as far back as when I first came to this country. They are still good food for older people (bananas are high in potassium and fiber), and they are easy to eat. I like mine cut up on top of Irish oatmeal, but of course you can eat them just as they are—but don't forget to peel them first." She laughs at the joke on herself, remembering her first banana at Ellis Island, when she ate it, peel and all.

For convenience, some centenarians drink liquid nutrition formulas in cans, which are sold in supermarkets and pharmacies. These cans of nutrition come in several flavors and contain nutrients and calories; some have added fiber. They can be consumed to supplement a person's daily diet or in place of a meal.

Nutrition experts and laypeople alike believe there can be a correlation between severe nutritional deficiencies and impairment in thinking and memory. Some consider even mild nutritional deficiencies to cause subtle impairments in thinking and memory. Protein, vitamin C, and various B vitamins—folic acid, niacin, pyridoxine, riboflavin, thiamine, and vitamin B-12—are generally credited as nutrients of special importance to a person's ability to think and to remember.

Current, but controversial, theories state that nutritional supplements may improve mental performance, with certain vitamins and mineral supplements specifically assisting with thinking and memory. Hopefully, the not-too-distant future will bring a much better understanding of the relationship between nutrition and brain function and more definitive findings. For now, some doctors do recommend a basic, multiple vitamin supplement daily (also available in liquid form). *The caution to heed, however, is to take vitamins under the supervision of a doctor, and in conjunction with your other health care. Attempting self-medication with vitamins can be dangerous.*

"Just keeping up with and sorting out all the nutritional information available is quite a task," concludes Billy Earley, who is all for keeping the body and brain working at its best. "I get all my nutrition from food; as I've said, I don't take supplements." For another easy meal for one, Billy recommends a baked potato with some cheese melted on top, a green vegetable or salad, and a little fruit. (Low-fat cheese and butter substitute can be used, of course.) "It's a nutritionally complete meal, I'm told. For dessert—often I have this later—I suggest a glass of milk with my famous homemade oatmeal cookies baked from my 100-year-old recipe. I'll send you a copy if you'd like."

❧

❧ 9 ❧

The Challenge of Surviving in Today's Complex Society

An old and frail grandmother, whose trembling hands would sometimes drop and break a china plate, was given a wooden bowl to eat from instead by her exasperated daughter. Seeing this change, the old woman's granddaughter asked her mother, "Why must Grannie eat from a wooden bowl when we all eat from china plates?" "Because she is old," the mother answered sharply. The young girl thought for a moment and said, "Then we must save the wooden bowl when Grannie dies. "Whatever for?" the mother asked. The child replied, "For you, when you are old."

—An American Folktale

IN other cultures and in earlier times in American society, when they were young, old people had more of a place in family, community life, centenarians say. Ida Fox, for one, tells throughout her story of growing up in a pioneer family in the West how her grandmother, great-aunt, and her mother remained integral and revered members of the family as they aged, each having both a place and a role in daily life and participants in community life. Many Native American cultures have a long history of honoring their elders, granting them respect and a place of authority within their tribes and holding open for them important roles in social and ceremonial life. At 102, Chief James Holy Eagle, the oldest living Sioux, attends Tribal Pow-Wows in South Dakota as a respected elder.

Many American immigrants also brought with them the belief that it was important for everyone in the extended family to have a place and to play a role. In expressing her wish for more compassionate and

✦ *James Holy Eagle at age 102, Grand Rapids, SD.*
Photo courtesy of the Holy Eagle family.

receptive treatment of elderly people today, centenarian Hedvig Peterson, who emigrated from Sweden in 1903 with her mother, tells that the lesson of the wooden bowl is repeated in many European cultures.

In modern times in our culture, it seems that the longer people live, the more likely they are to be shunned by society, and, tragically, sometimes excluded from their own families. Ageism is an unpleasant fact of life for many people of advanced age today; for centenarians, it is a cultural bias they have lived during their older decades. The word was coined in the late 1960s by Dr. Robert Butler, recipient of the Pulitzer Prize in 1976 for his book, *Why Survive? Being Old in America*. The word "ageism" is included in Webster's dictionary as coming into popular use in 1970 meaning "prejudice or discrimination against a particular age group and especially the elderly." The effects of ageism resound throughout the Centenarian Wish List: the exclusion from normal activities of family and society life, for whatever reasons.

If, in earlier times, old people felt more emotionally secure because of closer family and community relationships, and were not discriminated against *just* because they were old, those who were poor, alone, and could no longer "contribute" in a practical sense were apparently treated as callously as many of their counterparts today. Helen Cope, a former social worker, recalls the time, early in this century, when old people who had exhausted their own resources and had no family to turn to for help had no recourse but to appeal for charity from private groups and organizations. "Old people in those circumstances faced the dismal prospect of going to the poorhouse or almshouse," she tells.

Along with their hopes for love and acceptance, and for better vision, mobility, and mental health, the centenarians in this book continue their Wish List. They express their needs for a sense of belonging in today's society, and for the strengthening of family ties. And they seek workable solutions to meeting the challenges of basic survival, which include finances, housing, and health care.

❧

POVERTY AND LONGEVITY

It's harder to live nowadays—it takes so much money.
My money is running out; my big worry. Then what?

—Margaret Johnston, 102
Grand Junction, Colorado

In terms of basic economic survival, it is probably a better time to be old in America now, however difficult, than at any other time in this country's history. Foremost among today's advantages are social and financial assistance programs. The very old express their appreciation for such government assistance in statements such as that of centenarian Florence Eggleton of Sherril, New York, who says, "I'm grateful we have the Social Security program. It was much worse before."

During an era that spanned nearly half a century (the 1930s to the 1970s), America enacted legislation and established programs to address the needs of many disadvantaged persons, including the elderly. Among them were Social Security (begun in 1933 and expanded in the early 1970s); the Medicare and Medicaid programs (begun in 1965 and expanded in the early 1970s); and with subsequent periodic improvements to the basics of these programs came supplemental security income; housing and food stamp programs; and legislation, such as the Civil Rights Act of 1964 and the Older Americans Act of 1965.

Under the Federal Older Americans Act, which targets assistance to low income older adults, 670 Area Agencies on Aging have been established to provide information and referrals to community services for older people, and to allocate Federal funding to community agencies providing services. In some instances Area Agencies provide or coordinate service programs within the community. These programs vary from region to region and are frequently a collaboration with local government entities and private agencies serving the needs of older residents. One of the most visible accomplishments of the Older Americans Act has been the development of nationwide senior centers and the services provided through them, such as congregate meals, home-delivered meals, and transportation.

Together with improvements in private pensions, these government programs enable older people today to enjoy many advantages over previous times by augmenting limited resources for many and, for others, by providing a subsistence level of security. Unfortunately, the improvements—great as they are—have not kept pace with the rate of inflation since the 1970s or with the increases in healthcare and living costs or with the increase in record numbers of older people who need these services. Many Area Agencies on Aging, for example, currently have difficulty stretching their funding dollars to maintain programs and to meet the burgeoning need for home-and community-based services; meanwhile, the waiting lists for these services continue to grow. The frail elderly who need these services, though, are often not in a position to wait the several months that may be required to obtain the help. The likely result is premature or unnecessary institutionalization.

Adding to the burden of poverty and detracting from the quality of life in advanced age are other related problems and needs that affect this entire group. Among them, the baseline healthcare requirements of many older Americans far exceed their resources, even with the assistance of Medicare. Private pay nonmedical home care assistance is beyond the means of most people of advanced age, and medical home care services often are not covered by Medicare or are very limited and difficult to obtain. Medicaid spending for long-term care has so far covered mostly nursing home placement rather than home care assistance, and nursing homes, where one out of every four Americans age eighty-five and older live, can rarely be considered a "home" at all.

The American Society on Aging, recapping progress over the last forty years for older Americans, states in the program for its March 1994 annual conference: "There have been remarkable gains in the overall economic and health status of those over sixty-five, but huge pockets of poverty still exist, most notably among women and minorities." A large number of centenarians and others of advanced age, many of whom are women and minorities, are among those in the pockets of poverty. A recent report by Families USA Foundation in Washington, D.C., on healthcare costs of older Americans, states that "America's elderly spend more than twice as much money on healthcare costs than they did prior to the establishment of the Medicare program. In 1961, elderly out-of-pocket costs averaged $1,589 in inflation-adjusted dollars per elderly family. By 1991, out-of-pocket costs had reached $3,305 per elderly family." Concerned about the ability of many to meet the high costs of healthcare and other high costs of living today, Ron Pollack, executive director of the foundation, declared: "How can we turn our backs on the poorest, the oldest, the sickest, and the loneliest when they are struggling? In fairness, America must respond to the unmet needs of these Americans and their families."

In fact, many centenarians, speaking of having lived through all the decades of this century, say that, overall, growing old and living long have become more difficult because the world is now more complex, fast-paced, and expensive. Those who have lived the longest despair over how inadequate the money they do have is, when compared with the high cost of today's necessities. Louis Kelly remarks, "Every time I come out of a grocery store, I feel like I've left an arm and a leg." Centenarians, many of whom prudently saved all their lives, find that despite their best efforts their savings are running out. As Oscar Wilmeth often remarked, "I can't afford to live much longer—my money is going fast."

In a public television documentary, "Can't Afford to Grow Old," narrator Walter Cronkite pointed out that "although America's children are the poorest members of society (because they are dependent and without money or resources of their own), the elderly are the next poorest group in the country—they are worse off than any other adult group."

The oldest of the old are among the poorest of the poor. Most centenarians survive on very little income, less than $5,000 a year. In addition, there are approximately one million Americans eighty-five and over who are living on incomes at, below, or just a little above the official government poverty line (for 1993, $6,930 for an individual over age sixty-five; $8,741 for a couple). Important to note is that the poverty threshold differs for people over sixty-five, skewing the percentages of people living in and near poverty; if the threshold were the same, the statistics for older people would be even higher.

The struggle to survive on too little money is part of the daily life of thousands of centenarians—and a larger number of others of advanced age—numbers that will continue to increase in the foreseeable future and beyond. Those eighty-five and over belong to the fastest-growing age group in America. In 1980, there were 2.3 million Americans ages eighty-five and over; by 1990, there were more than 3.0 million; by the year 2000, it is predicted that this age group, sometimes referred to as the "old old," will include 4.9 million people. To put this in perspective, by the year 2050, 5 percent of the total U.S. population is expected to be eighty-five and over, compared with 1.24 percent at the present time.

In counting the oldest of the old, the census bureau in 1994 estimates the centenarian population to be 50,000 and expects this group to double to 100,000 in the next six years. *American Demographics*, a publication of Dow Jones & Co., Inc. of New York, estimates the centenarian population to be 45,000 at present. Whatever the exact number, which will never be known, the indisputable fact is that the ranks of this group are growing steadily. In 1980, the Census Bureau estimate was approximately 25,000 nationwide, ten times the number in 1950. By the middle of the next century, it is anticipated there will be between one million and two million centenarians in America.

The sad reality, then, is that longevity is all too often accompanied by poverty, and, for most, the longer one lives, the poorer one becomes. People eighty-five and older, for example, are twice as likely to live in poverty as those in the sixty-five to seventy-five age bracket. Furthermore, approximately three-fourths of the elderly poor are women, many of whom live alone. Centenarians and others of advanced age find that few in the mainstream are aware of the realities of their lives—and that fewer care. "People don't seem to care about a lot of things that used to be important," Margaret Johnston says. "It seems they just want to get all they can for themselves." Mrs. Johnston discerns with dismay an underlying attitude that seems prevalent in today's society: indifference toward elders in need and a concern for involvement only in causes that have popular appeal.

"Why shouldn't the cause of the elderly in this country be a popular one?" asks Judge Harry Fisher, 102, of Fort Scott, Kansas. "We old people feel we've paid our dues. We've helped build this country and have contributed generously in the past, when we could. We shouldn't be just thought of as obsolete or something to be gotten rid of. We have a place, too."

Perhaps what makes their plight an unpopular cause is that it is too easy to ignore the needs of our oldest citizens, who are often weak, alone, and vulnerable—without a voice. Mrs. Johnston's social commentary is echoed by other centenarians, many of whom are worried about their ability to survive in today's social and economic climate. Overarching is a sense of abandonment expressed by a great many of America's eldest citizens.

"America has got to get this straight," declares Vernon L. Greene, Ph.D., Professor of Public Administration at Syracuse University and president of the National Academy on Aging. In an editorial in *Aging Today*, a publication of the American Society on Aging, Dr. Greene stated, "The elderly are not a 'welfare burden' on our economy in either a technical or moral sense. They are in fact its principal investors, without whose determination to invest in human capital we would all be poorer."

❧

BELONGING

Nothing is more tragic than the man
who did nothing because
he could only do a little.

—Edmund Burke

The Role of Individuals

The Centenarian Wish List makes it clear that companionship is also
an important need in maintaining a good quality of life in old age.
Sadly, it is a need that is often overlooked or minimized by those who
have not experienced the isolation of elderly people. Numerous studies
show that older adults would like more social contacts and more opportunities for socializing than are presently available. Very elderly people,
even those who have some physical limitations, are no exception. Many
enjoy going out to restaurants, family gatherings, and to other events
where they feel comfortable and not physically overtaxed. "I wouldn't
suggest a rock concert," advises centenarian Billy Earley, "but going to
listen to a swing band or an orchestra would certainly be fun."

People make the mistake of assuming that a very old person would
not enjoy going out, thinking perhaps that impaired or limited mobility, sight, or hearing might make it too much of an effort for them.
Often this is not the case at all, as many centenarians tell.

Says Hattie McGuire, 103, of Phoenix, "I love going out, and as long
as I can keep going, I will." Hattie has her hair done weekly and is
always well-groomed and ready. Although she needs the assistance
of a wheelchair and now lives in a nursing home, her daughter sees
to it that she gets out on a regular basis to restaurants, family outings,
and other activities she enjoys.

Sharing in the older person's enjoyment is well worth the extra effort
it may take to make the necessary arrangements. Such simple pleasures as a ride in a car, with perhaps a stop for ice cream or a hamburger
even if eaten in the car, can brighten an older person's life. For those
unable to go out, a visit from friends and family, including neighbors
and children, has the same effect. Treats such as flowers, candy, or
something that might be considered a luxury adds joy to their lives.
When a visit isn't possible, letters, cards, and telephone calls can do

a great deal to bring pleasure and a feeling of staying in touch with the world. "I sure do enjoy receiving letters," says Ray Paul Nieto. "It makes me feel good all over, and I like to write back."

Here, too, people generally conclude that in advanced age a person would not have the interest in correspondence, but the responses from centenarians proved otherwise. "I enjoy having pen pals," centenarian Lillian Sawdy wrote in excellent penmanship. She lives alone in Clinton, Iowa, and included a picture of herself "because I thought you might like to see what I look like." (See the back of the book for information on the Centenarian Correspondence Club.)

Centenarians demonstrate in many ways that, just as people never outgrow or become too old for the need for love and intimate relationships, they continue to want close ties with family and friends, and fellowship with other people. Centenarians' feelings confirm what recent research has suggested: that connectedness with other people is good for us and can help maintain a person's physical and mental health, as well as quality of life. Further, centenarians suggest that the quality of life for people of all ages today would be improved if the values they grew up with were more in evidence, and were incorporated into modern life—values and beliefs such as those illustrated in chapter 5 by the family of centenarian Ida May Gilland Fox.

In short, centenarians bespeak the hope for more compassion, love, acceptance, and friendship for all older people from younger generations, which cannot yet imagine the effect of its absence. Based on their own experiences, far too many older people in our society would agree with the sentiment of Humanitarian Mother Theresa, who has said: "The greatest suffering is being lonely, being unwanted, being unloved. Just having no one." Caring individuals, either alone or as part of an organization, can do a lot to better the lives of the elders in our midst. With a little care and caring, great things are possible.

The Choice of Where to Live

INDEPENDENT LIVING

Among the most frequently mentioned wishes of centenarians is the desire to remain in their own homes or with family members. Centenarian James Hammond writes from his home in Cerro Gordo, North Carolina: "I think it would improve the quality of life for centenarians and others very old if they know they could remain at home until they were *totally* disabled. I do, and take part in many, many things, as always, organizations, etc. I'm still an active Mason."

Home care services can often help fulfill the wish to live independently. The Central Vermont Area Agency on Aging gives an example. "Mary was a client for the last five years before her death at 100," tells Ginger Thompson, the agency director. "She was a very independent woman, very feisty and very clear-minded. Her mind was made up to live on her own, and she succeeded. Through the home care services we provided, she was able to achieve her goal of remaining independent.

"Often just an hour's service a day may enable a frail elderly person to remain at home—that may be all they need. I've seen it so many times. Also, and this is very important but frequently overlooked when policymakers are deciding these things, the human contact of having someone there for a few hours a week is so helpful to keep their morale up. It gives older people some of the personal companionship they may need. It also gives them confidence that, if something really goes wrong, another human being will know about it and be able to get help for them. It saves the government money, too," Ginger adds, "for without home care services many of these people would be on Medicaid in a nursing home."

A surprising number of centenarians (estimates say around 25 percent) are living alone in their own homes or apartments; a larger number live with a family member. This suggests a strong need to refocus funding for long-term care away from institutionalization to create greater opportunities for home care for those who prefer to remain in the community. If, at age 100, people still retain the desire to keep their independence to the fullest extent possible, then surely others of advanced age, who are in far greater numbers, have this as their goal, too. The type of nonmedical assistance needed by people of advanced age can range from help with dressing and bathing, to cooking meals and housekeeping, to running errands and driving to the grocery store or doctor, to home maintenance and repairs. Often home healthcare is also required to help avoid unwanted or premature institutionalization.

With a combination of paid help, community services, and her family, Ruth Weyl, 101, of Skiatook, Oklahoma, is able to maintain the independence she prefers. "I still live alone in my own home, with good help," she says. "Meals on Wheels comes from the senior citizen center each noon, five days a week. I have a (paid) home care agency to provide transportation by sending a young lady each Wednesday morning to take me where I need to go, to the doctor, for groceries, whatever I need help with. I still prepare my Saturday and Sunday meals. My son comes each Sunday afternoon to do all the paperwork and business mail. We go to Tulsa to spend the rest of the day with my daughter, who is unable to drive because of poor vision. I plan to stay here in my home as long as the Lord allows, and we are looking into some retirement locations when I have to give up my home. I don't want to leave here until absolutely necessary."

"Independence is a goal they all will do anything to achieve," says Ellene Davis, director of the Northwest Kansas Area Agency on Aging, speaking of people eighty-five and over. "Even if it means moving into a high-rise (senior housing project) or going into a shared living arrangement or an assisted living arrangement." For the past fourteen years, Ellene has been the director of the agency that includes Smith Country, reputed to have the largest concentration of people eighty-five and over (per capita) in the country.

Ellene also speaks from personal experience, with her father, W.A. ("Ab") Earnest, living to be almost 107. "He would have made it, I'm sure," Ellene tells, "had it not been for a fall, hospitalization, and then complications. What he wanted most was to come home again.

"When he turned 100, my father sold his home and moved into a small apartment I had built for him on my property. He didn't want to live in my home with me. This was the ideal situation. I could check on him, sometimes take him food I'd cooked for dinner, and yet he had his independence, which he treasured. He had a microwave oven and prepared most of his own meals. He was reasonably self-sufficient with this arrangement, but he told me shortly after he moved in, 'If I ever need to go to a nursing home, I'll tell you. I won't fight it as so many old people do.'"

NURSING HOMES

For many people of advanced age, nursing home placement becomes an everyday possibility and a perceived threat to their desired quality of life and autonomy. Yet illnesses such as Alzheimer's disease or other debilitating afflictions can make it nearly impossible for some people to live anywhere but in a nursing home. Some have no alternative but to live in a nursing home on Medicaid or similar state programs, because they haven't the money to live anywhere else. This alternative sounds depressingly reminiscent of the poorhouse of long ago. Others, who do not suffer from dementia or a debilitating illness are placed in nursing homes as a result of falls or simply because they are frail or need some assistance with daily living. Centenarians who may only require some assistance with the activities of daily living, say that being placed in a nursing home, as a result, is one challenge they could do without.

"What hurts me the most is that I'll never get to go home again," says Josephine Sullivan, 101, of Sioux Falls, South Dakota. "I lived alone on my farm until I was ninety-nine and then I fell and broke my hip. After leaving the hospital, I was transferred to a nursing home—I thought it was temporary—but one day my doctor told me that I would have to stay here because my daughter could not take care of me at her home. Everyone was afraid I would fall again if I lived alone because my eyesight is getting bad. I guess it's true that I can't live alone without someone around, but it's a bitter pill to swallow.

"I'm resigned now to living in the nursing home, and, sure, I make the best of it. I try to be cheerful. I am even on the welcoming committee to meet with new residents and help them adjust. I participate in activities; I'm friendly to others and the staff. I have a telephone and I call my grandchildren and they call me. Everyone is pleased that I have 'adjusted.' I'm doing all the right things. But my farm was sold, and I have no place to go but here, and it hurts."

"It's rather like a prison," is one centenarian's description of his nursing home environment. "Particularly if you're being supported by Medicaid, there is almost no way to get better treatment. It's like a life sentence. There's nothing we can do about it, and no one to care. No one is watching what goes on in these places," he says. "The government is paying the money, but no one checks to see what's happening to the people they're supporting with it." This centenarian's experience has been borne out by studies showing that often those nursing homes that primarily serve Medicaid residents provide a poorer quality of care than do nursing homes where most residents pay on their own or have family members who pay for them. Of course, there are many outstanding exceptions to this generalization.

Nursing homes have their place: as an institution, they are here to stay. Reports of long waiting lists and difficulty getting into a good nursing home are common. The Hebrew Rehabilitation Center for Aged, in Boston, where 95 percent of the 725 residents are on Medicaid, is considered by many to be one of the national models for extended care, with a compassionate staff and community support. As one centenarian resident, Eva Akabas, tells, she moved there after her two daughters died. "There was no one, really, to look in on me when my daughters were gone—my grandchildren tried, but they are so busy with their own lives. It was hard to give up my home and most of my possessions. All I have left are a few clothes and my photographs; I brought as many with me as I could. There isn't much space for them here, I share a room, but they comfort me. "The Home is part of the Jewish community. A lot of us have volunteered here and made contributions over the years. We knew that one day, if we needed to, we could come here to live out our lives. It's a good place. For me, that's the way it is now."

It's also the way for Mrs. Chen, 106, who has lived at the Kin On Nursing Home in Seattle, Washington, since she was 102. Born in Mainland China, she speaks Mandarin and other Chinese dialects fluently, making this particular facility the perfect home for her. She prefers to conduct her life according to Chinese traditions and religion and follows the Lunar Calendar. "Although frail in appearance, Mrs. Chen is very alert and has a good sense of humor," the administrator, Sam Wan, says. "She is a very giving person and always is concerned about the well-being of other people. She gets along very well here."

San Francisco's Laguna Honda Hospital, also one of the country's largest long-term care facilities, has twelve centenarian residents (the oldest two are 107) and nine ninety-nine-year olds. "We're noted for our care here," says Virginia Leishman, Director of Nursing at the skilled nursing facility. "The majority of our patients are total care; we take them when other facilities in the area won't. No matter what their age, their quality of life and independence is going to be upheld; they don't lose any of their civil rights when they come into this hospital. We listen to what they have to say about their care and give them what they want." At its simplest, the most important factor of all is "they know that they are loved here. There's a lot of affection between patient and staff. Many of their minds are good, their bodies are just ailing."

Adds Maude Zea, a centenarian resident of the Bryans Care Center in Phoenix, Arizona, who also believes the skilled care facility where she has lived for the past six years is the best choice for her, "I'm in good health, and I could have lived with my family, but I prefer to be here.

I feel more secure. My family comes to visit often. I'm content here. I like it."

Assuming a proper level of care, what most often makes a difference in an elder's quality of life in a facility is the amount of contact the person has with the "outside world," so that they don't feel confined and forgotten. If their health permits, people can leave the facility, if they have someone to take them on outings. They can have frequent visitors; in fact, visits from family and friends are encouraged and welcomed in good facilities as contributing to the resident's well-being and satisfaction. All too often, however, it is the facility that tries to keep the resident's family involved and schedules events and activities to which families are invited; if the family members distance themselves from their elders, it is left up to the nursing home and its staff to fulfill all needs and aspects of the person's life.

We can speculate that part of the discontent of nursing home residency, and the unhappiness that some residents express, is due to the lack of continued contact with family members and the community—not the fault of their facility but the failure of some families to keep their elders involved in their lives and activities. "After all, this is where the responsibility lies," believes Robert Benzel of Lancaster, New York, whose great-grandmother, at 101, has been a resident of the Erie County Home for three years. "We keep in touch with her there as though she were still in her own home," Rob says of his family.

Edna Butler lived in her own home in this suburb of Buffalo until she was ninety-eight. "Then she began to fail," Rob explains. "We had no idea why and thought, well, maybe she was getting old." The family, headed by her daughter, Lois Benzel, and husband, Howard, Rob's grandparents, decided it was in Edna's best interest to move her to a nursing home where she would have more care and to prevent a fall. Once there, it was soon discovered that Edna's pacemaker was not functioning properly. "We were very concerned to have her undergo surgery at her age, but we finally agreed because it was imperative," Rob continued. "She came through with flying colors and almost immediately started to pick up again. Soon she was back to being herself, a strong, spirited, energetic, independent woman. It was the pacemaker that was wearing out, not great-grandmother.

"She's had three more good years, and a fantastic 100th birthday party, which we celebrated on Valentine's Day (1993) even though her actual birthday is February 11. It was a Sunday and we had a lot of

❧ *Edna Butler, with great grandson Robert Benzel and his bride, Jennifer,*
on their wedding day, September 11, 1993. Photo courtesy of the Benzel family.

people coming from out of town," Rob explains. "All five of her children came, Helen from England, Norma from Florida, and Patricia
from Texas. Her only son, Ronald, lives nearby, as does Lois, who
planned and hosted the party at the nursing home." The eighty guests
included fifteen great-great grandchildren, as well as many friends
from Edna's church and family friends from the community. "We're
very proud of her," Rob says as an understatement. "She knows she
is loved by her family and friends, and held in high esteem by the members of her church, of which she was a founding member in the 1930s."
As further evidence of the regard in which Edna Butler is held by her
close family, one of her grandsons, Jerry Caine, has visited her faithfully every Sunday since she's been at the Home.

Now no longer able to go out to attend large family celebrations,
Edna's family sees to it that she continues to feel included by bringing
the events to her. A recent example was Rob's wedding to Jennifer

Marrale. Following their reception, the bride and groom visited Edna, taking along roses from the ceremony.

The couple had planned to then visit Jennifer's grandparents, who are in their nineties and live at a nursing home thirty miles away. However, just as they were leaving their wedding reception, they were notified of her grandmother's fall earlier that day. As a result, the bride and groom visited her in the hospital instead.

This young couple's consideration illustrates the importance to them of keeping their elders, who are physically separated from their families, connected in some way. "Just because they are in another place doesn't mean they are forgotten," Jennifer says. "We want them to know that. Because they are not at home, they can tend to feel forgotten. It's up to the family to overcome this, we think."

A great deal has been written about the inadequate care, sometimes bordering on outright neglect and cruelty, in some nursing homes throughout the country; and, of course, there are many good nursing homes where the care is appropriate and the environment is good and where the older person is actually better off than the alternatives he or she has available. Anna Johnson, 105, of Roswell, New Mexico, voicing her view, summarizes: "Small, loving nursing homes at reasonable prices would improve the quality of life for centenarians who need the care and give them peace of mind that they had a good alternative. I tried a local one and found it too busy and impersonal and very expensive—$2,200 to $3,000 a month!"

In the book *Everyday Ethics: Resolving Dilemmas in Nursing Home Life*, Rosalie A. Kane, D.S.W., Professor of Social Work and Public Health at the University of Minnesota and Director of the National Long-Term Care Resources Center, states, "Without detracting from the dedication of the fine, often thankless work of many homes, we must acknowledge in plain language that nursing homes are not nice places to live. In many instances, they also are not nice places to work. . . . It is unnecessary and improper to accept these conditions as immutable. Rather, we need to give serious attention to liveability. . .to the maintenance of personal identity. . .[and to] the kind of personal autonomy that is wanted and wanting in America's nursing homes. . . . It is a challenge to determine what can and should be done about them, but surely they should not be ignored."

The challenge for nursing homes, then, is to make their facilities good places to *live*.

CONGREGATE LIVING

When living in one's own home is no longer practical or possible, and living with family not an option or not preferred, and nursing home skilled care is not needed, then retirement centers that provide assisted living and often increasing levels of care may be the answer. Also emerging as options to meet the growing need for assisted living are small group homes and foster homes, which are generally less expensive than other types of congregate housing.

One centenarian's granddaughter had the courage to stand up for her grandmother and help her move from a skilled nursing facility, where the treatment she was receiving was causing her great distress, to a retirement home, where she has her own room and can come and go freely yet receive help with personal care and daily chores. "Everyone in my family was against me, including my mother," she tells, "but they all live out of the area. I'm the only one who knows what goes on every day. My grandmother was right to want to find another place to live that was better for her rather than just accept where she was put. At 102, she still knows her own mind, and I support her in that. She's very happy where she is now and I'm happy for her. I don't know what the future will bring, but we'll handle it when it gets here."

Many religious and secular organizations, to their credit, offer retirement communities with options designed to alleviate the fears of moving from one's own home and the loss of independence associated with it. In these communities, residents may have separate apartments or private rooms, which they can decorate as they like, often with their own furnishings. Frequently, apartments come with a kitchen or kitchenette so that residents can prepare a meal or snack if and when they want to. The facility also has one or more main dining rooms where residents usually take at least one meal a day together. Most importantly, residents are free to make their own plans and to keep their own schedules, thus preserving their autonomy.

The Society of Friends, or Quakers, has been an innovating force in this field. Pennswood Village, for example, a Friends retirement community in Bucks County, Pennsylvania, was established in close proximity to a Friends boarding school to encourage the residents to participate in the school's activities and to bring the young students in touch with their elders.

Mary Brown chose to give up her home in suburban Chicago, where she had lived all her married life and where she had raised her four children, to move to a retirement community when, at the age of eighty-nine, she fell twice. The first time she broke her hip and the second time her arm. She moved to Pennswood Village to be near her daughters, deciding that it was more important to be near her children than to cling to the familiarity of her home.

What she liked about the facility was its three levels of life-care and the amenities available. At first, Mary moved into a three-room apartment with as many of her belongings as were practical and lived there for several years until she fell in the shower. After that, she decided to move to the next level of continuing care, a single room and bath where she has her own furniture. Here, she receives some assistance with daily grooming, takes her meals in the dining room with the friends she made while living in her apartment, and is free to keep her own schedule of activities. These include frequent visits from her daughter, Sally Zorn, and visits to her daughter's home to spend time with her many grandchildren and great-grandchildren. No longer able to read, Mary also enjoys daily two-hour visits from a professor's wife who reads books, magazines, and newspapers to her.

"Mother made it easy for us," Sally tells. "She made all the decisions to move herself. What I see here is that the people who are contented are those who made the choice themselves; the ones who are unhappy are those who have been 'put here' by their family. Mother knows that if she needs still more care, she can move to the nursing home wing of the facility. I hope she doesn't have to, but if she does, I'm sure she'll make that decision for herself, too."

Perhaps the resolution of the dilemma of where to live as one grows very old lies in this observation: "The decision to sell my house and move to a retirement center at age ninety-nine was the hardest I've ever made," tells Don Warren, Ph.D., of Fremont, California. But once I got used to it, I like it here. I'm free now to travel, which I enjoy, and I don't have to worry about someday having to move to New York City to be near my daughter for some assistance."

For many people as they grow old, congregate living, in its many variations, presents a reasonable alternative to living in one's own home, and a good alternative to unwanted institutionalization. At present, though, financial and health requirements constrain the wide use of some types of congregate housing: for the most part, retirement communities and other assisted living options are available to those who can afford to pay for them on their own or with help from their families. (Financial assistance is sometimes available through religious or secular organizations that provide the facilities. For example, a few not-for-profit retirement centers, such as Pennswood Village and the entire network of Friends Retirement Centers, offer financial assistance to those in need.) Also limiting access to some types of congregate housing is a requirement that residents be in relatively good health and ambulatory when they enter. With greater numbers of Americans living to advanced age in the near future, the need for innovative living environments will undoubtedly increase as well; hopefully ways of making congregate living accessible and affordable for more people will evolve.

FAMILY CAREGIVING

Contrary to popular thought, most older Americans who need help with daily living are not in nursing homes or assisted living facilities, they are cared for by their families. It is estimated that about 80 percent of what is considered long term care, including personal care and care for chronic illness, is being provided from within the family, usually by the women.

The scope of family caregiving ranges from occasional companionship, social visits, and assistance, such as Ruth Weyl enjoys in her own home, to total daily caregiving in the family's home, and all points in between. Throughout this book, there are numerous examples of families providing various levels of care and assistance, such as Helen Cope and Ted Gibson, who live with their children; Richard Johnson, whose granddaughter lives in an apartment in his home; Louis Kelly, who lives with his wife in their home; Mary Ogburn and Mary Gleason, who attend adult day-care centers while living with their daughters; Lizzie Davis, who has made her home with her daughter for many years; Tempa Robinson, whose four children "pitch in" to help her live in her home; Billy Earley, whose daughter lives at home with her; Alma Hauetter, who spends the winter months with her son's family in a warm climate; Clyde Ice, who spends the winters with his wife in his second home in close proximity to their daughter; and Nannie Cook Moree, totally cared for by her granddaughter and her extended family.

Centenarians are effusive in their gratitude for the family care they receive. As Elmie Steever, 101, of Stromsburg, Nebraska, says, she counts herself among the lucky ones: "I have lived alone since my husband died thirty years ago, but the days are not long for me nor are they sad. The time has passed quickly because my days are always occupied. I have a lovely family—we get along beautifully, and we do a lot of things together. Keeping occupied is important so that you don't have time to dwell on the things that have passed. I have an older brother, 104, who lives in St. Paul, Minnesota, but I've outlived all my friends. I'm fortunate to have a loving, caring family close by. They make it possible for me to stay here in the home I love."

At the other end of the spectrum, Marie Ozelia Ackman Lambert receives total care from her large extended family in Pierre Port, Louisiana, with additional help from an agency providing home care services. Better known as "Mama FeFe," she has the "100 percent" support of her family. "We love her so much," says her niece. "She is a loving and wonderful person. To look in her eyes you can see and feel the love of an old and dear friend. I know that in some homes it is very hard, probably, to tend to an elderly person, especially if they are sick and handicapped in some way, but Mama FeFe, at almost 103, is a love of a lifetime to us all."

It is often difficult for a person of advanced age or his or her family to learn about and gain access to the medical and social services that are available in the community, and that can be provided at home. As mentioned, one of the functions of the Area Agencies on Aging nationwide is to offer an information and referral service for assistance programs and community resources. In many communities, this information is also distributed through senior centers. In addition, doctors who make house calls are available in some areas once again; centenarians recall when this practice was the norm. Information on doctors in the area who are willing to make house calls may be obtained by calling the state medical association. Also, informally, home healthcare agency staff members and social workers may be familiar with doctors (including podiatrists and dentists) who will come to the home.

In-home assistance and home healthcare are growing industries, in response to the growing need for these services. Funding sources and programs are changing in many areas, and more services are becoming available. It often takes persistence and determination, though, to put together a workable and reliable home care plan. For families committed to honoring their elders' wish to "age in place"—the professional term for remaining at home or with a family member— the personal gratification of achieving this goal is, in the long run, worth the effort.

In addition to the financial considerations for caring for elders at home, there are important emotional factors that cannot be overlooked. Living at home, or living with a family member, provides a strong sense of security and comfort for many older people, more so than any other living environment. This sense of security is enhanced by the familiarity and continuous contact with family members, neighbors, and friends. The choice of where to live as one grows old, if one has a choice, is a highly subjective and personal issue.

FRIENDS AS CAREGIVERS

In some cases, it is not family but friends or neighbors who make it possible for an older person to remain at home, by giving them needed assistance or just reassurance they are not alone if they need help.

Dolly Stoppel of Sun City, Arizona, is a caregiver who is not a family member but who shares in the personal rewards of being a good samaritan. For Dolly, friendship with centenarian Grace Northrup covered many years and changes in circumstances as Grace went from living independently in her own home to living with some assistance in an apartment at Sun Valley Lodge, the first retirement center in Sun City, Arizona, and finally to the skilled nursing facility there. "I continued my friendship with Grace after my mother's death," Dolly explains. "Grace and my mother had been close friends. Grace was in her eighties at the time, had no children and no close family. I kept up my relationship with Grace as I had with my mother. I visited her almost every day, took her out for lunch occasionally, and participated in the family activities at the retirement center with her. Once a month I brought her checkbook so she could sign her own checks, which she liked to do. Gradually, as she needed more and more assistance, I took over more responsibility in assisting her, beyond just friendship and companionship.

"I wish I were able to befriend more of the people there who are alone," Dolly says. "Whenever I entered Grace's wing in the nursing home, I felt touched by so many of the other residents who would look up expectantly as I made my way down the hallway to Grace's room. These people became my daily acquaintances and I would stop and chat with them or give them a greeting as I passed by. It troubled me to see the visitors of other residents just come through and ignore those sitting alone in the hallways. It's so cruel to walk past them as if they don't exist—just because they aren't our personal responsibility."

Many centenarians and their families say it would be a big help to them both to have friendship from others outside the family. Simple old-fashioned neighborliness would do wonders, they suggest. "We need some outside contact," Frank Orneals's daughter, Gloria, comments. Frank has lived with Gloria in her home in Phoenix for almost twenty years since his wife's death. "You know, I guess it's human nature," Gloria says, "but we all tend to take family for granted, especially when we live together. Now that Pa has turned 100 and has attention and interest in him from others, it has renewed the family's attention and interest in him, too."

A good samaritan or a friendly neighbor can be a pleasant change, giving the elder someone to exchange greetings with or to chat with— someone to drop by with cookies or a meal they've prepared and would like to share or magazines, newspapers, and books they've finished reading or an offer to get something from the grocery store or drug- store. From personal experience, centenarians and their families acknowledge that it helps to cheer them and perks up their day. As Gloria candidly tells, "it's often just the family member and the cen- tenarian [or other of advanced age] who live alone together year after year. It can close in on you after a while."

❧

THE ROLE OF SOCIETY

> The moral test of government is how it treats those who are in the dawn of life—the children, those who are in the twilight of life— the aged, and those who are in the shadows of life—the sick, the needy and the handicapped.
>
> —*Hubert H. Humphrey*

With government as a reflection of society, then based on this humanitarian's premise, American society may be judged critically, for as people age, we turn away. Instead, it is incumbent upon us, to look after our elders by keeping them a part of society. The very old have been left behind with few, if any, means to stay involved. It's not that old people expect to be in the "fast lane," centenarians say, but they would like to feel as though they were still part of the social fabric of this country. Says Judge Fisher, "To a great many people, we oldsters don't even exist."

The feeling of living a "ghostlike" existence and of being on the out-skirts of society is articulated by many in the over-eighty-five age group, who feel it the most. "It's great when we turn 100—we get lots of attention for a little while," says centenarian Billy Earley. "But what about the years before, when we're just eighty or ninety or ninety-nine? And the days after, when all the excitement dies down? Personally, I would rather be known for who I am and be thought of as a worthwhile human being all along than to have this 'flash in the pan' and then be forgotten."

Other centenarians also question their place in society. "The saddest thing about modern life is that not many people respect old people today," remarks Essie Belle Montgomery, 102, of the Bronx, New York, "or wants them around." Woven throughout centenarians' comments and wishes are expressions of no longer feeling included. It is a recurring theme that the one thing they say they miss about the "good old days" is the slower pace of life back then, when family and friends had more time to visit and when communities had more activities to which elders were welcome.

Part of the reason for ignoring our elders no doubt stems from the youth-oriented culture for which America has become notorious over the past four decades, a culture in which old people are undervalued or devalued altogether. A related factor may be denial of the inevitability of the aging process. If as a society we are afraid to grow old, it follows that we would not want those who are old to be involved in everyday life, reminding us of this fear and of our own fate.

The encouraging side of aging, which a great many centenarians affirm, is that people are, in fact, never too old to continue an interest in the world in which they live. And the desire of some centenarians to participate in contemporary life and issues will change the mind of any skeptic who believes that all old people only want to sit on their front porches in rocking chairs. Despite their advanced age, a substantial number of our eldest citizens still want to participate to the degree they can. They want to be a part of society as a whole—of their families, of their neighborhoods, of their communities, and of their country.

At 100, Billy Earley continued her community involvement. She applied to the governor's office in Arizona for appointment to the Governor's Council on Aging. She did not get the appointment ("I hope it wasn't because they thought I was too old!" she says). Undaunted, she then applied for appointment to the Governor's Advisory Commission on Archaeology, based on her interest in Arizona's native cultures and her many decades of volunteer work encouraging communities to preserve their heritage. As a member of this commission, she attended regular meetings at various archaeological sites around the state. In the past five years since reaching the century mark, Billy has also remained involved in historic preservation projects in and around Florence, Arizona. She continues to receive statewide awards and recognition for her many years of service to her community and the state.

When he was 100, Dr. Henry Stenhouse of Goldsboro, North Carolina, made a bid for nomination as the state's Republican candidate for Congress from his district because, as he put it, "I think I have something to offer." He lost in the primary election, but was pleased to say, "I came in second!"

Frank Andersen, 101, who lives in Bridgeport, Michigan, a short distance from Saginaw, says, "I like modern times—it's progress. I have an interesting life." It's a statement typical of this entrepreneur who built a successful sand and gravel business in Saginaw, which he works at each day from 9:00 a.m. to 4:00 p.m. and who has continued his avocation of contributing to the community. Fifty years ago, "believing that local youngsters needed a place to go in the summertime," he became a driving force behind the construction of the town's first swimming pool. In his mid-nineties, still concerned about the town's children, he conceived a modern project for Saginaw and raised the money to have it built. A water park with a wave-producing swimming pool was completed and named after him in time for his 100th birthday.

At 102, well-known environmentalist Marjory Stoneman Douglas of Coconut Grove, Florida, was still at the work that had been the focus of her life for the past sixty-five years, crusading for the preservation of the Florida Everglades. In her centennial year, she traveled to Washington, D.C., to present the annual National Parks and Conservation Association award to its 1990 recipient. Named in her honor, the award recognizes others for their outstanding efforts in environmental protection of the country's national parks.

Author of *The Everglades: River of Grass*, a seminal ecological work, Mrs. Douglas was instrumental in creating the Everglades National Park in 1947. In 1969, she formed the volunteer activist group Friends of the Everglades. She continues to be active in the National Everglades Coalition, in efforts to protect several endangered species, to conserve

❧ *Marjory Stoneman Douglas at her home, sharing her views on advanced age.*
Photograph by Susan Greenwood, 1990.

the coral reefs of Key Largo, and to preserve the historic homes of Coconut Grove. At age ninety-eight, she completed her autobiography, *Voice of the River,* and began writing a biography of the English naturalist writer William Henry Hudson.

"At 100, I have a sense of achievement and a sense of leisure as well," she said. "I'm not pushed as much as I was. Old age can be more relaxing and more contemplative. I'm enjoying it more than middle age."

For people of advanced age, the heart of the matter of belonging in today's society is that they ought to be able to choose their lifestyle in later years, just as they were free to do when younger, and not be deterred or discouraged from doing so because of their age. If elderly people want to be involved in some aspect of community life or simply to be present at community events and social activities, they should be made to feel welcome and invited to participate to the extent they desire and that is possible for them. This is a moral imperative to be acted upon by society and individuals alike, on behalf of these deserving citizens who have contributed and been a part of so much of the greatness of America.

"Old people have been excluded, isolated, and ignored," asserts Judge Fisher. "All this strikes a responsive cord in me. It's time to bring about change for the better."

Public and private entities, as well as communities and individuals, can foster a sense of belonging, provide opportunities, and help meet the need for socializing and camaraderie. Eden Hospital Medical Center, a not-for-profit district hospital in Castro Valley, California, gives one example. The Geriatrics Department, under Director Sheryl Kramer, Ph.D., developed a program to reach out to centenarians in the area.

In May 1990, the department held a first annual event "to celebrate the accomplishments of local centenarians. We created the '100 Plus Celebration' and found sixty centenarians in Eden's service area," Dr. Kramer tells.

"As the planning progressed, the reaction by hospital staff, the media, and local community leaders was one of near-complete surprise. Few had imagined that there would be so many adults 100 and older living in the community or that two dozen of them would attend the luncheon in their honor. On the day of the event, people were also amazed to see many centenarians walk on their own, although there were a variety of walkers, canes, and wheelchairs in use. Also amazing to many was discovering that the centenarians were all alert and fully capable of enjoying the event."

In lively conversation with their new friends, the centenarians shared their memories and displayed their *joie de vivre*. Ann Simmons watched keenly as other centenarians began to arrive for the luncheon. Suddenly, she said, "Why, there's Jennie Schultz. I haven't seen her in ten years, ever since I stopped driving. We used to play bridge every Wednesday afternoon." Away she went, in her wheelchair, to greet her old friend. They were both delighted.

Heidi Ross, an enthusiastic young woman who handled many of the personal contacts with the centenarians, adds, "A souvenir Life History booklet was written for the event. Centenarians who weren't able to attend the luncheon received a visit from one of our staff and were presented with a copy of the booklet. I just love these people. They're wonderful!"

The following year's event was equally successful with an intergenerational theme. Students from a local high school worked with centenarians on an oral history project. They also attended the second annual luncheon with their new centenarian friends; the annual luncheon is now in its fourth year.

The townspeople of Bruning, Nebraska, gave their centenarian an exceptional birthday celebration. Carrie Hawks, who had lived in Nebraska for ninety-nine years, says, "I celebrated my 100th birthday with a weekend of festivities. The town really turned out for me. My church and civic groups worked with my family to plan the events, some of which were a surprise to me. At Sunday morning service, my birthday was announced and the children's choir sang my favorite hymn. Later, I was escorted from my home, where I still live alone, to the Opera House, riding in a 1929 Model A Ford, with the Legion Honor Guard and the Bruning High School Marching Band leading the way."

At a potluck dinner, 250 well-wishers helped Carrie celebrate 100 years of living. She was presented with a congratulatory letter from the governor and a plaque proclaiming her a member of the Nebraska Century Club. To top it off, the mayor presented her with a key to the city. Carrie adds, "I'm now finishing writing the story of my life compiled from diaries kept over the years." Her story includes a lot of the town's history, too.

Rhode Island was one of the first states to formulate a program to recognize and honor its centenarians. (See the state listing of centenarian programs at end of this book.) Terri Pare of the Department of Elderly Affairs in Providence originated a centenarian brunch at the governor's office more than a decade ago. "The brunch became an annual event, with centenarians and family attending from all over the state," says Terri. All centenarians receive a birthday letter from the governor during the year."

Ward Nance of Emporia, Kansas, is pleased to receive visits at Presbyterian Manor from schoolchildren in the area. On one visit shortly after he reached the century mark, Mr. Nance expressed his philosophy of life in a prose poem written for the children. He told the sixth graders of his childhood years growing up in Kansas and about his father, who was a veteran of the Civil War. He also told about his later life after retiring from the ministry at age eighty; he went on to remodel two houses and then to help his daughter with her business operating a nursing home for several years.

Among the many letters of appreciation he received from the youngsters following their time together, Ward was particularly touched by one young man who wrote: "I want to thank you for a gift that I will cherish for the rest of my life. Before I heard your poem I had always thought that after around seventy years of age you would get bored with life. . . .You have taught me that life can always be exciting and happy. . .even when you are of great age. . . .You have proved something very important."

Mr. Nance's son, Bob, adds, "Perhaps what the elderly need as much as anything else is to feel useful and appreciated. The children did that for my dad."

Centenarian Roy Miller took the initiative to implement his own intergenerational work by visiting schools in the area where he lived without a formalized program. Roy wanted to tell grade school students of his visit to the Statue of Liberty on her 100th birthday celebration in October 1987. With the help of his grandson, Roy tried for three years to persuade the U.S. Department of the Interior to include all Americans turning 100 in 1987 in "Miss Liberty's" birthday celebration. He failed to convince the planners; instead, he was invited to attend as the representative of all Americans reaching the century mark with him that year.

When I came back from New York, I wanted to tell children how beautiful "Miss Liberty" is—you can't really appreciate it in pictures. I looked way up and there—with a ray of sunshine illuminating her face—was the most beautiful sight I have ever seen. I wanted to tell the children what this symbol of liberty stands for. We centenarians grew up together with her in this great land. Many of us passed into this country under her watchful eye and welcoming light. We have seen glorious times and rocky times. I also told them what life was like in America when I was their age—they were pretty amazed. They, in turn, showed me the computer they were learning on. It looked interesting. I think I could do it.

Walter ("Pop") Talbot is another centenarian who counts youngsters as his friends. The entire fifth grade class of the Manzanita Elementary School in Phoenix turned out for his birthday celebration and helped him blow out 103 candles on his eight-foot-long cake. Participation at the senior center adjacent to the school is a regular part of the children's activities. They sometimes share meals, join in events, and invite their elders to attend parties and school performances. Many of the children stop by the senior center after school to get help with their homework assignments or to visit with an "adopted grandparent." Both young and old work on crafts together that they exchange as gifts on holidays. On his birthday, Pop received a handmade gift from the class as a reminder of his friends, which he proudly accepted and planned to take back to his summer home in Iowa. Driving his motorized "Amigo" scooter as he left his guests at the senior center, he turned, waved, and called out, "See you in September!" "Now, that's somethin'," a ten-year-old remarked.

✂

As people grow very old, the desire for independence frequently gives way to the reality of interdependence. Accepting the fact of needing assistance, yet without totally giving up one's individuality and personal autonomy in order to obtain the help, is a major challenge. For many it is the resolution of this challenge that makes it possible to achieve a good quality of life in advanced age wherever they live.

As individuals, we must become aware that, at some time, we all may have very elderly people in our lives and that one day we ourselves may be old and facing these same challenges. With this in mind, we should heed the wish of centenarian Cora Meek of Mattoon,

Illinois, who implores, "Treat us old people like we are human and be kind."

Some say it is a waste of time and energy to give attention to the old because they will die soon anyway, but centenarians say it is worthwhile for three reasons. First, while they are alive, they will enjoy the attention and the friendship and it will improve the quality of their years and mitigate somewhat the other, often unavoidable, physical changes that detract from the enjoyment of later years. Second, when they die, it will be with the peace of knowing that someone cared, which will bring comfort to the inevitable and give a feeling that one's life was noticed at its end. Third, by advancing this ethic, those giving the kindness will have the same to look forward to when they are old. This ethic goes beyond families just taking care of their own. We as a society need to help each other to care for our elders, and we must instill this in our younger generations for our own survival.

                                                 ❧

❧ 10 ❧

Moving Toward a New
Psychology of Aging

Let us recognize ourselves in this old man
or in this old woman. It must be done
if we are to take upon ourselves the
entirety of the human state.

—*Simone de Beauvoir*
The Coming of Age

WHAT can we learn from today's centenarians? From those who are actively engaged in life, we can see some possibilities for our own future, if we wish to live long. We can also see a rationale for moving from the commonly held view of aging as a time of dread and decline to a more enlightened view as a time of meeting challenges, coping with changes, pursuing personal interests, and enjoying the bonus years of life. Centenarians show us that despite the realities of old age, opportunities exist to create ways to maximize the last years of life, whether one lives to be seventy-five, eighty-five, or beyond. In this way, too, centenarians are redefining our ideal and idea of what it means to be old.

❧

HOW OLD WOULD YOU BE IF YOU DIDN'T KNOW HOW OLD YOU WAS?—Satchel Page

There seems to be a current consensus among laypeople and experts alike that, given reasonably good health, *feeling* old is largely a state of mind, making the quote from Satchel Page, the ageless baseball hero, prophetic. Ever so many people at 100 and over say they don't feel old in their minds and in their spirits. Mature, yes—in the sense of years lived and wisdom acquired and experience garnered—but not old in the sense of being worn out and used up.

Such a large number of centenarians say they do not consider themselves *old* that there must be something here for us to appreciate. Certainly, everyone's physical appearance and ability changes with the years; this fact of life, no doubt, contributes to the negative individual and societal conventions surrounding old age. Often not taken into account, though, because it is not readily apparent or discussed, and usually not revealed unless one gets to know people who have lived a long time, is the encouraging and equally important fact that a person's inner self—one's spirit—does not necessarily grow old, or age in keeping with one's chronological years or appearance.

"Perhaps people should be given an individual choice of when they would like to be considered old or a senior citizen," offers Billy Earley. She continues to declare, "I don't feel old and I don't think of myself as old (in a negative sense) at 105." Billy's viewpoint is a frequent refrain heard from active centenarians who insist that a person's inner self does not have to keep up chronologically with one's physical years. As one centenarian confided, "Over the years, I would be surprised when I would unexpectedly catch a glimpse of myself in a store window while passing or in a mirror to see that I looked older; but inside I felt about the same. I did not *feel* my chronological age, and I still don't. I feel young inside. There are times when I think to myself that I don't feel my age, and then I wonder, 'Well, what age do I feel?' I've determined it's around thirty. I don't think I've ever felt like fifty." Adds Billy, "To my mind, I'm sometimes thirty, fifty, or sixty. On bad days, I may feel like seventy, but whatever, I do not feel 100 years plus."

To Beatrice Wood, this is a familiar melody, and she adds her voice to the chorus. "I'm thirty-two at heart," she says and will brook no contradiction from those who remind her that she was born in 1893. "I'm a certain age to the rest of you but, thank God, to myself I am only thirty-two," she explains in the numerous interviews she is asked to give and graciously grants. Asked why thirty-two, the well-known and much-honored ceramic artist replies with humor, "Oh, I just like the sound of it. It brings back good memories."

From her home and studio in the beautiful Ojai Valley of California, Beatrice continues the work that has brought her critical acclaim for many decades in a unique pottery career she began at age forty while living in Los Angeles. Several of her pieces are displayed in museums, including the Smithsonian Institution in Washington D.C. and the Metropolitan Museum of Art in New York City. Over the last ten years, she has continued to have major exhibits and at ninety-nine flew to New York to receive the American Craft Council's highest honor, the Gold Medal Award. On her 100th birthday, which took a month to celebrate, she was swamped with engagements and accolades from the art world and women's organizations and was honored as an outstanding woman of our time.

Beatrice considers herself fortunate to be in good health and to be able to continue doing the work she loves in the place she loves and to live the life-style she loves. Her daily schedule begins at 7:30 a.m. in her studio and includes three to four hours each evening modeling and glazing her ceramic pieces, ending around 1:30 the following morning. During the day, she frequently sees visitors, answers mail, and continues to oversee her business with the assistance of her devoted staff.

The most noticeable change over the last few years has been the loss of her hearing, which Beatrice says she has learned to accept and to live with. Otherwise, she has changed little over the last many years, she tells.

As an artist, Beatrice continues to live a life of her own creation, far from the proper social world in which she grew up in Paris. Beatrice is a member of the Theosophical Society; she dresses with personal flair, wearing Indian saris, always artful jewelry—long necklaces, an armful of beautiful silver bracelets, or silver cuffs on each wrist—sandals, and red painted toenails; she wears her gray hair long.

"I'm very curious and interested in the world," she says, "and watch Ted Koppel's 'Nightline' regularly to get the lowdown on what is happening." To Beatrice, the advantage of living long is that it has given her the time to accomplish so much of what she wants to do, including writing her autobiography, *I Shock Myself*, published when she was ninety-two.

Addie Hutmacher attempts to explain this dichotomy of aging chronologically—even to 100 years—and yet not feeling as though one is old: At least, not too old! In a prose poem written for her 100th birthday celebration, to give to her family and friends, she shares her perspective on aging as it evolved over the years, and as she recalls perceiving herself. We might now term her thinking "New Age Aging".

~ *Beatrice Wood in her studio with assistant and friend*
Stephanie Dragovich. Photo used with permission
from the Ventura County Star, Ventura, CA.
Photograph by Robert St. John.
Photo courtesy of Beatrice Wood and Stephanie.

❧ *Aging* ❧

Twenty tomorrow—How old that seems. A
teenager no longer. Still, as long as I'm
not 25 I'll get by. And I know one thing:
I'm certainly going to make hay in the next
three years. After that I won't care!

Thirty tomorrow—How terrifying that sounds
now. I believe I'll go right out and buy
that lovely Jade dinner ring. After 50 I
won't care for those things!

Fifty tomorrow—Is that really old? No,
it's not even middle aged anymore. You're
all right as long as you keep your girlish
figure. Men don't quit admiring you until
you're 60!

Sixty tomorrow—Heavens I could rank as a
dowager. I don't feel it and I don't look
it. It's not your numerical age that counts
anyway. I think you're not old anymore till
you're 70 or even 80!

Eighty tomorrow—Well I don't mind being 80
as long as I'm not 90. As a matter of fact
you don't have much sense until you're 80.
You're much more interesting. I'll take that
trip to Bermuda, now. I might as well have a
good time till I'm 90!

Ninety tomorrow—I suppose it is all in the
way you look at it!

One Hundred tomorrow—But I'm still not too
old to keep looking!

—Addie Hutmacher

৯

THE FREEDOM TO *BE* IN OLD AGE

The "young at heart" feeling described by Beatrice, Billy and Addie, and many centenarians and others of advanced age is often accompanied by an inner sense of liberty. "I think we become less concerned about what other people think of us or how they view us, and so we are freer, in that sense, in old age," Hedvig Peterson suggests. "Our personal identity is not so tied to external things in life, such as work or raising a family or our spouse. We could look upon this time as we grow old, unfortunately often alone, as an opportunity to explore other ways of being, other facets of our personality, and other interests than those that have taken up the bulk of our years."

This newfound freedom as we age could mean a change from years of conformity, of doing what was expected. It could be expressed in unusual ways, such as wearing a particular style of clothing, as Beatrice does, or wearing trendy styles and bright colors like Billy, who wears a purple sweatsuit and black Reeboks when out on errands. Others like Addie may prefer to continue along the same path they always traveled because that's what pleases and suits them. For some, it could be a time of settling down, perhaps developing an interest in conservatism to try that out if they have lived their lives rather unconventionally. Whatever the style, the point is that there exists a freedom to be and to behave as one wishes in old age that should be encouraged and supported for our elders and for ourselves as we age because it's interesting, fun, and psychologically healthy.

"I think that's true," comments the psychiatrist, Helen Langner, M.D., of Milford, Connecticut. "In old age, there's often a sense of personal freedom because there's less pressure of a career or the responsibilities of work or raising a family. It can, and should, be a time for people to do the things that are important to them and a time to enjoy."

At 101, Dr. Langner enjoys the freedom to pursue interests of importance to her, in addition to the field of psychiatry, to which she has dedicated her life. She tells that the past twenty-five years since retirement from her full-time practice have afforded her the best of both worlds: continuing her vocation part-time and devoting time to her avocation as well. "Living long can provide an opportunity to do new things or to resume an interest one didn't have time for during one's working years or while being a homemaker. It's not only enjoyable and fulfilling," she reiterates, "it's also very good for mental health, and a good prescription for aging well."

Dr. Langner confirms what others have suggested: that these "bonus years" can be a time of accomplishment and achievement and creativity; a time to more widely expand what a person is capable of being or is interested in doing but wasn't able to develop in earlier years. For instance, there are interests that can be deferred until later in life, such as learning to paint or to play a musical instrument or joining a singing group or taking up photography or gardening or joining a discussion group at the library or doing volunteer work or taking a course of study, perhaps auditing courses at local colleges or traveling to Elderhostel programs that combine travel and learning. "There are so many choices that are appropriate to a person's later years and that take less physical effort yet at the same time are very good for keeping active and involved and mentally stimulated," Dr. Langner says encouragingly.

From her own experience, Dr. Langner knows how the pressures of a career and what it takes to succeed in one's working life can be all-consuming at younger ages. As only the fourth woman to graduate from Yale University's Medical School in 1922, she began her career "at a time when the field of psychiatry was new and when women in the medical profession were rare."

🙠

"I attended high school in Connecticut and wanted to major in the natural sciences in college, but no school in Connecticut would accept women in this course of study at that time," she explains. Family friends then invited her to live with them in New York City to enable Helen to attend Hunter College, an offer she says she gladly accepted. In 1914, she graduated and taught biology for four years to earn money for medical school. After completing her residency in psychiatry, she traveled to other states to find work, establishing child psychiatry clinics in Virginia and Indiana, moving on as the clinics subsequently became headed by male physicians. During World War II, she substituted for many of her colleagues who were called to military service.

Much of Dr. Langner's focus during her long career has been in the area of child psychiatry. She served for a time as school psychiatrist for the New York City Department of Education, taught clinical psychiatry at Cornell University Medical School, and was resident psychiatrist at

Vassar College. Beginning in the 1940s, she established a private practice in New York City, commuting by train each day from her home in Milford, until retiring from full-time practice at the age of seventy-six. Since then, she has continued to work part-time in psychiatric positions in Milford, including as a consultant to the Milford Health Department and the Milford Hospital.

Over the years, she has seen Milford grow to a small city. Given the "luxury of time," Dr. Langner then turned her attention to preserving the natural beauty and historic landmarks of Milford that have been threatened repeatedly by burgeoning commercial development of the area. "If you work for conservation, you are working for health," the centenarian believes. She has served for many years on the Milford Historical Society board and remains active in many conservation groups. Her success in achieving results in environmental and historic preservation has been a major contribution to the community. Presently, she is engaged in efforts to save that area of Connecticut from further commercial development. Dr. Langner attends meetings, writes letters in support of or in protest to current issues, and is an outspoken proponent for what she believes is right. "I am very strong about this," she says, then adds unpretentiously, "and I'm glad to be a little useful."

Dr. Langner continues to participate in alumni activities at both Yale and Hunter college, and regularly attends the annual alumni weekend at the Yale School of Medicine. "I am interested in the scientific symposia and lectures," she says. "I like to keep abreast of the current issues in medicine." Of her seventieth reunion in 1992, she remarked, "I was the only one left to represent my class, and since I had taught for four years before entering medical school, I think I was the oldest one in the class."

In June 1992, Hunter College observed her centennial year by awarding her an honorary doctor of science degree at its commencement ceremony. "The Alumni Association has been very good to me," Dr. Langner acknowledges. "They have a chapter in New Haven, and they called attention to the college of my 100th birthday. I am appreciative of the efforts of the grads of my alma mater for their interest." She tells this anecdote of the event: "The college sent a limousine to take me to New York for the ceremony. On the way, the dean called to ask if I were all right." In the long list of firsts in her lifetime, Dr. Langner says, bemused, "This was the first time I had ever talked on a car phone." At the ceremony, she was quoted as saying, "I am grateful to be alive and to have the wit to enjoy the occasion."

"To describe her personally, I would say she is the type of older woman as we think of Katharine Hepburn at her best—independent, strong-minded—not embittered by the male domination of her field during her career and very self-possessed and original." says Kathi McDonnell-Bissell, Executive Director of Milford Elderly Services. Dr. Langner is a centenarian who continues to exude intelligence and enthusiasm; she is another who is not jaded by life but who remains open to new experiences and who continues to live her life with integrity to her ideals while keeping a sense of humor. "Over the years, we have watched her walking purposefully through town and—although now with a cane—on her way to a meeting, perhaps, or to the library or up the hill to the hospital or to the Board of Health when called for a consultation," Kathi relates with admiration.

Helen Langner continues to live in her family home, where she grew up, within sight of Long Island Sound, in an area of the East Coast she wants to see preserved for others to know. "I enjoy my interests, but I don't have much time for leisure," she says. "It's a good time to be alive and to understand and be involved in what's going on."

To inaugurate her second century, Dr. Langner adds that she decided she should present a new image, so after all the celebrations were over, she got her hair cut, had a permanent, and bought a new dress.

THE CENTENARIAN JOURNEY

The first centenarian to attract real public interest was the American painter Grandma Moses, whose achievements at an advanced age received national recognition. Both her life and her painting have come to exemplify the possibilities for personal fulfillment in later life. Grandma Moses, whose given name was Anna Mary Robertson, began painting in her mid-seventies and continued producing and selling her work until the age of 101. At the time of her death in 1961, today's centenarians were just embarking on their own journey into advanced age.

"Grandma Moses could have been what people today would term our role model," says Billy Earley. "The thought occurred to me after seeing a dramatization of her life in the spring of 1989 when I was one hundred and a half, a play called *Grandma Moses: An American Primi-*

❧ *Dr. Helen Langner at age 100. "This is an award winning photograph,"*
she remarked. "I think it won an award because it caught every wrinkle!"
Photograph by Bill Treloar. Photo reprinted with the permission of
The Milford Citizen, Milford, CT.

tive. Sixteen of us from the Arizona Century Club got together to attend a matinee performance in Scottsdale at the beginning of the play's nationwide tour.

"Cloris Leachman was outstanding in the role of Grandma Moses. She is an Academy Award-winning actress, so we didn't expect a poor performance, but we were surprised by how well she portrayed the positive side of living long. During the play, Ms. Leachman aged from forty-five to 101 years; in fact, she looked older than I do.

"Coincidentally, it was her sixty-third birthday, so we gave a birthday tea in her honor after the play and invited the audience to attend. We presented her with a 'future centenarian' T-shirt (pink with white letters) and a plaque designating Ms. Leachman as an honorary member of our group. She said it was her best birthday celebration to date."

As a special surprise, the Century Club invited octogenarian Rose Schwartz, Ms. Leachman's first dance instructor from her early years as a performer, who now lives in Sun City. She and Cloris embraced and reminisced, with Cloris crediting Rose for having taught her "all her moves." When they did an impromptu dance routine, they were still very much in unison.

As a result of studying and performing this role, Cloris Leachman remarked: "I've changed my attitude about what it means to age. Some people, even at a very great age, bring color and mastery to their lives. That's what I've tried to do, too. I'm looking forward now to my next stage of life."

❧

The mastery in later life that Cloris Leachman refers to is part of what geriatrition Dr. Walter M. Bortz II calls "self-efficacy." He considers it to be the "final identifying element to aging successfully.

" 'Self-efficacy' is having confidence in what you are doing at any age and having a coping capacity to keep on doing it while adapting to changing circumstances," he explains. The term was coined by the psychology professor Albert Bandura of Stanford University, a pioneering researcher and teacher in the psychology of behavior. Although he developed the "self-efficacy theory" and has written extensively about it, he has not focused his study on aging, where an understanding of self-efficacy is most helpful, Dr. Bortz believes. Dr. Bortz has incorporated it into his formula for aging well in his book *We Live Too Short and Die Too Long: How to Achieve and Enjoy Your Natural 100-Year-Plus Life Span.*

✃ *Arizona Centenarians celebrating Cloris Leachman's birthday.*
From left to right: Marie Puls, Billy Earley, Katherine Case, Esther Johnson.
Behind from left: Hedvig Peterson, Mabel Shaw, Cloris Leachman, Lizzie Davis.
Photograph by Jim McHugh, used with permission from PEOPLE Weekly, 1989,
''Painting a New Face on Old Age.''

"Just as a biomedical understanding of muscle loss and regeneration necessitates a physical program for minimizing such losses during aging, for example, self-efficacy calls for establishing principles for successfully coping with changes at the psychological level," Dr. Bortz says. "Bandura's research explores how each of us develops and maintains self-efficacy. As centenarians illustrate, it is never too late; we need to continually renew the skills of self-efficacy over an entire lifetime if the challenges of aging are to be met."

Billy Earley stands out in this regard. Over the past few years she has become legally blind, but that hasn't stopped her. Billy has been able to accept this limitation and adjust her life so that she may continue to be active volunteering and in other pursuits that interest her. Billy asks her daughter to keep her closet arranged so that each outfit is separated from the next—"so I can keep the colors straight," she tells. She wants to be able to dress appropriately on her own and leave as her schedule dictates. With Angie's help, she keeps her thick address book updated so she can keep in touch with a wide range of acquaintances and friends and has memorized several of the telephone numbers so she can make calls herself while Angie is at work. Billy can call upon many friends for transportation to get where she needs to go. "I do these things so I can keep being Billy," she says. In that one sentence, she shows us what self-efficacy and some centenarians are all about.

Centenarians are long-distance travelers, speaking to us from the pinnacle of old age. Researchers, medical scientists and laypeople are all learning from them.

Leonard W. Poon, Ph.D., director of the Gerontology Center and Professor of Psychology at the University of Georgia, is at the forefront of current scientific research regarding centenarians. Dr. Poon and colleagues at the University of Georgia and the Medical College of Georgia have been studying a group of approximately ninety-six centenarians living independently in the state; this in-depth and interdisciplinary study is funded by a grant from the National Institute of Mental Health. Many of their carefully researched findings bear out what laypeople and caregivers have observed from personal associations with centenarians and what people working the field of aging services, who have spent time with centenarians, have come to know through experience.

"The traits that centenarians have in common, which seem to contribute to their longevity, are not as might be expected," Dr. Poon reported in a "20/20" television interview with Hugh Downs in 1992. It's not so much having physical characteristics in common, say the researchers, such as coming from a family of long-lived persons, or certain dietary habits or exercise regime. Rather, the common traits have to do with what could be considered part of a person's personality and psychology: "optimism, engagement or commitment to something they are interested in, activity or mobility, and the ability to adapt to loss."

Discussing these findings in a July 1993 "20/20" follow-up to the program, Barbara Walters commented, "You know, the thing that interested me the most, because we always hear diet and exercise, is that it's optimism and good humor and keeping busy, engagement, and accepting loss." Added Hugh Downs: "Flexibility and loss acceptance. It may be difficult to do, but these people do it."

It is very useful and encouraging to have this major study by Dr.

Poon and prominent researchers. Their work calls attention to and supports the importance of a person's individual psychology in living. This is great news, indeed, since personality and psychology are something each of us can do something with and about, adding another piece to the puzzle of longevity.

Taking all of this into account, along with many examples of centenarians in this book and the stories of their lives, what seems to be the most pronounced attribute of centenarians' personalities is self-determination: self-efficacy and a sense of self-worth and self-esteem that gives people of advanced age the incentive to find the reasons, the courage, and the will to continue living in the face of challenges or circumstances that could, instead, incline a person to give up. Centenarians, in general, hold many values dear, as we have seen, including a concern for others. What is so outstanding and illuminating is that even at very great age, centenarians also exhibit a healthy regard for themselves.

Elva Sholes of Glendale, Arizona, is representational. A bright, lively, sociable woman, this petite 100-year-old is far from frail, but she does have a vision impairment, so common in centenarians. Nevertheless, she has lived alone in a trailer park since her husband's death several years ago, and she lives nicely. She cooks and cares for herself, with some assistance in cleaning. "My niece calls every afternoon to check if I need anything. Every Saturday, she comes to help with things I can't see to do; she handles the bill paying and drives me to the grocery store. Her husband is a big help, too. He makes repairs when needed and does the outside work."

Elva is in control of her life. Her self-determination is evident in her life-style; it's something she has been working at for quite some time. She has cultivated a wide range of friends and makes new friends also, by reaching out to others. For example, Elva calls—she doesn't sit and wait for people to contact her; she invites people for lunch or for a visit. In short, Elva is pro-active and yet she handles her social life in a very refined, ladylike manner, successfully combining the current mode of action with the "old-fashioned" mores of her youth.

"I've never had a lot of money," she tells, "but I've lived comfortably." Elva, who was born in the Ozarks of Missouri, lived in several states throughout the Midwest and Southwest before retiring to Arizona with her third husband. "When we met, I was working as a governess for a family in Texas," she says. Although she has no children of her own, Elva has the support of her two stepchildren, who live in neighboring states and visit frequently. The closeness of their relationship is reflected in her speaking—she refers to them as her son and daughter and to their children as her grandchildren. Her favorite birthday gift, made by her granddaughter, was a white T-shirt with "Happy 100th" written in gold glitter. She wears it proudly.

Elva is a contemporary woman, both in her demeanor and her thinking. "I go out someplace everyday," she says with enthusiasm. "I always have something planned. On Fridays, I go for dinner with a friend of many years. We go for pizza or a taco. On the other days, I go to luncheons given by my church or here at the clubhouse at the trailer park or to a restaurant with friends or to their homes; at times, I entertain here. I also attend meetings of the organizations I'm involved with, and every Sunday, without fail, a friend picks me up and takes me to church.

"I belong to a church circle," she continues, "and I go to every gathering. I've had many a member—twenty and thirty years younger—tell me that she has gotten up on the day of the meeting and felt achy and not felt like going but would then think of me, knowing that I would be there, and say to herself, 'If Elva can do it at her age, I can too.' So many people have told me I am an inspiration to them in this regard. I'm glad. I love people."

There are numerous models of living a good life at 100 plus: centenarians who are in good health, who pursue interests, who maintain a curiosity for the world and a concern for others, and who enjoy contemporary life. These factors, coupled with their particular brand of self-determination, make a powerful life force.

Extending this concept, we can draw inspiration, too, from recognizing that a feeling of personal inner freedom can be enhanced with age, and, moreover, that a person's essence—and spirit—and life principle can remain vital to a very great age if mental and physical health hold up reasonably well. Centenarians demonstrate that they continue to feel emotion, happiness, enthusiasm, and passion for their causes and interests for as long as health permits: for many to the very end of their lives. This further refutes the depressing, discouraging and frightening stereotype of only apathy and disinterest in living in advanced age. In turn, centenarians' personal psychology, it seems, distinguishes many of these survivors, bolsters their courage, and fuels their will to live.

✤ *Elva Sholes dancing with her stepson at her*
100th birthday celebration. Photo courtesy of Elva Sholes.

Certainly there are and will continue to be people for whom old age is a burden or a bane. Conspicuous by their absence from this book are the greater numbers of centenarians who unfortunately are too frail or who were not able, mentally or physically, to respond or to take an interest in participating. Also noteworthy, however, are a few who although healthy, said they were simply to busy too give any time to participating or who had already given so many interviews that they were tired of doing them!

While it is true that centenarians today who are actively engaged in life and living are the exceptions for their generation, given their examples of what is possible, our goal could be for a time to come when living long and living well is the rule, not the exception.

ॐ

EXCELLENCE IN AGING

Future centenarians, nonagenarians, octogenarians, and septuagenar-
ians (those in their nineties, eighties, and seventies, respectively)
consider going beyond aging gracefully—to aging excellently!

We are inundated nowadays with information telling us how to
achieve excellence in various aspects of our lives with an abundance
of self-help books, "how-to" books, magazine and newspaper articles,
audio and video tapes, and lectures and seminars. In a society that
prides itself on seeking the best of human potential—from our personal
lives to careers to marriage to parenting—why stop there? It's time to
add aging to the roster and to seek excellence in the way we live our
lives in our later years: beyond the traditional retirement years, and into
the new-found bonus years of advanced age.

The current interest in health and longevity has spawned an out-
pouring of information and material, too, on the physical aspects of
aging and what we can do to take the best possible care of ourselves
as we age. Armed with this knowledge, we are all more aware of the
potential for living longer and healthier lives; and if we choose to try,
our chances to succeed in living long may actually be increased.

If we aspire to longevity, then we owe it to ourselves to also strive
to be comfortable with aging and to strive to be happy in old age. Our
third age of life is a time to be utilized and to be made worthwhile, not
just to be dreaded and lamented, many who have lived the longest
advise us. By approaching it with gusto and spirit and realism—neither
glorifying nor vilifying this time of our lives—we can make the most
of our longevity. To do otherwise is selling ourselves short.

Along with the awareness of the potential for living longer lives and
even living to very advanced age, in order to be content with ourselves
as we age, we need to develop an acceptance of aging as a natural part
of life's process in which we will be playing a major role by living long.
As one centenarian put it: "Throughout my life, I have always tried to
be happy with where I'm stopped at."

To help us prepare for a good old age, we also need to develop a cultural mind-set in our society, as well as an individual one, of an acceptance of aging and of old age, itself; and an acceptance of the presence
of old people in our society. At present, we Americans seem to be living
a paradox. On the one hand, we are interested in and are searching for

ways to live longer, healthier lives, and we lead the world in biomedical and genetic research in longevity. On the other hand, we are unwilling, individually and collectively, to recognize the old age that comes along with the achievement of living long. We decry the process of aging, are bored by the serious side of it and the challenges to be met, are scared to think about our own later years, and secretly abhor the reminders before us of our years to come. It is as though we harbor a romanticized notion of living long, thinking it will be an extension of how we have lived in previous decades or that somehow we will escape or be spared the downside of longevity.

This wishful thinking runs contrary to what those who have experienced living long advise. "Face the facts early," and prepare, both physically and financially, for the possibility of living to advanced age, centenarians recommend. "To most of us in my generation, living long came as a surprise," Louis Kelly remarked. "Younger people today have the advantage of preparing for their futures—and that includes old age."

As a nation we need to start thinking about living to advanced age and devising was to make these years pleasurable. This is important to each of us because our own lifestyles in old age may be influenced by how society views us. Accepting a cultural view of old age as a miserable time, for instance, a person growing older could adopt that position, behave accordingly, and come to believe it is true. Figuratively speaking, it would be like wearing a mask and then having your face grow to fit it, further perpetuating the image. Many centenarians, however, seem to have never accepted this line of reasoning, or they have moved past it to achieve a greater individualism that refutes society's negative view of old age. Through the examples of their daily lives, many centenarians are saying "NO!" to the negative stereotype of people of advanced years. They are breaking the mold—surpassing the expectations—and are enjoying doing it.

The manner in which some centenarians have continued to enjoy life in advanced age suggests a trend to a positive approach to aging for the 1990's and the next century. "Perhaps what we need is an age revolution," quips Billy Earley, only half in jest.

Participating in shaping this trend is something to contemplate for those now in their fifties, and the baby boom generation following immediately behind them. "The Times They Are A-Changin'" (Bob Dylan, 1963) is again an apt concept (this time around at the other end of life's spectrum) for these two generations of Americans who wit-nessed and influenced so much social and political change in their youth.

Recently, encouraging illustrations of a nucleus of this trend, and a shift away from a narrow societal focus on youth, have come from the industry most obsessed with youth and most intolerant of aging; to wit: Fashion designer Calvin Klein has stated that the 1990s are about "being healthy, accepting lines and wrinkles"—accepting one's aging; older models are now appearing in fashion ads and magazines; women in their fifties, instead of being ignored by advertisers, are now being hailed as in their "Prime Time" and at "the Age of Elegance"; and supermodel Lauren Hutton, at fifty, is in demand once again. She says she is "headed to ninety" and offers herself as a role model through the next four decades. Along with others, Ms. Hutton predicts a cul-tural change in America in its acceptance of aging and the aged because of the demographics (and the proclivities) of her generation and the next.

Bear in mind these statistics: By the year 2000, nearly thirty-four million Americans will be over sixty-five and will make up 25 percent of the population. In the next thirty years there will be a 100 percent increase in the number of Americans eighty-five and over. And predic-tions continue to abound that at least half of the baby boom genera-tion (seventy-six million strong, who once had as their motto: "Don't trust anyone over thirty!") can look forward to living into their eight-ies and nineties—with a million or more living to be 100.

People in their early fifties are often just beginning to be concerned about health, security and the quality of life that will accompany their future years. Perhaps they are beginning to have an inkling, too, of the need also for social and policy changes that will improve the well-being and welfare of older Americans. This new awareness is sometimes brought about because of their experience with their own parents who are grappling with growing old with little outside assistance or interest—and no road maps to this new era of longevity in America.

From the Wish List of contemporary centenarians, we see that the basics for a good old age are potentially lacking for a great many Americans. Our eldest citizens have done us a service by alerting us to what needs our attention now and what we should prepare for, both individually and as a society, for the future. At the very least we need to begin with a realization of what old age is like today, so we can bring about a change for the better. Many very old people show us that the will and the spirit to live long endures. What is not so evident is that we as a society need to supply the support and the resources as our contribution to their old age, and ultimately to our own.

An improved quality of life in old age for Americans is possible to attain with a committed effort from individuals, communities, policymakers, the medical profession, and, of course, from elders themselves. From the medical profession we need a variety of help, including addressing the care and treatment of older adults and the development of the specialty of geriatric medicine as one on a par with other specialties in importance, training, research, and expertise. From government and policymakers, America needs a long-term care policy that provides security and options for the kinds of care often required in advanced age, and healthy and creative and affordable living environments. From family members and caregivers, we need understanding and compassion and often assistance with daily living as we grow old. And from our communities and society at large, we need acceptance and a place of respect and welcome. Is it worth this effort? Once again, the answer from all of us who seek longevity must be a resounding *yes*.

Americans could develop a cultural ethic of excellence in aging: of living long and also enjoying a good quality of life, and happiness, in old age. To do so would be to thwart the doomsayers who predict that the aging of America will be a disastrous time. To do so would be to produce a new phenomenon for the twenty-first century. If you will, suspend your skepticism for a moment and—Imagine.

☙

Old age holds the potential for being an interesting time of life, centenarians report. Given the right circumstances, it can be wonderful to live long, many say. The wisdom they share is that we should all live life to the fullest, regardless of how many years we live, and do so with enthusiasm. If we live as though we were going to live for 100 years, we will improve whatever time we do have by taking good care of ourselves and by not giving up on life along the way. And in the process of improving our own years, we will set a good example for younger generations to follow. To accomplish all this, Americans need to develop a new psychology of aging along with a new persona in old age, modeling the centenarian spirit.

❧ 11 ❧

Triumph of The Spirit

THERE are thousands of contemporary centenarians giving inspiration for our future. In every part of the country, present-day centenarians, who remain in good health, are living engaging lives. It is their *spirit* comprised of the desire and the courage and the determination to keep going, that is the hallmark of those who live long and who continue to enjoy life. These centenarians exhibit a spirit that is leading us toward a new definition of old age itself and that is pointing toward a new life-style in advanced age. This spirit is the elixir, the essential principle, that when coupled with good health, makes longevity viable and vibrant.

❧

THE CENTENARIAN SPIRIT

The spirit of these centenarians is their spark of life. It is their spirit that enables them to make the most of the days and years God has given them. It is their spirit that creates aliveness out of everything they do, both big and small things of daily life: whether being with family, reading the newspaper or watching the news or "the soaps," gardening, a morning at the hair salon, exercising, reading books, visiting with friends, taking trips, taking care of their health, volunteering for community projects, or sharing their lives with others through oral histories and family chronicles, to name a few. It is their spirit that keeps these 100-year-olds creatively living and that accounts for the unexpected in people of great age. Centenarians are full of surprises.

It is heartening to learn what some of those introduced in this book have been doing while its writing was in process. Also, new centenarians have made themselves known along the way.

❧

As the highlight of her 100th birthday celebration in February 1994, Myrtle Little attended a Phoenix Suns basketball game at the city's American West Arena. The tickets and a Suns' T-shirt were gifts from her church congregation. Myrtle's birthday was announced and her picture was telecast on the stadium screen while the crowd sang "Happy Birthday" to this special fan. "I never knew my mother liked sports until five years ago," her son Wayne, who accompanied her, said.

"The first thing I do when I get the paper every morning is pull out the sports page and read it," Myrtle countered. "I watch every game that is televised and the others I listen to on the radio. I always have, with the Suns, since before they had a good team and became popular." Myrtle has made her home for the past seventeen years in an apartment at a city housing complex for seniors. "Sometimes a friend comes over and we watch together. I would have to say that Charles Barkley is my favorite player," she adds. "I think Paul Westphal is a good coach and a gentleman, and he's good looking, too."

❧

To 103-year-old Ollie Pike, the best looking man is her idol, country singer Merle Haggard. "He's as handsome as all get out! I got the surprise of my life," she says, "when my granddaughter, Jessie, came home with tickets to his concert right here in Klamath Falls [Oregon]. I've been in love with him and his music since I was about eighty." Ollie has memorized all of Haggard's songs. "I have all of your records," she told the amazed singer when they met backstage just before the concert, early in 1994. "I play your records all the time, and my room is decorated with your pictures." Ollie is hard of hearing and her eyesight is poor; as she patted his knee, she explained, "I just wanted to touch him." Merle took her hand and held it while she repeated all her favor-

❧ *Myrtle Little at the America West Arena, rooting for her favorite basketball team—the Phoenix Suns, February 1994. Photo courtesy of Myrtle Little and her son Wayne.*

ite song titles to him. Then he was off, saying, "I gotta go play now." But shortly after beginning his performance he stopped and told the audience: "I dedicate this whole show to Ollie, my oldest fan."

"I just couldn't believe it, it was so exciting to meet him," Ollie said, sporting a new dress and shoes for the event. Was she attracted to his country music because it reminded her of her roots in the Ozark mountains of Arkansas? "No," she recalls, "I got to liking him when I lived for a while with my son; my grandson played his records all the time.

I became a fan and later got my own collection after I moved in with my granddaughter, Jessie. Everyone in the family now gives me records or pictures of him for gifts 'cause they know I'll like 'em." Jessie adds, "I had a hard time convincing her to leave—she wanted to stay for the second show."

⁊

Billy Earley took a trip to Memphis, Tennessee and Graceland in April 1994 with her daughter Angie. "I liked Elvis Presley's music," she explained, "but I would never have thought of going there. But when I asked Angie where she would like to go for a week in the springtime, she said Graceland, so off we went. I'm glad we did, we had a good time. Angie had never seen the South and it was in full bloom and beautiful. We took a river boat cruise on the Mississippi and just enjoyed a leisurely week. As 105, I'm still wheeling and dealing," she reports.

Billy confides how she raised the money for her "big trip" to the 1993 presidential inauguration by foregoing gifts on her 104th birthday in December 1992. "As soon as President Clinton was elected—I voted, of course—I decided I wanted to attend his inauguration, so I told all my friends and family that I would rather have the money toward the trip to Washington than gifts and a party for my birthday. I called it my inaugural fund," she says with satisfaction. "I told everyone a contribution would be much nicer and more meaningful than another nightgown or bottle of perfume. I had a wonderful birthday and had something great to look forward to."

As is her custom each year, during the summer and fall of 1993, Billy took several smaller trips around Arizona to visit friends. "I also spent a few days at the Grand Canyon and I went to New Mexico," she tells. "We flew to Albuquerque and then went on to Taos and Los Alamos. My friend there has a Ph.D. in anthropology, a fascination of mine; he showed us all around the area. It was a wonderful experience."

Billy continues to be active in her church, the Woman's Club, the Historical Society and the Town Improvement Committee. "She's the pride of Florence," friends say as she continues to receive awards and honors for her contributions to historic preservation and the community. "I'm the volunteer of the century," Billy responds. "I continue to do the kinds of things I've always been interested in—maybe a little differently—but I'm still doing!"

In July, 1994, Billy was selected as one of the recipients of the annual *12 Who Care* award, to be presented at a black tie gala by Phoenix Channel 12 TV and a volunteer organization of business and professional men affiliated with St. Luke's Medical Center, one of the oldest in the Southwest. This prestigious tradition honors twelve individuals who have contributed outstanding volunteer service to improve the quality of life for people in their Arizona communities. Coming as a complete surprise to Billy, this recognition is the culmination of her many decades of significant volunteer efforts.

Billy is planning her "big trip" for 1994 to New York City in the fall. Included in her agenda is a special day "for old time's sake. I used to love to take the afternoon ferry to Staten Island when I was young," she reminisces, "and then ride back, watching the lights come on in the city. Although I won't be able to see them clearly now, I'll still feel the thrill. Then we're going to the Rainbow Room for dinner; it's been re-done and is back in vogue. It should exciting to be there."

❧

Meanwhile, in New York, catching up with Claire Willi at 103, she reports that a fall has caused her to change her exercise pattern. Claire now rides a stationary bicycle instead of attending the exercise classes near her apartment, but she still works on her balance by doing deep knee bends and keeps her posture erect with shoulder rolls. "Exercise gives you life," Claire says. "And besides, it's fun." She still takes walks in nearby Central Park in good weather and is as particular as ever about her appearance, going to the hairdresser regularly and her manicurist. "It's a hard job looking nice," she says jokingly. Claire's sense of humor and fun are as lively as ever. "She loves to laugh," a friend tells. Claire adds, "I'm a happy old lady."

❧

In honor of his 100th birthday, Angelo Maltas took a day trip from his home in Connecticut to visit the recently constructed Ellis Island Memorial in New York harbor. He found his name on the wall commemorating those who passed through the immigration center to the United States when both he and the country were much younger. "Ellis Island looks very much the same as I remembered it," Angelo says. "I found the bench where I sat. It brought back a lot of memories, including that of my first American food. A lady gave me apple pie and coffee."

❧ *Angelo Maltas standing next to his name at the Ellis Island Memorial, 1991.*
Photo courtesy of the Maltas family.

Angelo enjoyed the trip with his family but says he would like to have seen the dates of arrival included along with the names on the memorial. "I suppose that because there are so many names, it would have been difficult to find room for the dates," he surmises, "or perhaps it would have cost too much. Yet, I believe that anything's possible, if you believe in God and work to make it happen."

Angelo is still very involved in the Greek Orthodox Church services and other activities in the Greek community in Bridgeport, Connecticut. At 102 and no longer able to stand for long periods of time by the candle offering, the church has made a new place for him, seated by the door to greet people as they arrive for Sunday Mass.

At home with his daughter, Katherine, and son-in-law, Nick, Angelo tells, "I continue to have the run of the house. My family is very good to me." Ever considerate and sensible, though, he adds, "I try to avoid making any trouble. I stay out of the way, at times, and I keep quiet when I should. After all, they're a married couple and they have their life too. It shouldn't all revolve around me." For Angelo and his family, including his son, John, who visits frequently and is an active participant with his father in the church and Greek community, this is a perfect working out.

Angelo looks forward to the future. "If I live to be 120, I'll learn something new every day."

ꙮ

In nearby Milford, Connecticut, Dr. Helen Langner continues to live alone in her family home. With the assistance of an aide/secretary, each morning she participates in the aspects of the work that has captured her attention since she was young. "To me, medicine is the most interesting thing in the world," she declares. Dr. Langner continues to consult at the Milford Hospital once or twice a week. "I guess I'm an institution there," she says with subtle humor. "They have my portrait hanging in the corridor." She also works tirelessly on her avocation, environmental causes to preserve the beauty of the Connecticut coastline and the historical buildings in her hometown for future generations. For diversion, Dr. Langner enjoys attending book discussions at the public library, a busy, modern building a hundred yards or so from her home. Her brother, Gus, who is ninety, lives across the marsh, just a short walk from her home. "Since I now have to use two canes to get around, he most often comes to visit me," she says, adding, with pride, "He still swims three times a week.

"I'm never bored, and I don't get lonely," Dr. Langner says of her life.

ꙮ

Richard Johnson has made two trips since turning 100 to visit his sister in Bermuda for her "ninetysomething" birthdays. At 103, he was an extra in the 1992 movie *School Ties*, and enjoyed the opening party at a theater in Natick, Massachusetts, where he continues to live in his own home.

ꙮ

In Idaho, Irene Hazelbaker, at 100, was busy writing her autobiography on her personal computer; Frank Kleminski, meanwhile, spent the summer fishing at his cabin in a remote section of Wisconsin and flew back to Tucson for the winter. Ray Paul Nieto, at 101, sent a Valentine with a note saying, "I feel as good as I did fifty years ago." From Hazel Herring we hear, "Just wanted to let you know that at 103 I'm alive and well and looking forward to the book."

ॐ *Richard Johnson, age 103, at the local opening of the movie ''School Ties''*
in September 1992. Photograph by Ed Hopfmann. Photo reprinted with
permission from the Middlesex News, Framingham, MA.

·❦

Clyde Ice, at 101, attended the Reno Air Show for the eleventh year in a row. "As always, he stood out there near the field from the time the first plane took off in the morning until sundown," his son Howard tells. In the fall, Clyde again went hunting with his sons for deer and elk in Wyoming, and then settled down for the winter with his wife, "reading books, mostly." The following summer, he set out once again for South Dakota visiting with his sons and looking forward to more adventures with "the Flying Ices."

·❦

At 105, Alma Hauetter, an Arizona "snowbird," returned again to spend the winter with her family. Her friend, Mary Ogburn, at 105, continued to enjoy the friendships made at the adult day-care program at the Mesa Senior Center.

·❦

North Carolinian Dr. Henry Stenhouse, who ran for Congress in 1990 at the age of 100, was a guest on "The Tonight Show" before Johnny Carson retired and then finished writing a book based on his experiences in China before World War I. "I still go to parties at night and am planning a reunion in Denver with some old navy buddies," he said.

·❦

Hattie Allen, 103, addressed the annual convention of the Pioneers of Alaska in Palmer; she received a standing ovation. Hattie is proud to say that she still doesn't need glasses, takes no medication, and gets around by herself. She told the audience at the Hotel Captain Cook, "Young people need remember there's no such thing as 'can't.' Just make up your mind and work, and you can do anything."

·❦

In her 1990 Christmas letter, Helen Cope wrote from Connecticut: "This year I've been reaping the benefits of being a centenarian and it certainly is fun. I love all the interviews from different sources. Tomorrow, for instance, someone is coming to ask me about women getting the right to vote. I've also been interviewed about my experience as a social worker in Detroit during the Depression. I like to give these interviews because I don't think people understand how much motivated women could do in the early half of this century."

Her centenarian brother, Ted Gibson, joined Helen in Arizona in the spring of 1991, where she was visiting her stepson, and told of his travels by car with his son and daughter-in-law. They then went on to Lake Tahoe. The postcard he sent read: "It's all parties and picnics and fun up here!" Later in the year, both Ted and Helen had surgeries to correct medical problems. "I don't let it faze me," says Ted. Adds Helen, "I fell in June and cracked my hip, which kept me grounded for a couple of months. My wonderful young surgeon put a pin in to hold me together and now I'm on the go again, but carefully."

However, in her 1991 Christmas letter, in addition to an update on her activities for the year, Helen had to include: "I'm sorry to say I must give you sad news about my brother, Theodore. He died at home in Los Angeles at the age of 103. We'll all miss his loving presence among us, but everyone who knew him has such wonderful memories of him that we can comfort each other in our gratitude for the joy and love that he brought into our lives. I'm especially grateful that I had the first dance with him at my 100th birthday party. He always loved a party and his kindness and gallantry made every woman he talked to feel very special indeed."

·ᵡ·

Hedvig Peterson has arranged for the proceeds from her million-dollar lawsuit settlement to be used for charitable causes. At 101, her newfound wealth has not changed her life-style. She still carries on community activities, including her lifelong work with children in the public school. "I visit with them in their classrooms so they can meet someone who has lived 100 years," she says. "Being with the children makes me feel several years younger."

·ᵡ·

Gladys and Ben Pruitt of Springfield, Oregon, at 102 and 103, respectively, celebrated their seventy-ninth wedding anniversary with their children and other family members.

·ᵡ·

Pearl Sprague, 104, has been a widow for the past twenty-four years and lives alone in an apartment in Phoenix. She enjoys spending her time quietly, reading romance novels and watching "the soaps" on television. When her daughter recently moved her into a new apartment because the neighborhood where Pearl lived had become unsafe, she first asked her mother to move in with her. Pearl protested. "No way!" she replied emphatically. "I'm just not ready for that. Just let me live by myself. I enjoy my own company."

❧ *Pearl Sprague, as she appeared on the front cover of a special section*
on aging of the Arizona Republic shortly before her 104th birthday in February 1994.
Photograph by David Petkiewicz. Reprinted with permission from
The Arizona Republic.

❧ *Susie Cook with her son David, 1991. Photo courtesy of her daughter Margaret.*

Shortly before her 100th birthday, Suzie Cook of Elmswood, Nebraska, moved in with her daughter, but after a fall that broke her hip, she moved to a care center, where she has been a resident for the last three years. Nevertheless, Suzie has stayed active, walking for exercise, playing Scrabble, and gardening. Her eyesight is poor and she can read only with a magnifying glass, but she enjoys books on tape supplied by the Library for the Blind. Suzie entered one of her quilts in the county fair last year in the senior division, and won first prize. She takes delight in visits from her family and great-grandchildren, as well as trips by car with her daughter; she has made local news by flying with her son in his private plane to visit relatives in other areas of the state. At 103, Suzie says she is interested in participating to the fullest extent possible in whatever comes her way.

At 103, Robert Cushman of Yuma, Arizona, could be found knitting beautiful woolen scarves and other accessories, some of which he sold

✤ *Dr. Donald Warren at World Poultry Conference in Japan.*
Photo courtesy of Dr. Warren.

and some of which he gave away. He was still driving and lived alone in a trailer at the California border. A big man and a former U.S. Marshall, he seems an unlikely candidate for needlework. When asked how he learned to knit, this World War I veteran explained: "I was shot down during the war and was flat on my back for three months in a hospital in France. I had to do something, so I learned to knit. Now it's a hobby."

✤

For centenarian Donald Warren, Ph.D. of Fremont, California, no hobby generates quite the same spark as his seventy-year career as a poultry geneticist. He says, "I like to keep up-to-date with what's going on, even though I'm no longer doing research myself." At the age of ninety-nine, Dr. Warren traveled alone to Nagoya, Japan, where he was a special guest at the World Poultry Congress. "The congress takes place in different cities around the globe every few years," he explained. Dr. Warren has been attending them regularly for the past sixty years.

One of the leading figures in the field of poultry science, Dr. Warren recalls, "Chicken used to be a luxury; eggs, too, were dear." It is thanks in large part to Dr. Warren's work that poultry and eggs can be mass-produced, making them an affordable staple today. In September 1992, at the age of 102, he flew to Amsterdam to attend yet another World Poultry Congress. Since then he has continued to maintain contact with others in his field and follows their scientific progress.

·⁊⁰

Frederick Pohl, 101, of Westfield, Massachusetts, rather than continue an involvement in a lifelong career, chose to develop a second career. "I had been a teacher for many years, after graduating from Amherst College in 1911. I always urged my students to look beyond what they were doing and to look toward the future with the goal of excelling beyond their own expectations. At the age of fifty-four, I began living my own philosophy—I began to write."

During the second half of his life, Mr. Pohl became a recognized scholar and historian. He received critical acclaim for his latest book, *The New Columbus*, published in 1986 when he was ninety-seven. He then began work on a historical novel.

·⁊⁰

Eli Finn, 102, of Norwalk, Connecticut, continued taking history courses each semester at Fairfield University in Fairfield, Connecticut, successfully completing the spring semester of 1992. He looked forward to the fall but was disappointed that his scheduled August trip to Moscow, through the university, was canceled for lack of student participation.

·⁊⁰

At 103, Marjory Stoneman Douglas, the ever-conscientious environmentalist, publicly requested in the summer of 1994 that her name be removed from the Marjory Stoneman Douglas Environmental Act because recent proposed amendments, affecting farmers, would change the law in a way she does not approve.

·⁊⁰

The Delaney sisters, Sarah, 104, and Elizabeth, 102, have made news by becoming best-selling authors with their 1993 book, *Having Our Say: The Delaney Sisters' First 100 Years*, written with Amy Hill Hearth.

⁂

At 106, the theatrical producer/director George Abbott spent several months actively consulting on the Broadway revival of his 1955 hit play, *Damn Yankees*. He then attended several of the preview performances, participating in the final production and the opening night performance in March 1994, almost thirty-nine years after first directing the play. He has now accomplished his 125th career production, including those in his early days as an actor and a writer. Mr. Abbott is best known for hits such as this and for *Pajama Game* and *Pal Joey*. In a CNN interview, he told that he recently had the batteries in his pacemaker replaced. In June 1994 he celebrated his 107th birthday with a round of interviews regarding his work.

⁂

And finally, "future centenarian" Cloris Leachman again portrayed Grandma Moses in a new play, *Joy Ride: The True Story of Grandma Moses*, in Los Angeles in May and June of 1994. In it she aged from fifty to 100; a reviewer called Ms. Leachman's performance "magnificent." Of related interest, Rose Schwartz, now ninety, appeared as a guest on the television show *Live with Regis and Kathy Lee* where she did a dance routine with Kathy Lee similar to the lively steps she danced with her early student, Cloris, at their reunion five years ago. Rose still teaches aerobics classes three times a week. When Kathy Lee asked if it is difficult for older people to get into doing mild aerobic dancing after many years of inactivity, the vivacious Rose replied, "Not at all—people pick it right up."

⁂

The centenarian spirit shows through not only in action but in quiet ways too—in the very being of many centenarians. The great variation in the activities of centenarians depends on their circumstances: first, on their health—both physical and mental—and on their physical ability; second, on their financial resources and living environment; and third, on their life experiences. Given these qualifiers, they are doing what they can do. What matters is that they still want to do it.

⁂

After surviving a heart attack at eighty-one, Martha Knoke of Atlantic, Iowa, retired from the clothing store where she had worked for many years. She continued to work for the next six years baby-sitting for families in the neighborhood where she lived in her own home. As more and more friends her age went into nursing homes, she would visit them and then return home to mow her lawn, tend her flowers and garden, or bake bread. At ninety, she sold her home, had a garage sale of her belongings, and moved to Littleton, Colorado, to live with her only daughter, Anella. Throughout her nineties, her life in Colorado continued to be busy. "I love the mountains and I still enjoy working with my plants and flowers and I still bake bread," she said at 100. "The altitude affected the results at first, but I finally got the hang of it."

"Her favorite pastime is visiting with the neighborhood children," her daughter comments. "It's no accident that she enjoys a good life; she just keeps on the move and carries on to the best of her ability."

ॐ

When she was ninety-four, Anna Barth moved from Quincy, Illinois, where she had been living for twenty years with her two younger sisters, caring for their older brother. In her new home of Lincoln, Nebraska, she knew no one except her son and his family. Anna moved into an apartment building where there were several widows. She began cooking and inviting them for lunch or coffee, although she was much older than they were, and made new friends.

At 103, now a resident of Lincoln Lutheran Home, Anna keeps busy knitting for needy children. She also knits baby caps for hospitals and other charitable projects the home supports. Like many centenarians, Anna enjoys writing and receiving letters and corresponds regularly with about fifty people all over the United States, only a few of whom are relatives. Her daughter-in-law says, "She has always been a kind, helpful, considerate woman. I guess that's why she has so many friends. She always adjusts to every situation."

ॐ

As she has been all of her adult life, Mary Vandewege at 100, of Firth, Nebraska, continues as a homemaker and in doing things for her family. She lives in her own home and says, "I do my housework and cook dinner every day and my son comes and has dinner with me, which I enjoy. I also enjoy making my own dresses and crocheting afghans for my family." However, before thinking of Mary as a home-body, she adds that she can often be lured away from the home front by a fishing trip with any one of her eight children or by grandchildren and other members of her large family. "The last time we went this summer," she says, "I was the only one to catch a fish, and that's not a fish story."

∙ॐ

Bertha Bliven, of Salem, Oregon, has also been a homemaker all her life, as have many centenarians. Like Mary Vandewege, she continues to live alone in her own home. The mother of six children, her family, too, has been her focus. On her 100th birthday she presented each of her children with handwritten booklets giving the highlights of her life. As was her habit, Mrs. Bliven was up early on that special day. One of her daughters tells, "Mother still treats me like a little girl whenever I come to visit. How many kids can say that on their mother's 100th birthday she came to the bedroom door at 6:30 a.m. to announce, 'Breakfast is on the table!'"

∙ॐ

THE DAWNING OF THE AGE OF CENTENARIANS

The potential for so many Americans to reach the century mark in the foreseeable future prompted Jane Shure, information officer for the National Institute on Aging, to ask rhetorically in connection with the first national recognition day for centenarians in 1987, in Washington, D.C., "Is this the dawning of the Age of Centenarians?" The possibility of this new age of longevity is enticing for the generation that experienced the "Age of Aquarius" and others who would like to be able to look forward to a few or several more decades of living. An "Age of Centenarians" offers possibility as a philosophy of life, an approach to living long.

A number of scientists believe that people in general have the genetic potential to live to 100 and beyond. Presently, the upper life span is thought to be between 115 and 120 years. Over the last few years, the oldest person living at any given time in the United States has been between 114 and 118; the oldest person ever documented was 120 in Japan.

Although the quality of their *spirit* is a constant in the centenarians who are enjoying life at the pinnacle of old age, as discussed before, there is great variation in the physical and mental health of people who have reached the century mark. Many are no longer physically or mentally functional; others are in good health for their age; and an increasing number are in good health, period. Of the latter two groups, some have lived long because of medical interventions, usually during the past twenty to twenty-five years of their lives; for others it is a combination of their genetic makeup and a healthy life-style. And for some, there seems no explanation at all. Active centenarians do not espouse living long for its own sake, of merely adding length to life. To be alive without cognitive function, without "their marbles," or to be desperately ill or deteriorated is not living, most believe. They feel that staying healthy to be able to enjoy the extra years is what counts.

Overall, the future for longevity in America looks good; and, along with it, the means for maintaining the adequate mental and physical health to enjoy living long. The knowledge of the benefits of living healthier lifestyles—not smoking, eating healthy foods, and getting good nutrition, perhaps augmenting it with vitamin supplements, regular exercise, and getting enough relaxation and sleep—contributes significantly to an individual's opportunity to live long and well, doctors and researchers say. Many Americans are starting now to make these changes in favor of a healthier life. The near certainty of continued advances in medical science also bodes well for increased longevity. These anticipated advances include the promise of life extending drugs, genetic repairs for faulty disease-causing genes, hormone therapy, more drugs to combat and to slow the effects of Alzheimer's disease, the development of memory-enhancing drugs that would help people suffering from neurological disorders such as Parkinson's disease and strokes that impair mental functioning, "smart drugs" that would help retain mental acuity in healthy aging brains, and ever-improving surgical and diagnostic techniques such as laser surgery and MRI (magnetic resonance imaging).

This forecast of an increased life span is supported by numerous researchers. The only difference in their views seems to be over how long we can expect to live in the coming few decades. An in-depth article in *Fortune* magazine (February 21, 1994), "Why We Will Live Longer," summarizes, ". . .the way to bet is on lives that will increasingly stretch out toward ninety and beyond in the years ahead—with considerable potential on the upside."

Improvements in life-prolonging devices, such as pacemakers, are sure to come, along with high-technology assistive devices to help ameliorate the disabilities caused by vision impairment, hearing loss, and hindered mobility. According to inventor Raymond Kurzweil, who designed the music synthesizer used by blind musician Stevie Wonder,

  ⌐ৎ *Billy Earley at home on her exercise bicycle.*
Photograph by Tina Romano. Photo courtesy of Billy Earley.

in a speech "The End of Handicaps" delivered at the American Society on Aging's annual meeting in 1993, "Within the next two decades...the handicaps associated with the principal physical and sensory disabilities will be overcome through the judicious application of artificial intelligence." These high tech assistive devices will have a tremendous impact in alleviating some of the profound and common challenges to people of advanced age, and offer a significant improvement in the quality of life for those who live long. Some of the devices he foresees are hand-held reading machines (personal readers) to read printed text out loud (available by the end of this decade at a cost under $1,000), special glasses or lapel pins that will describe what comes into view, listening machines able to convert spoken words into visual displays, and "exoskeletal robotic devices" that will allow the wearer to walk and climb stairs.

In addition, the inventor believes that with the use of such devices, "prejudicial behavior toward persons with disabilities [and this applies to older people] such as treating them as incapable will disappear as technology makes disabilities less apparent. For example, in ten or fifteen years, when a deaf person can read what you are saying in their glasses, you may not even realize the person is deaf."

This is wonderful news. However, in order to take advantage of the present and future advances in medicine and in technology, older people need to have access to them and be able to afford them. This is, in part, a government policy and medical ethics issue. Suggestions of possible healthcare rationing based on age are chilling to the hopes of those who would like to live long and who might need medical intervention to enable them to do so. And, of course, both medical interventions and assistive devices need to be made affordable to help older people continue to function as independently as possible—an almost universal wish of people who live long.

Dr. Paul Rousseau, Chief of Geriatrics at the Veterans Medical Center in Phoenix, himself a member of the baby boom generation, says he would like to live to be 100. Like many of his colleagues, he thinks that while a person's genetic makeup is a factor, only half of a person's potential for longevity can be ascribed to it; the other half is within our control. He, too, believes that the objective should be to live healthier longer, so that a good quality of life can be maintained. What people need to do is develop a lifetime program of healthy living, he advises. With such an emphasis on healthier habits and life-styles, Dr.

Rousseau is optimistic that they will pay dividends in the years to come. This harkens back to what Billy Earley and other centenarians opined in chapter 1: "You start with what you inherited, and the rest is what you make of it."

Thomas J. Katsenes of Phoenix, who turned 100 on March 24, 1994, concurs, saying he owes his life and longevity to completely changing his life-style after a heart attack forty-four years ago. Prior to 1950, Thomas had been a hard-driving, success-oriented businessman, pursuing his goal of a better life for himself and a good life for his family,

·❧ *Thomas Katsenes shares a private moment with his wife Fannie, following the marriage of their son. Photo courtesy of Lori and Paul Katsenes.*

a goal he set out to achieve at the age of fifteen when he left Greece, alone, for America.

Thomas succeeded in building a successful insurance and real estate business with his wife, Fannie, and later their three sons. Following his recovery from the near fatal heart attack, and taking his doctor's advice, he shared the business responsibilities with them, relieving his stress, he tells. Thomas then limited his business activities to managing the family's real estate interests and devoted his energies to learning about and living a healthier lifestyle. Always active in the Greek church, where he was a cantor, Thomas became more involved and refocused his activities to non-business pursuits within the Greek community. He also made time for a social life, participating, with his family, in Greek national and regional organizations.

"Dad has always been a pretty accommodating guy," his son Paul tells. "If someone he respected said, 'This is what you need to do,' and he was convinced that the advice was right, he would do it. He's never been rigid in his thinking. He changes his mind to do the right thing." Looking back on his decision and his life since then, Thomas doesn't regret it and doesn't think he missed anything important. "I had many good years of working hard and I've had many good years with my family since then. I gained a lot," he says, with satisfaction.

.᠙᠊

Current research also buttresses the long-held position of Dr. Walter Bortz II and others that a lifelong program of physical exercise is as important a factor as any to aging well and healthfully. The new thinking postulates that it is never too late to start exercising to realize some benefits from it and that exercise should include some weight lifting (light weights) to increase muscle strength, along with aerobic exercise.

Collister Wheeler, D.D.S., of Portland, Oregon, is a centenarian with considerable experience in this area. Dr. Wheeler joined the Multnomah Athletic Club when he was eighteen. "I've been a member for eighty-two years," he says, "since 1911. Between 1912 and 1921, I was a championship canoeist and swimmer," he tells. "I first participated in the Master's tournaments [national and international competitions for amateur athletes] in 1912. Over the years of my dental practice, I exercised moderately, but did not participate in athletic competitions."

Then, after a fifty year hiatus, at the age of eighty-two, Collie, as he is known to his friends, began competing in the swimming and track and field competitions once again. He set world records for his age group, holding thirty-one in all, during his eighties and nineties. To Collie, his most relished victory came at the age of ninety, when he won the 220 yard dash over a former professional athlete in his age group.

"We went to New Zealand to the Master's ten years ago," says Frances, his second wife twenty years his junior, whom he married when he was eighty. He won medals in the swimming and track and field events, she tells with a great deal of pride and love in her voice. "At ninety-one, he was the oldest athlete there," adds Becky Nelson, membership director at the club. "He continues to be an inspiration to club members of all ages."

"At ninety, Collie could still do one-armed push-ups, at ninety-five he could still do chin-ups," says long-time friend and trainer at the club, octogenarian Joe LaPrinzi. "He has kept up swimming, too. Then at ninety-seven he stopped competing for lack of other participants and because his own performance disappointed him."

Realistically, Collie assesses his physical condition at 100. "I figure my strength is about 40 percent of what it used to be," he says. Disappointed? Sure. "But," he adds optimistically, "I've beaten the average life span by twenty years or more. I figure ten years of that is due to exercise and the other ten years to moderation," a principle he firmly believes in. "I've always been a middle-of-the-road person in my behavior," he explains. "I've never gone in for long-distance running or swimming. I'm not a fanatic about exercise, either. An hour two or three times a week is good. You keep in good shape, sleep better, eat better, and it helps your digestion. Frances and I are not fanatics on diets, either. We stay away from salt, sugar, cholesterol, and fats as much as possible and have a drink or two every night. I don't hesitate, though, to eat cake or pie or candy once in a while. It won't hurt you, it just won't help you, and it's a couple more calories to take off."

Collie is proud of his weight control. He weighs only three pounds more than he did when he enlisted in the navy in World War I. "I spent most of the war in a U.S. Navy training station in New York State," he tells. "By the end, I was a commissioned officer and ensign." During World War II, he was a commander in the navy. In 1950, he was on active duty in Washington, D.C., serving as a consultant during the Korean War, with the rank of captain. "In all, I had fifteen years of active service in the navy," he says. Collie and his friend, Biddle Combs, are the only two World War I veterans remaining in the Portland area.

❧ *Collister Wheeler at his 100th Birthday Party, 1992.*
Photo courtesy of Dr. and Mrs. Wheeler.

"Biddle still works in his insurance office every day," Collie says. "He'll turn 100 in October [1994]."

Speaking of his life at 100, Collie says, "I have a beautiful, loving wife, good friends, a club to go to for social events, as well as exercise [with 19,000 members Maltnomah is one of the largest in the country], and I'm spry enough," he adds with a laugh. "Frances sings in the club chorus, which performs at many of the nursing homes and retirement centers and at the VA Hospital."

From their apartment, a two-minute walk from the club, they over-look downtown Portland, with a clear view of snowcapped Mount Hood, fifty miles away. "If you can stay healthy and active, living to 100 is terrific!" Collie says. "I'm in good health generally, but I've had the flu twice since my birthday [June 1993] and it's really taken the starch out of me. When I reached 100, I decided to try for a comeback, competing again in the Master's Tournaments [swimming and track and field]. I really think I would have been able to, if it hadn't been for getting sick. I wanted to set some age group records for 100-year-olds because there aren't any. Well, maybe I'll feel up to it by the time I'm 101—I've only got four months to go!"

"One of the things I admire so much about Collie is his mind is so sharp—it's like a computer," Joe LaPrinzi shares. "His only problem is his hearing. He works out, two or three times a week, using light weights and swimming. People see him and say to me, 'If I exercise like he does will I live longer?' I tell them, you may not live longer but you'll feel better while you're alive."

✤

At 100, Anna King, known as "Speedy" to her friends at the New Age Hair Salon in Scottsdale, Arizona, where she is a regular client, believes that "keeping busy keeps you healthy and helps you live long." The petite, lithesome, joyous centenarian doesn't have an exercise routine. She tells: "I get my exercise helping out with the housework and keeping up with my three-year-old great-great-grandson. I do the laundry, ironing, and the dishes and keep my room tidy, and I spend time with little Carter every day." Anna has lived with her granddaughter, Barbara, for the past twenty-eight years, helping to rear Barbara's two daughters while Barbara ran a retail business.

Anna was one of eleven children born to Norwegian immigrants. "I particularly liked watching the [1994] Winter Olympics in Lillehammer," she says. "I stayed up later than usual every night so I didn't miss a thing. It was wonderful to watch them." Anna's father was a lighthouse keeper; she grew up on the Sheboygan River in Michigan. "We had a lovely life," she remembers. "My father was stern, but my parents were very loving. They believed in education, and I went to college and earned a teaching certificate. I graduated in 1912 and taught elementary grades in Indian River, Michigan, for sixteen years, in all. I raised my two girls and then moved to Fort Lauderdale, Florida where I worked as the head of housekeeping for a hotel right on the beach. It was very nice, and the owners were good to me. My husband had been in the navy in World Wars I and II and was injured and later disabled. He spent many years in a veterans home in Michigan, so I had to support myself. After the hotel was sold, I stayed on for another two years, but I became lonesome without any family. So I thought, where can I be of help to younger ones—and I moved to Arizona at the age of seventy-two, where one of my daughters lived, and helped with her daughter [Barbara] and then later moved in with Barbara to help with her girls. I learned to like living in Arizona."

Anna's 100th birthday party on February 25, 1994, was celebrated by all of her family and several friends at an outdoor party at a Phoenix landmark restaurant. Barbara invited four of her high school friends and their mothers. "We reminisced about being teenagers and all the normal things kids do—things that Nanna had to contend with with us," she said with a laugh. "Everybody loves Nanna. One of Barbara's friends hired a limousine to take "all the girls, including the birthday girl" to the restaurant. "We've always had a lot of fun with Nanna," she said.

Anna says her health has always been good and she's never been hospitalized. "I take medicine now for high blood pressure and for my kidneys," she informs us, "but after all these years, that's not too much to expect. When I was going to school, I think I was in the eighth grade, I was walking with my friend along the river and I asked her how long she would like to live," she reminisces in a light, lilting voice. "She said she didn't know. I said I'd like to live to be ninety, and that was my thought throughout my life. I wanted to live long, but I never thought I'd live to be 100; it just came naturally. And then I thought, 'I'm 100 years old and there's nothing really wrong with me, I'm not sick. I think I could live for a while. . .as long as I keep well, maybe I'll live another ten years—that's not very long.' I've already lived another ten years from ninety—time goes by fast."

"You know how when you first wake up in the morning or during the night, you are thinking about something or someone in your past—it's on your mind. I was thinking a lot about my mother and my brothers and sisters, all gone, for a while before my birthday, and I was a little down. And then with all the parties and friends and well-wishers, and Barbara's encouragement, it cheered me up. Barbara gave me a new bedroom set as one of my presents, and I'm looking forward to moving soon into her new home. I stay by myself in the summer while she goes back to Michigan, to our family home there. I'd like to go back and see it again. I made up my mind that I am going to keep busy, keep living. It's important to be optimistic—I learned that. I do the best I can—I always have and I always will. I decided I won't quit now.

"I love to talk over the things that happened in my lifetime," she says with eagerness. "Imagine, there were no planes or cars or anything.

I got to see all of that. I've really enjoyed it—I've really seen a lot of things and it's been good." Anna's project now is to begin recording her life story for her family. "My great-granddaughter, who is a television anchorwoman in Wisconsin, gave me a recorder and tapes for me to start writing my story. I have hundreds of pictures, starting from the time I was young, and I received big albums for my birthday to put them in. It'll keep me busy for quite some time. I even have a picture of myself with the basketball team I formed and played on when I was teaching, when girl's basketball first started. We are all wearing bloomers with headbands holding our hair. It's funny. We used to travel all over the little towns in Michigan."

There is no doubt that the emotional support and motivation Anna receives from her family, especially her granddaughter, Barbara, helps

✑ *Anna King on her 100th Birthday with her granddaughter Barbara,
February 1994. Photo courtesy of Anna and Barbara.*

maintain her spirit and adds appreciably to her enjoyment of living. Her family provides a sense of belonging and purpose. "We love having her," Barbara says sincerely. Barbara is upbeat and young at heart. "I learned it from Nanna," she says with a big smile.

.❧

IN CELEBRATION OF LIFE

To catch the spirit of active centenarians such as these is to affirm life. To develop this spirit within oneself can add life to years and, perhaps, even years to life. The centenarian spirit is a combination of the desire to continue to live and to enjoy living and the courage to meet the challenges of advanced age; it includes the ability to cope with losses and adapt to changed circumstances, and the determination to continue beyond them and renegotiate life at every turn. In sum, it is the will to see life through to the very best of one's abilities.

The centenarian spirit can be applied to living excellently at any age. It means living each day well and looking forward as though we would live to be 100. It means keeping one's outlook positive, realistic, and yet optimistic. To embrace the centenarian spirit is to discover the fountain of youth within ourselves: the culmination of one's will, and the interest to tap into whatever else is available—medical miracles as they come along, and life-style measures for good mental and physical health as we age. Centenarians reiterate that the most important thing to do in life is to take care of your health and to be self-reliant and vigilant in this pursuit.

The centenarian spirit is an animating force—a spark of life. The traits, attributes, and characteristics centenarians possess show their spirit.

It's the *enthusiasm* of Myrtle Little to go to a basketball game, and the *get-up-and-go* of Billy Earley to attend the presidential inauguration and to continue to travel, which she loves. It's the *playfulness* of Beatrice Wood in shaping both her art and her lifestyle, and the *joie de vivre* of Claire Willi, dressing up and going out for lunch in Manhattan.

It's the *sprightliness* of Roy Miller in refusing to conform to society's stereotype of old age, and the *sociability* of Elva Sholes in making new friends. It's the *innovation* of Helen Cope by participating in this book "for posterity!" and the *openness* of Thomas Katsenes in wanting to share his life story.

It's the *individualism* of Ida Gilland Fox, following her father's loving admonition to "always carry your own freight in this world," in choosing to live in a nursing home rather than with her daughter. It's the *integrity* of Marjory Stoneman Douglas to remain true to her ideals, protesting a government action she believes is wrong.

It's the *good will* of Frank Andersen in his philanthropy for children in his community, and the *patriotism* of Richard Johnson in raising the American flag each morning. It's the *ingenuity* of Ruth Weyl to create a workable plan of assistance to enable her to stay in her own home, and the *good sense* of John Langham to know his limits.

It's the *spunk* of Hazel Herring to live as she wants to live, and the *stick-to-itiveness* of Oscar Wilmeth in maintaining a healthy life-style, alone and without anyone else to care. It's the *dedication* to weekly exercise of Collister Wheeler even though he can no longer "do like he used to do," and the *wit* of Louis Kelly in writing and telling his memories.

It's the *dignity* of Hedvig Peterson to forgive a grievous harm, and the *appreciation* of Edna Butler for her family's continuing regard. It's the *stalwartness* of Mabel Correa in keeping a positive attitude while living under adverse conditions, and the *fortitude* of Mary Gleason in carrying on despite her physical impairment.

It's the *good nature* of Lizzie Davis in rolling with life's punches, and the *eagerness* of Ray Paul Nieto corresponding with pen pals. It's the *romanticism* of Pearl Sprague that keeps her reading romance novels, and the *composure* of Mary Brown in her decision to relocate to a retirement center near her children.

It's the *loyalty* of Frank Rowels in visiting his wife daily at a nursing home, and *love and commitment* that prompted Ben Pruitt to move into a nursing home with his ailing wife. It's the *peace of mind* of Angelo Maltas secure in his spirituality, and the steadfast *belief and faith* in God of Nannie Moree at life's end.

It's the *determination* of Michael Heidelberger to undergo life-saving surgeries and continue his work, and the *resilience* of Ted Gibson in facing life-threatening illnesses. It's the *optimism* of George Abbott to upgrade his pacemaker and look forward to his 107th birthday, and the *motivation* of Helen Langner to keep current in her professional field of psychiatry.

It's the *adventuresomeness* of Clyde Ice to fly a plane again at 100, and the *charisma* of Henry Stenhouse in running for public office. It's the *initiative* of Eli Finn in taking college history courses, and the *social conscience* of Harry Fisher in expressing his convictions.

More over, it is a clear set of old-fashioned values, a sense of self-worth, and a touch of pride that also show in the centenarian spirit. These traits and the theme common to many centenarians of striving for the maximum amount of independence and autonomy as possible, are epitomized by Tom Beston.

❧

At 101, Tom watches the sunsets from aboard his twenty-eight foot powerboat docked at the Port Royal Marina at Redondo Beach, California. He has made his boat, the *Wiki Wiki*, home for the past twenty years, after moving to California from Detroit. He and his wife moved to be near their daughter, but two weeks after they arrived, his wife died. "I tried living in my daughter's home for a while and spent some time visiting relatives in Canada," he tells, "but I knew I had to be on my own. I looked around at apartments, but in this area, they're hard to afford." Tom didn't like the idea of being struck with only four walls and other apartments to look at. "My daughter's home was up the hill from the marina in Palo Verdes. On one of our visits to the marina, as I watched the boats, I thought, 'Why not?' I bought an old one for $6,000 and rented a slip."

As the boat rocks gently on the water's swells, Tom admits that some people think it's odd he lives year-round on a boat, in what seems to some as little more than camping out. "But I like it," he says cheerfully. "I've got everything I need in here—a telephone, TV, and a brand-new microwave oven. There's a wonderful sense of freedom being on the water and being among people who like boats and the sea. There's always something going on. I like the people, the activity, the comings and goings. I like being a part of it all. You couldn't wish for a better way of living. It's never lonely here; I have lots of friends."

Tom spent his early life by the water, too, in view of the Irish Sea. Born the youngest of five children in Brea, County Wicklow, Southern Ireland, he immigrated to Canada as a young man with his mother and all the children. In Calgary, the family opened a restaurant, but Tom was bored by the enterprise. Fascinated by the stories of American cowboys, he tried his luck on a ranch in Montana for a year. Finding the life wasn't for him (or vice versa, he says), Tom went to Alaska and worked for a short time as a surveyor.

"Everyone was talking about the big money to be made working for

ஃ *Tom Beston with his boat, 1993.*
Photo courtesy of Tom Beston and his daughter Audrey.

Henry Ford," he recalls. "We were all going to get rich." So Tom went to Detroit but was disillusioned by the treatment of the workers on the assembly line. "It wasn't right," he maintains. So Tom became an early union organizer and stayed with it through the bloody times of the 1930s. "The unions served a very useful purpose at that time. Workers needed someone to negotiate for them," he tells. Working with labor leaders such as Walter Reuther, Tom's involvement in the labor movement lasted until his retirement in 1958. He became a tool and die maker first at the Ford plant and later at Borg Warner. "I was an active Democrat, my wife was a Republican," Tom says with a smile. "She hated my involvement with the union," especially the fact that he would take his young daughter, Audrey, along with him to Saturday meetings and to help hand out sandwiches and coffee on picket lines.

During these years, Tom was also involved in furthering other social causes. "I am always for the common good," he says with a trace of pride. "I worked with Norman Thomas, the Socialist party candidate in the 1928 presidential race, getting signatures on petitions to create a social security system in this country. FDR is credited with starting the Social Security Program, but it was actually Norman Thomas. The concept of Social Security was a good one, and needed," Tom tells. "There were poorhouses then, and that's where old people likely ended up. They were terrible places.

"The original idea behind Social Security was that everyone who was working would contribute a little to help those in need who were too old to work. They didn't take much out—it was a tithing. It was meant to offset the poorhouse, so old people could remain independent and keep their dignity. It wasn't for everyone, just for those who needed it. I think it's been overdone in the past years and spread around to too many who didn't need it." Tom says he's always been very interested in national politics and is active to this day. He attends campaign meetings and listens to speakers whenever they come to his area. He expresses favor of President Clinton's proposed reforms to the Social Security system. "I think he is trying to take it back to more like what it was intended to be. He's coming under a lot of fire, but I think people ought to give him a chance. He's got a tough job to do. There are a lot of things to be fixed that have gone wrong in this country, and it takes time."

Tom enjoys talking and reminiscing, especially with his young friends, about the historic events in which he participated. He feels strongly that the past is important to understanding the present. "How can we understand ourselves if we don't understand our history and heritage?" he asks rhetorically. "Old people often feel alienated from the future," he continues philosophically. "Young people often feel divorced from the past; the only common meeting is in the present, where both future and past can be shared. That's what I enjoy doing."

Tom is also concerned by what he sees today as a life-style for younger generations that appears void of any vision of greatness, void of a vision of one's own. And he is disturbed by what he sees as a world that will be rich for a few in material comforts but a world poor in moral, intellectual, and spiritual strengths.

The years have not dampened Tom's passion for causes, his independence, his interest in others, or his spirit. He strides purposefully from his home at the water's edge several miles into town to do his grocery shopping, often refusing rides from well-meaning passersby. "I like to walk," he says. "I walk several miles every day. It's good exercise and keeps me strong."

For his 100th birthday on December 16, 1991, Tom's friends gave him a surprise party at the marina yacht club, with an honorary membership as his gift, one Tom makes good use of on rainy days, he says. "I'll go up there and sit for a while and have a cup of coffee or maybe a beer."

"Well, the party was supposed to be a surprise," daughter Audrey says, "but Dad called me [in Arizona where she had moved several years before] and said, 'Something's in the wind. I think they're giving me a party. You'd better get over here.'" At the party, the mayor of Redondo Beach presented Tom with a proclamation declaring it "Thomas Beston Day," and the U.S. Coast Guard inducted him into its auxiliary. "It was quite a party," Tom says.

He was honored again the following year by his appointment as Grand Marshall of the traditional Parade of Lights, in which boats from yacht clubs and marinas are decorated with Christmas lights and cruise along the California coast for the enjoyment of onlookers along the shore. Again, Audrey joined him for the event. Tom sat next to the captain of the lead boat, a large three-decker, while the festive armada made its way up and down the coastline for several miles. To get onto the boat, Tom had to climb a six-foot ladder straight up the side of the hull. "There was nothing down there but water," Audrey tells. "Dad made it all right without assistance."

Whether consciously or not, living near water has been a theme in Tom's life. For all the years in Detroit, as a young man, his married years, and rearing his family of three children, Tom lived on what was originally a farm on the banks of the Detroit River, near the Canadian border, between the Great Lakes of Erie and Huron. "It was a lovely area," he recalls. Tom feels that in later years it's equally important for people to be in an environment they enjoy. "I think the people who are happiest and most satisfied are those who have some say over the way they live when they are old."

Tom still thinks of the poorhouses and is concerned that with our modern-day predilection for institutionalizing many things, that it is being extended to old people, as well. In a country like this, he feels there has got to be a better solution. "People need to feel their lives are lived with integrity and to keep with the present, using the past only as a guide. I am independent and that's the way I have to live. For others, it may be different, and God bless them. Each person should have the right to a sense of dignity as they grow old. To rob them of that, even if not meaning any harm, is to rob them of life.

"I've seen in the newspaper lately there are now foster homes for old people, like they have for children, where they can live with a family for much less than it costs in an institution. If they're well treated, I think this is a good alternative for some who aren't able to live on their own."

In quiet times, Tom loves to listen to music, from classical to rock 'n' roll. His small living space is crammed with sound equipment: radio, stereo recording equipment, speakers, headsets, records, and tapes. He often records songs he hears on the radio or has on records and tapes for people he has met and sends his friends songs he knows they like. His most recent acquisition was a CD player. "I had to have one of these, as soon as I heard the quality of the sound—it's beautiful," he says. Tom walked the several miles to the electronics store and made his selection. Without it being a contradiction, he enjoys the present and at the same time appreciates the past. He also looks ahead. "I put money in the bank each month," he declares, "for the future."

Tom Beston has been a touchstone for many people over the last twenty years; younger people feel there is something very life-affirming in talking with someone who has lived as long as he. "People come and tell me their woes and leave feeling better. I like that. I tell them to find pleasure in every day. I'm an optimist," he says with a twinkle in his brown eyes. "Encapsulate the good memories and let the others go."

In September 1993, Tom received yet another honor, this time not for having lived a century but for the person he is. One of his young friends, and part owner of the marina, named her baby boy after him. In appreciation, Tom recites the familiar Gaelic Blessing for his namesake:

> *May the road rise with you,*
> *and the wind be always at your back.*
> *And may the Lord hold you*
> *in the hollow of his hand.*

For his 102nd birthday, Tom visited Audrey in her home in Arizona, and she prevailed upon him to stay for the winter. "But only if I stay in an apartment on my own," Tom said as he reluctantly agreed to being landlocked.

"I know I'm living on borrowed time," he muses, "and I'd like a little more of it. We will all be here as long as God intends us to be, so we should make the best of what we have."

A Toast To Future Centenarians

The centenarian voice tells us, "Live each day; each day is a new day; value each day; each day is precious." This affirmation of daily quality increases in importance as we age. In persons of great age, this affirmation can assume a higher, philosophical level, one in which the qualitative dimensions of life are what matter most. In other words, it is not how many things one can do in a day, for example, but rather the enjoyment of the things one is able to do and wants to do that makes life meaningful.

The spirit portrayed by the centenarians in this book, and thousands more like them, enables them to go beyond survival to achieve personal fulfillment and personal accomplishment in advanced age. One needs only to spend time with them to sense it. This spirit is part of their personalities, a strong life force that can be felt in their presence, seen in their actions, and heard in their voices. Centenarians themselves define this quality in their unique, individual ways. It is this spirit that makes centenarians extraordinary. It is this spirit that crowns their longevity.

The unifying message heard from centenarians who are active and participating in life is that it is possible to create a good and worthwhile life for oneself in advanced age, with some help from family, friends, and society. Centenarians have shown that there is no age limit on happiness. Yet, as with anything worth having in life, they have shown also that achieving happiness, contentment, and a good quality of life as one lives long often requires effort, perseverance, knowledge, patience, and compromise. This is the ultimate drama of aging, and active centenarians are playing a leading role. Their presence in society spotlights those who are aging. The pioneering centenarians of today are at the frontier of human aging experience, and what we can draw from their examples is that which they have most in common—their *spirit*.

It is a great distinction to live to celebrate 100 years or more. It is a victory to have done so with the spirit and zest for life that so many centenarians share. As Americans continue their quest for longer and healthier lives, myriad advances in medical science will most certainly result in greater numbers of people living long and greater numbers of people living to be 100. These improvements will result in ways to make our later years healthier and more problem-free. More people will thus be able to truly enjoy the bonus years of living long.

If future centenarians and others who live long can match the spirit of today's centenarians, they will do well. The centenarian spirit is a precious gift—it is their legacy. Integrating this spirit into our lives will strengthen our own resolve to live well, help in meeting our own challenges, and help make the most of our later years. In this spirit there is triumph.

ஃ

Epilogue

FOR those nearing the century mark, Rose Tackles tells of her journey to the pinnacle of old age.

"I met Grace Northrup [the centenarian introduced in the Prelude of this book] when she moved into the skilled care wing of Sun Valley Lodge, the retirement home where I live in an apartment. I have always believed in helping others, so after my husband died, I volunteered to help residents who needed some assistance with their evening meals. Since I am a registered nurse, a graduate of the University of Michigan School of Nursing in 1912, I was permitted to do so.

"After meeting Grace, I began thinking about living to be 100 myself—I only had five more years to go. As I got closer, I actually started looking forward to reaching the century mark."

Rose kept busy over the next five years, leading an active and interesting life-style socializing with friends and her family. "I realized years ago when I moved to Sun City, Arizona, that I also needed a hobby that would give me pleasure. I started with lapidary and just loved it—finding stones, polishing them, and making jewelry. But when arthritis took over my hands, I was no longer able to do such fine work. That's when I decided to take up painting. At first I tried painting with acrylics and a pallet knife, but I had difficulty holding the knife and so I switched to oil painting and brushes. I took lessons and eventually was able to produce recognizable landscapes. I painted from pictures or postcards or from my memory—whatever struck my fancy. Since I was about the same age as Grandma Moses when she started painting, my family began calling me 'Grandma Roses.' I would paint pictures and give them as gifts to family and friends. I did this until I was about ninety-nine and then I stopped, figuring I'd done about all there was to do with this.

"I don't hear or see as well as I did, and my arthritis in my hands is pretty bad, and for a while I had to use a walker after I fell and broke my hip. But I go out and have lunch with my daughter and frequently go to her home for dinner, and I attend all the activities and parties here at the lodge. I have my hair done regularly and keep up my appearance; it has a big effect on how I feel and on how others feel about me.

"I enjoy letter writing to friends and family both near and far away. Sun Valley Lodge is so homey it gives me a lot to be thankful for and I don't miss being alone in my own home. For some people, it's better to live in a retirement center where they have activities and there are people to be friends with rather than staying home alone. We each have to do all we can to help ourselves throughout our lives, and old age is no exception. When we get old that changes somewhat and we become more dependent on others, but it's still important to keep constantly in mind that saying I and others of my generation grew up with, 'The Lord helps those who help themselves.' I would add that other people are more inclined to help those who at least try to help themselves in whatever ways they can."

Six months before the "big day," Rose began planning her 100th birthday celebration and sent the invitations. She also began housecleaning, in anticipation of out-of-town guests. While cleaning out a closet, Rose came upon an old unused canvas that she'd started painting on years before. "I had stopped after filling in the background because I didn't particularly like the shape of the canvas," she recalls. "I didn't want to throw it away, though, because it was still good. Undecided, I left it near the door, ready to be sent to the trash.

"Then one day the old canvas called to me. I got out my paint box, but many of the tubes had dried up and some of the colors were missing altogether. The brushes were worn and frayed. At first I decided to paint on that old, out-of-shape canvas using the colors I had left that

∽ *Rose Tackles: Happy at 100!*
Photo courtesy of Sun Valley Lodge, Sun City, AZ.

were not completely dried up and with the fine brushes that were in better condition. That took a while and was rather tedious, but as I worked on it a little, day after day, the canvas was taking form and I began to like it more. I decided I'd mix some turpentine in with the dried-up paints and use them again. They were a little thinner and the colors not so vibrant, but it was working out all right, especially since I had soaked the bigger brushes to straighten out some of their bristles and could use them too, after a fashion. It was easier going then because I had more to work with. Finally, I began making new colors altogether by combining the ones I had left. The result wasn't quite perfect, but it still worked.

"I painted a landscape—my favorite subject—with trees and water and sky, which is what I'd done best in all the hundreds of pictures I'd painted over the years. It was a beautiful view, and when I'd finished—by my birthday—I was quite pleased with it. I decided to have it hung in the art room at the lodge; perhaps it will encourage someone just beginning."

On September 21, 1990, Rose was jubilant. All three generations of her family attended her centenary birthday celebration, along with dozens of friends and all of the residents of the retirement home, whom Rose had personally invited. "My family was surprised that I have so many friends. It is dear friends and my loving family that have helped me along the way," she acknowledged. If a picture is worth a thousand words, then this one of Rose at 100, at her party, is an inspiration for a whole new generation of centenarians.

Rose announced that her five-year plan was to keep active, continue to be creative in every avenue open to her, and to be alive. "I think people miss something if they say they don't want another birthday," she believes. "Every day is important. I enjoy the simple pleasures of being alive."

At 103, Rose's spirit is as joyful as ever. "When I awaken and see the sunshine, it puts me in a happy mood to start the day. My arthritis is there, but has to be lived with, and talking about it makes it worse. After breakfast, I go to exercise class and then get ready to go out or do whatever activities I have planned for the day. I don't just sit around, unless there is something I want to read—but usually I save reading for the evenings. It is important to talk to others about your interests instead of your ailments. It makes more friends that way. I try to encourage other people by my example."

Grace Sumner Northrup, Rose's inspiration, passed away shortly before her 105th birthday. She left a wonderful successor in Rose Tackles, who says with confidence, "It is great to live to be 100 years old or more and still be active and loving life. I enjoy every day of my life."

☙

❦ Appendices ❧

CENTENARIAN PARTICIPANTS

Following are the centenarians who wished to have their names listed; many other preferred to remain anonymous and some prefer to have only their names listed, without their locale.

Abbott, Elizabeth M.　Brewster, MA
Accardo, James　Union, NJ
Akabas, Eva　Boston, MA
Alexanderson, Wilmont Esther
　Kingsford, MI
Allen, Mann　Columbia, LA
Allen, Hattie　Palmer, AK
Andersen, Frank　Saginaw, MI
Andersen, Gus　Prescott, AZ
Andre, Ann　David City, NE
Andrews, Reba　Gillispie, IL
Arley, Paul, D.C.,　Greenwich, CT
Arneet, Will Tom　Saylersville, KY
Arnelli, Carmela　Jamestown, NY
Arrington, Beatrice　Akron, OH
Arrington, Jacob F.　Twin Falls, ID
Asher, Julia　Brooklyn, NY
Aucoin, Clema　Delambre, LA
Axtell, Claire R.　Thermopolis, WY
Ballard, Mary Owen
　Gray Gables, MA
Barker, Paul W.　Utica, NY
Barth, Anna　Racine, WI
Bates, Jennie J.　Cambridge, MN
Batiste, Olivia Page　Slidell, LA
Becker, Anna T.　Freeman, SD
Beston, Thomas
　Redondo Beach, CA
Bevelhymer, Emma Agnes
　Adrian, MI
Bidwell, Mary E.　North Haven, CT
Biegert, John J.　Shickley, NE
Billings, Virginia　Sun City, AZ
Brooks, Emma Bird　Creston, IA
Birk, Selma C.　Kalispell, MT
Black, Carrie Thomas　Oakland, CA

Bliven, Bertha Kalb　Salem, OR
Blubaugh, Christine　Wichita, KS
Boyajian, Setrak K.
　Los Angeles, CA
Brende, Karen　Sioux Falls, SD
Brigham, Vella V.　Forest Grove, OR
Brown, Mary　Newtown, PA
Brown, Jay　Soldotna, AR
Brown, Richard M. Sr.
　Martins Ferry, OH
Brown, Bertha M.　Utica, NY
Brownell, Gary　Woodus Hill, CT
Burch, Blanche Orpha　Blufton, OH
Bushee, Bessie Lyon　Scotia, NY
Butler, Edna　Lancaster, NY
Butler, Gertrude　Indianola, MS
Campbell, Frances M.
　Lewiston, Idaho
Canion, Ola　Prescott, AZ
Canter, David L. Clifton, TN
Carlson, Maude　Bismark, ND
Carter, David Lipscomb
　Waynesboro, TN
Case, Katherine　Glendale, AZ
Chapman, Mayme
　Leavenworth, KS
Chen, Chin　Seattle, WA
Cheney, Clarence　Sun City, AZ
Choitz, Elizabeth
　Arlington Heights, IL
Christian, Luna Lee
Christopher, Harris C., M.D.
　Des Moines, WA
Clark, Anna E.
　Grand Junction, CO
Clark, Cora Alice　Salem, OR

Clark, William O.
  Salt Lake City, UT
Cleveland, Ethel Donohue
  Twin Falls, ID
Cloughly, Hermine M.   Union, NJ
Colaianni, Antonio   Pocatello, ID
Colbert, Magna   Warmonster, PA
Collins, Lena   Amarillo, TX
Conley, Mary Melvin
  Harriman, IN
Cook, Suzie   Elmswood, NE
Cope, Helen Gibson
  Greenwich, CT
Correa, Mabel   Oakland, CA
Cuttino, Maggie Rose   Florence, SC
Davis, Elizabeth   Yuma, AZ
Davis, Isabel   Hamilton, NY
Denny, Anna T.   Granite Falls, NC
Derowski, Joseph   Allendale, NJ
Dexter, Selma   Caledonia, MN
Di Berardo, Frank   Columbia, NJ
Ditler, Prinella   Portland, OR
Dittman, Pauline Louise   Miller, SD
Doran, Lulu T.   Deshler, NE
Dorsey, Emma Gleich
  Delaware, OH
Douglas, Josephine Penn
  Lubbock, TX
Douglas, Marjory Stoneman
  Miami, FL
Dudley, Mabel   Florence, CO
Duran, Margarita Padilla
  Phoenix, AZ
Earley, Mrs. Lynn (Billy)
  Florence, AZ
Eggleton, Florence S.   Sherrill, NY
Elliott, Emerson M.   Hamilton, OH
Ellis, Effie R.   Colfax, LA
Empey, Mary Catherine
  Victorville, CA
Engh, Peter   Northwood, ND
Ensinger, Mary   Ravenna, OH

Epperson, Clara Knoch   Alma, KS
Eschner, Henrietta G.
  Lockport, NY
Essenmacher, Tillie Lambert
  Edgewater, FL
Essmus, Bessie   Racine, WI
Fangler, Emma   Plainfield, CT
Farrington, Maude T.   Eugene, OR
Feagins, Ben E.   Selma, AL
Fengler, Emma   Plainville, CT
Fenske, Ottelia   Glencoe, MN
Fergus, Hazel Akely   Juneau, AK
Fessenden, Margaret Mae
  Salem, OR
Filter, Lena C.   Adrian, MI
Finn, Eli   East Norwalk, CT
Fintus, Mae Belle   Montrose, CO
Fisher, Harry W., Esq.   Ft. Scott, KS
Fisher, R.   San Bernadino, CA
Foster, Ann   Grand Junction, CO
Foster, Anna Barker
  Grand Junction, CO
Fox, Ida Gilland   Cheyenne, WY
Franke, Clara   Zanesville, OH
Gates, Maude P.   East Haddon, CT
Gates, Henry C.   Marlboro, MA
Gere, Laura B.   Buzzards Bay, ME
Gewecke, Ida   Geneva, NE
Gibson, Theodore T.
  Culver City, CA
Gilardine, Annie Volkel
  Thermopolis, WY
Gilbreath, Mrs. Ollie A.
  Denver, CO
Gillespie, George
  Colorado Springs, CO
Gleason, Mary   Columbia, SC
Goldberg, Abraham
  West Palm Beach, FL
Goule, Harry   Salt Lake-Ogden, UT
Graham, Euphemia
  Bellingham, WA

323

Greb, Augusta   Racine, WI
Greenwald, Viola
   Niagara Falls, NY
Griswold, Mary   Phoenix, AZ
Grosse, Magdalena Harley
   Cedar Bluffs, NE
Groves, Rev. Tom   Buffalo, NY
Gustafon, Johannah
   Colorado, Springs, CO
Guthrie, Jessie   Appomatox, VA
Hadrath, Ernest C.
   Montevideo, MN
Haller, Lillian May   Freeport, IL
Hammond, James Palmer
   Gerro Gordo, NC
Hancock, Vita   Homeland, FL
Handyside, James   Akron, OH
Hanson, Lula Mae Reid
   LeHarpe, IL
Harvat, Mary   Chippewa Falls, WI
Hathaway, Bessie   Johnson City, TN
Haubach, Helen R.   Gilman, IL
Hauetter, Alma   Kansas City, KS
Haughawout, Mary Elizabeth
   Ponca City, OK
Havlovic, Mary   Wilber, NE
Hawkins, Margery C.
   Sweet Home, Oregon
Hawks, Carrie M.   Bruning, NE
Hayes, Henry   Barnswell, GA
Haynes, Effie Dallas
   Alamogordo, NM
Heidelberger, Michael Ph.D.
   New York, NY
Heimgartner, Mystie Belle
   Juliaetta, ID
Hendrickson, Carl   Jamestown, NY
Hensley, Mary Donaldson
   Murphy, NC
Herring, Hazel   Lawton, OK
Hertzka, Hattie Mai
   Brentwood, TN

Hettinger, Mary C.
   West Carrollton, OH
Hinton, Grace   Kansas City, KS
Holman, Jessie   Dodson, MT
Holy Eagle, James   Rapid City, SD
Horacek, Anna   David City, NE
Hoss, Esther M.
   Medicine Lodge, KS
Houston, John Leslie   Nashville, TN
Howe, Myrtle H.   Bradenton, FL
Howes, Grace   Bristol, CT
Hummel, Pearl C.   Louisville, KY
Hutchins, Nellie   Lincoln, NE
Hutmacher, Addie   Freemont, IL
Ice, Clyde W.   Spearfish, SD
Ingle, Sara   Watford City, ND
Itava, Mary Ann   David City, NE
James, Isabel   Wilmington, NC
Jenkins, Evelina   Shannon, MS
Jerons, Mrs. Francis   Bethleham, PA
Johnson, Lettie   Bertrand, NE
Johnson, Viva Pearl   Corning, IA
Johnson, Richard Berry
   Natick, MA
Johnson, Lettie   Nebraska
Johnson, Anna Elizabeth
   Roswell, NM
Johnson, Fannie Sipe
   Flagler Beach, FL
Johnston, Margaret K.
   Grand Junction, CO
Jones, Bertha N.   Perry, IA
Jones, Elizabeth Ann   Denver, CO
Jones, Mark William   Eugene, OR
Jones, Maude Elizabeth
   Santa Maria, CA
Jones, Hazel   Twin Falls, ID
Kandel, Oma   Marysville, OH
Kannerker, Gustave   Waterbury, CT
Kasper, Anna   Grand Junction, CO
Katsenes, Thomas J.   Phoenix, AZ
Kastanek, Rose   Crete, NE

Keithler, Anna   Grants Pass, OR
Keller, Mollie Tueller   Sandpoint, ID
Kelly, Lewis   Scottsdale, AZ
Kemp, Arthur R.   Englewood, OH
Kessel, Marie   Westlake, OH
Kiene, Margaret Annetta
   McGrann, PA
Kietzman, Agnes   Miller, SD
Kilburn, Cecile   Kent, OH
King, Anna   Scottsdale, AZ
Kinnison, Susan Larird   Kelly, LA
Kipfer, Mary   Stephenson, MI
Kirshbaum, Anna   Waterbury, CT
Kleminski, Frank   Tucson, AZ
Knoke, Martha   Littleton, CO
Kyzar, Myrtle Ann
   Brownwood, TX
Lambert, Maria Ozelia Ackman
   Pierre Port, LA
Lamont, Elizabeth   Plainsville, CT
Langham, John   Prescott, AZ
Langner, Helen M.D.   Milford, CT
Lax, Ida   Paris, TN
Laymance, Letta Dryman
   Harriman, TN
Lee, Bennie   Nashville, TN
LeStourgeon, Ethelbert
   Bridgeton, NJ
Lindholm, Ida
Lindsey, George   Fortuna, CA
Little, Myrtle   Pheonix, AZ
Lohoefener, Adolf   Oberlin, KS
Lolakus, James K.   Gillespie, IL
Lowenstein, Dr. George
   Clearwater, FL
Lowry, Marie   Lamar, CO
Lynn, Susanna   Kansas City, KS
Lyon, Grace   Burbank, CA
Mack, Thannie Marie   Rahway, NJ
Mack, Lula Bell   Selma, AL
Majors, Grace   Lincoln, NE
Maltas, Angelo   Huntington, CT

Martindel, Ruby
Matzigkett, Ollie
May, Charlie   Aitkin, MN
McCleneghan, Anna
McDavitt, Lavern   Galesburg, IL
McDonald, Agnes Wendt
   Bridgeport, CT
McFarland, Harry   Abilene, KS
McGlochlin, Wilma   Kellogg, ID
McGuire, Hattie   Phoenix, AZ
McMahon, Mary   Boise, ID
McSwain, Johnsie Kirkman
   Chesterton, MD
Meek, Cora   Matoon, IL
Mercier, Marilda Juneau
   Plainfield, CT
Michael, Peter   Walker, IA
Miller, Emma
Miller, Stella Fancher
   Audobohn, IA
Miller, Rev. Roy   Glendale, AZ
Miller, Mary I.   Sioux Falls, SD
Millsaps, Earl   Murphy, NC
Minnis, Marie   New York, NY
Molkie, Ella   Sherwood, OR
Montgomery, Essie   Bronx, NY
Moore, Manira
   Arlington, Heights, IL
Moore, Louise Taylor
   Des Moines, IA
Moore, Rev. David E.   Roswell, NM
Moree, Nannie Cook   Athens, TN
Moss, James Lee   Lewisburg, TN
Moulton, John A.   Jackson, WY
Mullen, Matilda   Westlake, OH
Mygrant, Daisy Marguerite
   Paradise, CA
Nafe, Donald O.   Ypsilanti, MI
Nail, Mary A.   Dallas, OR
Nance, Ward   Emporia, KS
Nelson, Fritz Otto   Clarkson, NE
Nessman, Louise   Union, NJ

Nielson, Tina   Sioux Falls, SD
Nieto, Ray Paul   Yuba City, CA
Northrup, Grace   Sun City, AZ
Otoole, Mae   Phoenix, AZ
Ogburn, Mary   Mesa, AZ
Orneals, Frank   Phoenix, AZ
Ortega, Virginia   Chimayo, NM
Overton, Edith G.   Somers Point, NJ
Page, Effie Johnson   Crete, NE
Paisley, Oscar C.   Coeur d'Alene, ID
Palmer, Annie L.   Lewiston, ID
Parcell, L.W.   Montrose, CO
Parsons, Mattie   Stratford, CT
Passmore, Anne M.
   Boulder City, NV
Paukert, Elizabeth   Faribault, MN
Paul, Anne Laurie Kant
   Sioux Falls, SD
Paulson, Carl J.   Hoople, ND
Paulus, Lena B. Collins
   Sheridan, WY
Penn, Rev. Joseph   Phoenix, AZ
Petersen, Hedvig   Tempe, AZ
Pike, Ollie   Klamath Falls, OR
Pohl, Julius Frederick
   Westfield, MA
Porter, Amy   Phoenix, AZ
Powell, Sidney   Stuart, FL
Preheim, Marie   Freeman, SD
Pugliese, Marie   Niagara Falls, NY
Puls, Marie Mae   Sun City, AZ
Quigg, Ellen Gertrude
   Brewster, MA
Radeke, Marguerite   Milbank, SD
Ragan, Pansy M.   Loveland, CO
Raiter, Elizabeth   David City, NE
Ramsey, Martha Browning
   Alkol, WV
Randall, Mina C.   Las Vegas, NV
Raske, Ellen E.   Warrenton, OR
Rider, Seymour   Hart, MI
Rieger, Mildred   Evanston, IL

Riggs, Alice Cassie   Salem, OR
Ritz, Anna   Brewster, MA
Roberson, Ethel Pace   Arcadia, LA
Robinson, Tempa   Lenoir City, TN
Ross, Marie   Highland, KS
Rossi, Irving   MI
Ruffin, Irene Halsell   Lisman, AL
Rusley, Bessie C.   Minot, ND
Russell, Tillie   Grants Pass, Oregon
Rust, Nina Amanda   Roseburg, OR
Ruttman, Edna   Klamath Falls, OR
Sales, Nellie   Roseburg, OR
Samanie, Diana T.   Houma, LA
Santree, Georgiana LaFleche
   Fitchburg, MA
Sawdy, Lillian   Clinton, IA
Schneiden, Elizabeth
   Boca Raton, FL
Schrock, Pearl Edith   Goshen, IN
Seibert, Martha   Spirit Lake, ID
Severson, Rebecca Mae   Presha, SD
Severson, Mae   Presho, OH
Shaw, Mabel   Sun City, AZ
Shepherd, Margery Bellinger
   Silverton, OR
Shere, Edith   Tabor, IA
Sholes, Elva   Glendale, AZ
Shopbell, Veleda   Tucson, AZ
Siers, Flora Ann   Aitkin, MN
Simmons, Pearlie   Pontotoc, MS
Simon, Cipora   Phoenix, AZ
Smith, Fred A.   Carrolton, OH
Smith, Julia   Clarksdale, MS
Smith, Bertha   Glendale, AZ
Smith, Johanna Sellnick
   Manitou Springs, CO
Smith, Elizabeth Barrett Browning
   Marietta, GA
Smith, Sadie C.   Washington, MO
Soltwedel, Minnie Devantier
   Effingham, IL
Souther, William H. Blairsville, GA

Spears, Leona   Greensburg, LA
Sprague, Pearl   Phoenix, AZ
Starks, Cora May   Sioux Falls, SD
Starr, Bessie   Phoenix, AZ
Stava, Mary Ann   David City, NE
Steele, Harold   Sun City, AZ
Steeves, Fred Wellington
   St. Helena, CA
Stenhouse, Henry M.D.
   Goldsboro, NC
Stenson, Minnie   Turtle Lake, SD
Stevens, Fannie E.
   Medicine Lodge, KS
Steves, Fred Wellington
   St. Helena, CA
Straley, Wilda   Phoenix, AZ
Strand, Anna   Crosby, ND
Sullivan, Josephine
   White Lake, SD
Sutton, William F.   Stockdale, TX
Tackles, Rose   Sun City, AZ
Tagliere, Maggie   Grants Pass, OR
Talbot, Walter G.   Williamsburg, IA
Tappe, Agnes   Freeport, IL
Taylor, George H.   Arizona City, AZ
Taylor, Anna Marie   New Castle, IN
Thomas, Carrie   Oakland, CA
Thompson, Benjamin Harrison
   Coeur d'Alene, ID
Thompson, Katie   Reading, PA
Tidwell, Maggie   Snellville, GA
Timm, Will   Herington, KS
Tuttle, Otis   Norway, IA
Unger, John
Unkel, Eva Lee Gregory
   Dayton, TX
Valle, Brullio   La Pryor, TX
Vandewege, Mary   Firth, NE
Vangones, Ingelborg
   Dell Rapids, SD
Van Hooser, William   Yuma, AZ
Vannata, Ada   Gillespie, IL

Van Spanckeren, Ethel
   Phoenix, AZ
Venhorst, Josephine M.
   Cedar Rapids, IA
Vestal, Edwin Ray   Elyria, OH
Wagner, Eldred L.   Kingston, TN
Wallace, Esther Davis
   Salt Lake City, UT
Waller, Elizabeth   Rochester, MN
Warfield, Roger   Tampa, FL
Warmer, Inez Mae   Center Point, IA
Warren, Donald Ph.D.
   Fremont, CA
Watkins, Willie Moss   Liberty, KY
Wells, Laura   Hartford, CT
Wetsch, Elizabeth   Kildeer, ND
Weyl, Ruth   Skiatook, OK
Wheeler, Collister, D.D.S.
   Portland, OR
Whiting, Mary Sullivan
   Mapleton, UT
Willi, Claire   New York, NY
Willis, Lillian May   Tolna, ND
Willoughby, Mrs. Ebon   Liberty, TX
Wilmeth, Oscar   Phoenix, AZ
Wilson, Sarah D.   Lake Worth, FL
Wilson, Hattie Mae Buchanan
   North Little Rock, AR
Wilson, Gertrude   North Platte, NE
Windesheim, Ernest M.D.
   Kensington, CA
Wine, Margaret   Covina, CA
Wolfe, Rosa Mae   Boise, Idaho
Wolfe, Adelheit Eveline
   St. James, MN
Wood, Beatrice   Ojai, CA
Wood, Clark S.   Levan, UT
Woodside, Iona   Fontanelle, IA
Wright, Ruby L.   Phoenix, AZ
Yax, Mabel   Mesa, AZ
Zea, Maude   Phoenix, AZ
Zeitz, Isidor   Monteclair, NJ

NATIONAL CENTENARIAN RECOGNITION

To receive birthday greetings from the President and First Lady:

Write to:
Greetings Office
The White House
Washington, DC 20500

Allow at least two weeks in advance of the date you want the greeting received. In your letter, put what the occasion is, a 100th birthday, the date of the birthday, the centenarians name, and exactly how you want the envelope addressed including zip code. Also, for clarification purposes, include the name and address and phone number of the person sending the request.

For more information call:
(202) 456-1111

Note: If you are planning to present the card framed, allow enough time in advance to receive the card. Also, explain your intention in the letter and ask to have the greeting sent to you rather than to the celebrant.

To contact Willard Scott write to:
Willard Scott TODAY
30 Rockefeller Plaza, Room 352
New York, New York 10012
For more information call:
(212) 664-5488

Send the request three to four weeks prior to the birthday and send a recent photograph (it will not be returned). Include the person's name and date of birth and address. Also, give a contact person's daytime telephone number. About twenty requests are received each day, and of course not everyone can be mentioned. The oldest are chosen first and after that by geographic location The policy is to not mention two people from the same state on the same day. A week before, the contact person will be called if the centenarian they submitted is to be mentioned on the air. All others will receive a birthday letter from Willard Scott.

RESOURCE AGENCIES

The following are national agencies to contact for general information and to locate local chapters of these organizations. To obtain information on federal government programs and community services in your area, contact your nearest Area Agency on Aging, listed in the telephone directory or contact:

Administration on Aging
330 Independence Avenue SW
Washington, D.C. 20201
(202) 245-0724
(general information)
(202) 245-0641 (publications)

National Association of Area Agencies on Aging, Inc.
1112 16th St. N.W.
Washington, D.C. 20201
(202) 296-8130
Eldercare Locator: 1-800-677-1116

Publications: *Where to Turn for Help for Older Persons* is available free of charge; a directory listing the local Area Agencies on Aging that provide assistance in finding local services to fulfill specific needs is also available and a list of other materials available will be sent on request.

A Resource Director for Older People is published by the National Institute on Aging (9000 Rockville Pike, Bethesda, MD 20892 (301)496-1752)

Health

Aging Network Services
4400 East-West Highway, Suite 907
Bethesda, MD 20814
(301) 657-4329

AARP Pharmacy Service
P.O. Box NIA
1 Prince Street
Alexandria VA 22314
(703) 684-0244

Alzheimer's Disease and Related Disorders Association, Inc.
919 North Michigan Avenue, Suite 1000
Chicago, IL 60611-1676
(312) 335-8700

American Diabetes Association
Two Park Avenue
New York NY 10016
(212) 947-9707

American Dietetic Association
216 West Jackson Boulevard, Suite 600
Chicago IL 60606
(800) 366-1655

American Heart Association, National Center
7272 Greenville Avenue
Dallas TX 75231
(214) 373-6300

American Federation of Home Health Agencies
1320 Fenwick Lane, Suite 100
Silver Spring, MD 20910
(301) 588-1454
For Nutritional Questions and Registered Dietician Locator Nutritional Hotline:
1-800-366-1655

American Red Cross Daily Care
5615 Pershing Avenue
St. Louis, MO 63112
(314) 454-3941

American Speech-Language Hearing Association
10801 Rockville Pike
Bethesda, MD 20852
1-800-638-8255

Cancer Information Service
National Cancer Institute
9000 Rockville Pike
Building 31, Room 10A18
Bethesda, MD 20892
(800) 4-CANCER

Families USA Foundation
1334 G Street, NW
Washington, DC 20005
(202) 628-3030

Food and Drug Administration
Consumer Affairs Branch
(HFN-365)
5600 Fishers Lane
Rockville, MD 20857
(301) 295-8012

High Blood Pressure Information Center
120/80 National Institutes of Health
Bethesda, MD 20892

The Lighthouse
1-800-453-4923

National Center for Vision and Aging
111 East 59th Street
New York, NY 10022
(212) 355-2200

National Council on Alcoholism
12 West 21st Street
New York, NY 10010
(212) 206-6770

National Health Information Clearinghouse
P.O. Box 1133
Washington D.C. 20013
(800) 336-4797

National Hospice Organization
1901 North Moore Street, Suite 901
Arlington, VA 22209
(703) 243-5900 or (800) 658-8904

National Information Center on Deafness
Gallaudet University
800 Florida Avenue NE
Washington D.C. 20002

National Safety Council
444 North Michigan Avenue
Chicago, IL 60611
(708) 285-1121

Presidents Council on Physical Fitness and Sports
450 5th Street NW, Suite 7103
Washington D.C. 20001
(202) 272-3421

Resources for Rehabilitation
Living With Low Vision
A Director for Resources for Finding Equipment and Services for Independent Living
33 Bedford Street, Suite 19A
Lexington, MA 02173
(617) 862-6455

Self-Help for Hard of Hearing People
(301)657-2248

The Skin Cancer Foundation
245 Fifth Avenue
New York, NY 10016
(212) 725-5176

Visiting Nurse Associations of America
3801 East Florida Ave., Suite 206
Denver, CO 80210
(303)753-0218

Housing/Nursing Homes

American Association of Homes for the Aging
1129 20th Street NW
Washington D.C. 20036
(202) 296-5960

National Association for Home Care
519 C Street NE
Stanton Park
Washington D.C. 20002
(202) 541-1424

National Citizens Coalition for Nursing Home Reform
1424 16th Street NW, Room L2
Washington D.C. 20036
(202) 797-0657

Nursing Home Information Service
National Council of Senior Citizens
Education and Research Center
925 15th Street NW
Washington D.C. 20005
(202) 347-8800

Home Care Information

AARP
601 E. Street NW
Washington D.C. 20049
(202) 434-2277
Or contact your local chapter of AARP

Assisted Living Facilities Association of America
9401 Lee Highway, 3rd Floor
Fairfax, VA 22031-1802
(703) 691-8100

General Information

Directory of Aging Resources Business Publishers, Inc. 1-800-274-0122 (Check with your local library to use this detailed reference guide, organized by states and updated annually.)

American Association of Retired Persons
1909 K Street NW
Washington D.C. 20049
(202) 872-4700

American Society on Aging
833 Market Street, Suite 512
San Francisco, CA 94103
(415) 882-2910

Association of Jewish Family and Childrens Agencies
3086 State Highway 27, Suite II
Kendall Park, NJ 08824
(800) 634-7346

National Council on the Aging
409 3rd St. SW
Washington D.C. 20024
(202) 479-1200

National Institute on Aging
Public Information Office
Federal Building, Room 6C12
Bethesda, MD 20892
(301) 496-1752

Office of Veteran Affairs
941 Capitol Street NE,
Room 1211-F
Washington D.C. 20421
(202) 737-5050

Social Security Administration
Office of Public Inquiries
6401 Security Boulevard
Baltimore, MD 21235
(301) 594-1234

Women and Adult Children

**American Association of
University Women**
2401 Virginia Avenue NW
Washington D.C. 20037
(202) 785-7700

**Association of Jewish Family
and Childrens Agencies**
3086 State Highway 27, Suite II
Kendall Park, NJ 08824
(800) 634-7346

Children of Aging Parents
1609 Woodbourne Road
Levittown, PA 19057
(215) 945-6900

**Displaced Homemaker
Network**
1411 K Street NW
Washington D.C. 20005
(202) 628-6767

**National Women's Health
Network**
224 Seventh Street SE
Washington D.C. 20024
(202) 223-6886

Older Womens League
1325 G Street NW, Lower Level B
Washington D.C. 20005
(202) 783-6686

Support and Companionship Groups

**National Group Self-Help
Clearinghouse**
Graduate School and University
Center
CUNY
33 West 42nd Street-Room 1227
New York NY 10036
(212) 840-7606

Senior Companion Program
Older American Volunteer
Programs Office
1100 Vermont Ave. NW, 6th Floor
Washington D.C. 20525
(202) 606-4855

Education

Elderhostel
80 Boylston Street, Suite 400
Boston, MA 02116
(617) 426-7788

**Older Adult Service and
Information system (OASIS)**
7710 Carondelet, Suite 125
St. Louis, MO 63105
(314) 862-2933

Senior Net
399 Arguello Blvd.
San Francisco, CA 94118
(415) 750-5030

Legal

Commission: American Bar Association on Legal Problems of the Elderly
1800 M Street NW
Washington D.C. 20036
(202) 331-2297

National Senior Citizens Law Center
2025 M Street NW, Suite 400
Washington D.C. 20036
(202) 887-5280

Other Resources

For information on the two fitness methods shared by participants in the book contact:

Milton Feher School of Dance and Relaxation
200 West 58th Street
New York, New York 10019
(212) 246-4144

Booklet: *The Art of Walking: Walk Correctly for Health, Voice, Sports, and Figure* by Milton Feher. ($3.00)

Video cassette tapes: *Relaxing Body and Mind*, a stretching and standing exercise tape, and How to Walk. ($10.00 each)

STRONGPUT® This is a new hand-weight founded on the principle of Non-grip Technology®, which means that the weights can be used without gripping to hold them. They have been reported to be easier to use by people with physical limitations, such as arthritis, or those whose hands are weak and who have difficulty holding on to a weight for strengthening exercies.

Available in one pound to ten pounds, it is a cantaloupe-size sphere that allows the individual to place his or her hand inside in an at-rest position. In this position the weight stays on the hand while strength-building exercises are performed. Sold in pairs at $59.95 (senior discount $10.00 per pair) or individually at $34.00 (senior discount 10%).

To order:
1-800-TRY-ONCE (879-6623)
STRONGPUT, INC.
110 Saint Paul Street, Suite 702
Baltimore, MD 21202

New York Times, Large Type Weekly to order: 1-800-631-2580
Reader's Digest, Large Type Publications
To Order: 1-800-877-5293

STATE AGENCY LISTINGS

*Indicates a centenarian recognition program in that state. Please note that some states, such as New York and Connecticut, have recognition programs through the regional Area Agency on Aging and many states through the Governor's Office. If you experience difficulty contacting the appropriate office in your state for centenarian recognition, call 1-800-243-1889 and the National Centenarian Awareness Project will assist you.

Alabama*
Commission on Aging
770 Washington Avenue, Ste. 470
RSA Plaza
Montgomery, AL 36130
(205) 242-5743   (800) 243-5463
Contact: Claude Hooks, Jr., Director

Alaska*
The Division of Senior Services
Alaska Commission on Aging
333 Willoughby Ave.
P.O. Box 110209
Juneau, AK 99811
(907) 465-3250
Contact: Pat Denny, Director

Arizona*
Aging and Adult Administration
1789 West Jefferson, #950A
Phoenix, AZ 85005
(602) 542-4446 or (800) 362-3474
Contact: Richard C. Littler, Director

Arkansas*
Division of Aging and Adult Services
Department of Human Services
7th and Main St.
P.O. Box 1417, Slot 1412
Little Rock, AR 72201
(501) 682-2441
Contact: Herb Sanderson, Director

California*
Department of Aging
1600 K St.
Sacramento, CA 95814
(916) 322-3887
Contact: Robert Martinez, Director

Colorado
Aging and Adult Services
Department of Social Services
110 16th St., 2nd Fl.
Denver, CO 80202
(303) 620-4147
Contact: Rita A. Barreras, Director

Connecticut*
Department of Social Services
Elderly Services Division
25 Sigourney St.
Hartford, CT 06106
(203) 424-5292   (800) 443-9946
Contact: Thomas Corrigan, Director

Delaware
Division of Aging
Department of Health & Social Services
1901 North DuPont Hwy.
New Castle, DE 19720
(302) 577-4791
Contact: Eleanor Cain, Director

District of Columbia*
Office on Aging
One Judiciary Square
441 4th St. NW, 9th Fl.
Washington D.C. 20005
(202) 724-5622
Contact: Jearline F. Williams, Director

Florida*
Florida Department of Elder Affairs
1317 Winewood Blvd.
Building E, Rm. 317
Tallahassee, FL 32399-0700
(904) 922-5297
Contact: E. Bentley Lipscomb, Director

Georgia*
Division of Aging Services
2 Peachtree St. NW, 18th Fl.
Atlanta, GA 30303
(404) 657-5258
Contact: Judy Hagebak, Director

Hawaii*
Executive Office on Aging
Office of the Governor
335 Merchant St., Ste. 241
Honolulu, HI 96813
(808) 586-0100
Contact: Jeanette C. Takamura, Director

Idaho*
Office on Aging
700 W. Jefferson, Rm. 108
P.O. Box 83720
Boise, ID 83720-0007
(208) 334-3833
Contact: Ken Wilkes, Director

Illinois*
Illinois Department on Aging
421 East Capitol Ave., #100
Springfield, IL 62701
(217) 785-2870   (800) 252-8966
Contact: Maralee Lindley, Director

Indiana*
Aging/In-Home Care Services
Department of Human Services
402 West Washington St.
P.O. Box 7083
Indianapolis, IN 46207-7083
(317) 232-7000   (800) 545-7763
Contact: Bobby Conner, Director

Iowa*
Iowa Department of Elder Affairs
914 Grand Ave., Ste. 236
Des Moines, IA 50309
(515) 281-5187
Contact: Betty Grandquist, Director

Kansas*
Department on Aging
150 Docking State Office Bldg.
915 S.W. Harrison
Topeka, KS 66612-1500
(913) 296-4986   (800) 432-3535
Contact: Joanne E. Hurst, Director

Kentucky*
Division of Aging Services
Cabinet for Human Resources,
5th West
275 East Main St.
Frankfort, KY 40621
(502) 564-6930
Contact: S. Jack Williams, Director

Louisiana*
Governor's Office of Elderly Affairs
P.O. Box 80374
Baton Rouge, LA 70898-0374
(504) 925-1700
Contact: Robert Fontenot, Director

Maine
Bureau of Elder and Adult Services
Department of Human Services
State House Station #11
35 Anthony Ave.
Augusta, ME
(207) 624-5335
Contact: Christine Gianpoulos, Director

Maryland*
Office on Aging
State Office Bldg.
301 West Preston St., Rm. 1004
Baltimore, MD 21201
(410) 225-1100   (800) 243-3425
Contact: Rosalie Abrams, Director

Massachusetts*
Executive Office of Elder Affairs
1 Ashburton Place, 5th Fl.
Boston, MA 02108
(617) 727-7750
Contact: Franklin P. Ollivierre, Director

Michigan*
Office of Services to the Aging
P.O. Box 30026
Lansing, MI 48909
(517) 373-8230
Contact: Diane Braunstein,
Director

Minnesota*
Board on Aging
444 Lafayette Rd.
St. Paul, MN 55155-3843
(612) 296-2770   (800) 652-9747
Contact: Jim Varpness, Director

Mississippi*
Division of Aging and Adult Services
750 N. State St.
Jackson, MS 39202
(601) 359-4929   (800) 948-3090
Contact: Eddie Anderson, Director

Missouri*
Division on Aging
615 Howerton Ct.
P.O. Box 1337
Jefferson City, MO 65102
(314) 751-3082 or (800) 235-5503
Contact: Don Howard, Director

Montana*
Department of Family Services
Aging Office
48 N. Last Chance Gulch
Helena, MT 59604
(406) 444-7780   (800) 332-2272
Contact: Charles Rehbein, Director

Nebraska*
Nebraska Department on Aging
P.O. Box 95044
301 Centennial Mall, South
Lincoln, NE 68509-5044
(402) 471-2306
Contact: Dennis Loose, Director

Nevada*
Division for Aging Services
340 North 11th St., Ste. 203
Las Vegas, NV 89101
(702) 486-3545
Contact: Suzanne Ernst, Director

New Hampshire
Division of Elderly and Adult Services
115 Pleasant St., Annex One Bldg.
Concord, NH 03301
(603) 271-4680   (800) 852-3345
Contact: Ronald P. Adcock,
Director

New Jersey*
Division on Aging
Department of Community Affairs
101 South Broad St., CN 807
Trenton, NJ 08625
(609) 292-4833
Contact: Ruth Reader, Director

New Mexico*
State Agency on Aging
228 East Palace Ave.
Santa Fe, NM 87501
(505) 827-7640 or (800) 432-2080
Contact: Michelle L. Grisham,
Director

New York*
New York State Office for the Aging
2 Empire State Plaza
Albany, NY 12223
(518) 474-4425
Contact: Jane Gould, Director

North Carolina*
Division on Aging
693 Palmer Dr.
Caller Box 29531
Raleigh, NC 27626-0531
(919) 733-3983
Contact: Bonnie Cramer, Director

North Dakota*
Department of Human Services
P.O. Box 7070
Northbrook Shopping Ctr.
Bismarck, ND 58507-7070
(701) 328-2577   (800) 755-8521
Contact: Linda Wright, Director

Ohio*
Ohio Department of Aging
50 West Broad St., 8th Fl.
Columbus, OH 43215-5928
(614) 466-5500
Contact: Judith Brachman, Director

Oklahoma*
Department of Human Services
Aging Services Division
312 North East 28th St.
P.O. Box 25352
Oklahoma City, OK 73125-0352
(405) 521-2327
Contact: Roy R. Keen, Director

Oregon*
Senior and Disabled Services
Division
Human Resources Bldg.
500 Summer St. NE, 2nd Fl.
Salem, OR 97310
(503) 945-5811
Contact: Jim Wilson, Director

Pennsylvania*
Department of Aging
400 Market St., 7th Fl.
Harrisburg, PA 17101-2301
(717) 783-1550
Contact: Sharon Alexander-Keilly,
Director

Rhode Island*
Department of Elderly Affairs
160 Pine St.
Providence, RI 02903-3708
(401) 277-2858   (800) 322-2880
Contact: Barbara Rufino, Director

South Carolina*
Governor's Office,
Division on Aging
202 Arbor Lake Dr., #301
Columbia, SC 29223
(803) 737-7500   (800) 868-9095
Contact: Ruth Q. Seigler,
Director

South Dakota*
Office of Adult Services and Aging
Kneip Bldg.
700 Governors Dr.
Pierre, SD 57501
(605) 773-3656
Contact: Gail Ferris, Director

Tennessee*
Tennessee Commission on Aging
500 Deaderick St., 9th Fl.
Nashville, TN 37243-0860
(615) 741-2056
Contact: Emily M. Wiseman,
Director

Texas*
Department on Aging
P.O. Box 12786
Austin, TX 78741
(512) 444-2727   (800) 252-9240
Contact: Mary Sapp, Director

Utah*
Division of Aging and Adult Services
P.O. Box 45500
Salt Lake City, UT 84145
(801) 538-3910
Contact: Jim Quast, Director

Vermont*
Department of Aging and Disabilities
103 South Main St., Osgood 1
Waterbury, VT 05671-2301
(802) 241-2400   (800) 642-5119
Contact: Lawrence Crist, Director

Virginia*
Virginia Department for the Aging
700 East Franklin St., 10th Fl.
Richmond, VA 23219-2327
(804) 225-2271   (800) 552-3402
Contact: Thelma Bland, Director

Washington*
Department of Social and Health
Services
Aging and Adult Services
Administration
P.O. Box 45050
Olympia, WA 98504-5050
(206) 586-3768   (800) 422-3263
Contact: Charles E. Reed,
Assistant Secretary

West Virginia*
Commission on Aging
Holly Grove-State Capitol Complex
Charleston, WV 25305
(304) 558-3317
Contact: William E. Lytton, Director

Wisconsin
Bureau on Aging
217 Hamilton St., Ste. 300
Madison, WI 53703
(608) 266-2536
Contact: Donna McDowell, Director

Wyoming*
Wyoming Division on Aging
139 Hathaway Bldg.
Cheyenne, WY 82002
(307) 777-7986   (800) 442-2766
Contact: Morris Gardner, Director

REFERENCE LIST

Bortz II, Walter M. *We Live Too Short and Die Too Long: How to Achieve and enjoy Your Natural 100-Year-Plus Life Span.* Bantam Books, New York, 1991.

Butler, Robert N. *Why Survive: Being Old in America.* Harper & Row, New York, 1975.

Douglas, Marjory Stoneman. *Voice of the River.* Pineapple Press, Sarasota, Florida, 1988.

. *The Everglades: River of Grass.* Pineapple Press, Sarasota, Florida, 1988.

Frankl, Viktor. *Man's Search for Meaning: An Introduction to Logotherapy.* Beacon Press, Boston, 1962.

Freidan, Betty. *The Fountain of Age.* Simon & Schuster, New York, 1993.

Fries, James. *Aging Well.* Addison-Wesley Publishers, Reading, Massachusetts, 1989.

Kane, Rosalie. *Everyday Ethics: Resolving Dilemmas in Nursing Home Life.* Springer Publications, New York, 1962.

Peale, Norman Vincent. *The Power of Positive Thinking.* Prentice-Hall, New York, 1952.

. *The Tough-Minded Optimist.* Prentice-Hall, Englewood Cliffs, New Jersey, 1961.

Sedgwick, Rhonda Coy. *Sky Trails: The Life of Clyde W. Ice.* Quarter Circle A Enterprises, Newcastle, Wyoming, 1988.

Wood, Beatrice. *I Shock Myself.* Chronicle Books, San Francisco, 1985.

Suggested Reading

Beard, Belle Boone. *Centenarians: The New Generation.* Greenwood Press, New York, 1991.

Delany, Sarah and A. Elizabeth, and Amy Hill Hearth. *Having Our Say: The Delany Sister's First 100 Years.* Kodansha International, New York, 1993.

Heynen, Jim. *One Hundred Over 100: Moments With One Hundred North American Centenarians.* Fulcrum Publishing, Golden, Colorado, 1990.

Poon, Leonard W., ed. *The Georgia Centenarian Study.* Special Issue of the International Journal of Aging and Development (ed. Robert J. Kastenbaum). Baywood Publishing Company, Inc., Amityville, New York, 1992.

Segerberg, Jr., Osborn. *Living to be 100.* Charles Scribner's Sons, New York, 1982, (This is an analysis of Social Security Administration interviews: "America's Centenarians" from 1963 through 1972.

Carter, Rosalyn with Susan K. Golant. *Helping Yourself Help Others: A Book For Caregivers.* Times Books, New York, 1994.

Index

AUTHOR'S NOTE TO READERS

I hope you enjoyed this book. If you have any thoughts or comments you would like to share, I'd be delighted to receive them. If you want to send a copy of the book as a gift to a special person in your life, I would be happy to autograph and personalize it for them.

If you know of a centenarian (or soon-to-be-centenarian) who would enjoy corresponding or just being included on my personal list for correspondence including greeting cards, birthday wishes, and holiday greetings throughout the year, let me know and I will be pleased to keep in touch with him or her. We all like to receive mail and to be remembered. (The centenarian correspondence club)

Address all correspondence to me at:

Centenarian Awareness Project
c/o Health Press
P.O. Box 1388
Santa Fe, NM 87504

Further, if you would like to participate in my continuing effort to bring positive attention to America's elders, I would like to hear from you.

One last note: My grandmother would have been 100 in May 1992. I laud those of her generation who have achieved this distinction and others who follow. I dedicate my efforts of bringing recognition to all those who have reached the century mark, in her memory.

I am often confronted with the question,
Why bother with old people?

To that, I reply:
Because it is the right thing to do.

I stand for this. If you feel the way I do, that our elders deserve better treatment and regard, I invite you to write to me with your comments and opinions.

If any of this has touched a responsive chord, I would welcome hearing from you.

~

ABOUT THE AUTHOR

Lynn Peters Adler is a graduate of Sarah Lawrence College and holds a law degree. Formerly of New York City and Connecticut, she has lived for the past nine years in Phoenix, where her husband is a partner in a national law firm.

An advocate for older adults in Arizona, she is a member and past chairman of the Phoenix Mayor's Aging Services Commission and a member of the advisory board for the Senior Companion Program; she served for three years as a member of the Governor's Advisory Council on Aging. In 1985 she founded the Arizona Centenarian Program and in 1989 the National Centenarian Awareness Project. All of her work with centenarians is as a volunteer, and represents a labor of love on her part.